Dining on the B&O

Dining on the
B & O

··

RECIPES AND SIDELIGHTS
FROM A BYGONE AGE

··

Thomas J. Greco and Karl D. Spence

IN ASSOCIATION WITH THE B&O RAILROAD MUSEUM

THE JOHNS HOPKINS UNIVERSITY PRESS, BALTIMORE

The Johns Hopkins University Press
2715 North Charles Street
Baltimore, Maryland 21218-4363
www.press.jhu.edu

*Special discounts are available for bulk purchases of this book. For
more information, please contact Special Sales at 410-516-6936 or
specialsales@press.jhu.edu.*

The Johns Hopkins University Press uses environmentally friendly
book materials, including recycled text paper that is composed of
at least 30 percent post-consumer waste, whenever possible. All
of our book papers are acid-free, and our jackets and covers are
printed on paper with recycled content.

LIBRARY OF CONGRESS CATALOGING-IN-PUBLICATION DATA

Greco, Thomas J., 1947–
 Dining on the B&O : recipes and sidelights from a bygone age /
Thomas J. Greco and Karl D. Spence ; in association with the B&O
Railroad Museum.
  p. cm.
 Includes bibliographical references and index.
 ISBN-13: 978-0-8018-9323-0 (hardcover : alk. paper)
 ISBN-10: 0-8018-9323-2 (hardcover : alk. paper)
 1. Cookery, American. 2. Railroads—United States—Dining-car
service—History. 3. Baltimore and Ohio Railroad Company.
I. Spence, Karl D., 1940– II. B&O Railroad Museum. III. Title.
 TX715.G8114684 2009
 641.5973—dc22   2009006033

A catalog record for this book is available from the British Library.

FRONTISPIECE
DINNER ON THE CAPITOL LIMITED.
Baltimore and Ohio Railroad Museum

CONTENTS

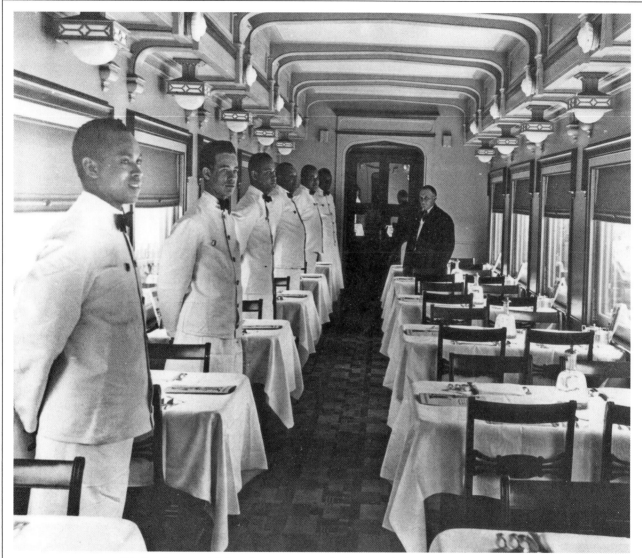

STANDING PROUD. B&O rules required that dining car crews be "on guard" at their stations by the time passengers began boarding or whenever the train was stopped in a station. A photo taken at the same time as this one, which appeared in the *Baltimore and Ohio* magazine (October 1942), identified the waiters *(from left to right)* as Russell D. Wood, Joseph S. Hines, Adolphus Lewis, Wesley T. Parker, Louis Lowman, and Alfred S. Cauthorne. Waiters Wood and Hines look eager to welcome guests to the world of fine B&O cuisine. Baltimore and Ohio Railroad Historical Society

An Eastbound Trip on the Capitol Limited, Autumn 1957

The huge sign—almost the length of two railroad passenger cars—sits atop a dark Norman fortress of a building exhorting Chicagoans to ride the Baltimore and Ohio Railroad's Strata-Dome Dieseliners Capitol Limited, Columbian, and Shenandoah to Washington, D.C. The large letters on each side of the building's clock and bell tower identify the B&O as its owner. The clocks read 3:20 as you approach Grand Central Station at Harrison and Wells streets. You're looking forward to a relaxing overnight ride to Washington aboard a Pullman sleeping car on B&O Train 6, the Capitol Limited.

You already have your tickets so you use the time before the train's 4:30 p.m. departure to buy a copy of the *Saturday Evening Post* and get a snack at the Murphy Company lunchroom. You enter the concourse in time to see the B&O's all-coach Columbian clear the platform following its 4:10 departure. The heavy iron gate to Track 7 is rolled back and people surge ahead as an announcement is made for the boarding of the all-Pullman Capitol Limited. It is a daily ritual that dates back to the train's inaugural in 1923.

As redcaps scurry by with carts of luggage, you leisurely pass the *Nappanee,* an observation, lounge, and sleeping car, its illuminated Capitol Limited tail sign appearing as a ghostly apparition amidst wisps of rising steam. Several cars ahead is your sleeper—the *Tygart,* named after a river flowing through the coalfields of West Virginia. This train presents itself as conservative, dignified, almost regal in its livery of dark blue and gray with gold lettering and trim. Even the touches of stainless steel carry themselves well in this environment. The *Tygart's* porter assists you aboard and directs you to Roomette 4 ("second door on the right") and promises to return after departure to explain the features of your home for the next fifteen and a half hours and get your wake-up call for the morning.

Walking forward through the train you enter the dining room of the twin-unit diner 1092-1093. You're struck by how spacious, colorful, and inviting it is. The main section has fifty-two seats at tables for two and four. An adjacent area that doubles as a cocktail lounge or intimate dining room is furnished with angled banquettes for two people, with total seating for twelve. The car immediately forward of the dining room contains a large kitchen and dormitory quarters for the crew.

The dining room is empty now except for the several waiters standing at attention by the tables and the steward who is easily identified by his gray slacks, white vest with gold buttons over a white shirt and maroon neck-tie, and well-tailored dark blue sport coat. You pause to admire the main dining room's decor and furnishings in multiple shades of rose, gold, and pale green. The tables are set with pressed linens and silver-plated flatware. The steward introduces himself as Alan Felmar and, in answer to your question, says he likes working these cars. The greater seating capacity has almost eliminated the problem of passengers waiting in line to be served or the need to operate two diners. The car's crew varies in number between nine and thirteen, depending on the passenger load. In addition to Mr. Felmar, there are generally three to five men in the kitchen and five to seven waiters, one of whom is likely to spend much of his time providing room service. Frequently, some of the extra personnel will be used to cover just one heavy meal period and then "swing" back from an interme-diate point such as Willard, Ohio, or Cumberland, Maryland.

On your westbound trip aboard the Shenandoah, the single-unit dining car—a modernized edition of one of the B&O's famous Colonial series diners of the 1920s—had a crew of six: a steward, two cooks, and three waiters. You speculate that the waiters would favor that diner over a twin-unit car since they would not have to walk as far, but the steward counters that the higher capacity of the new cars actually reduces the distance each waiter has to walk during a meal. You read recently that the B&O serves about a million and a half meals a year and look forward to one later on in this attractive setting.

The Capitol Limited is under way as you climb the stairs of sleeper-dome car *Moonlight Dome* and the train lurches through the switches leaving Grand Central. You take the front seat on the engineer's side of the car, the next-best vantage point to being up in the engine itself. An hour later it is dark but still too early for din-ner, so it seems an opportune time to have a cocktail in the lounge of the *Nappanee.* This is a handsome and convivial room furnished with comfortable lounge chairs, banquettes, and booths upholstered in blue, as well as handy tables and magazine racks. Mirrored pier panels, Venetian blinds, wood-veneer paneling, fluorescent lighting, and a photo mural contribute to the appeal of the lounge, which is now playing host to a mostly male crowd in business suits and military uniforms.

You pick up a Chicago newspaper and Western Union telegram form, find a seat, and order a Haig and Haig Scotch, tin of peanuts, and pack of Old Golds from the Pullman attendant. After skimming the paper and composing a brief telegram to a business associate, you settle into your drink and smoke just as the B&O and Pullman conductors arrive to collect their respec-tive tickets. With them is an attractively uniformed stewardess-nurse who introduces herself as Katherine Ivelic and offers to give your telegram to the agent at Garrett, Indiana, for sending. She also has you fill out a card listing your Pullman room accommodation and home address in the event a message needs to be deliv-ered to you.

A dining car waiter enters the lounge at 7:00, ringing chimes and announcing the third call for dinner in the diner five cars ahead. It's time to eat. Before leaving the lounge, you pick up some of the train's stationery for a letter to be written later and buy a package of razor blades from Pullman's supply of toiletries. En route to the diner, you stop briefly at your roomette to freshen up. Your porter asks if you wish to leave a morning wake-up call. You request 6:00 a.m.

The train is slowing for Garrett, Indiana, when you enter the diner and are greeted by Steward Felmar, who reminds you to set your watch ahead to eastern time. Suddenly it is 8:15, a bit later than you usually have dinner! After being seated, you are handed a menu, guest check, and pencil. In common with the practice on most railroads, the B&O requires that guests write their order on the check. You decline the steward's suggestion of a cocktail and are taken aback when you recognize Chicago Mayor Richard J. Daley at a table across the aisle engaged in animated conversation with an associate. You quickly return to the business of selecting dinner.

Waiter Clover Street—recognized from previous trips—arrives at the table with a china butter chip with a pat of butter, plus an iced glass into which he pours from a decanter containing Boiling Spring water from the B&O's own facility at Deer Park, Maryland. You exchange greetings and, recalling that he has a son in the military, ask how Clover Junior is doing. The proud waiter produces a photo of the young first lieutenant, who recently received the Soldier's Medal for heroism.

The waiter reads back your order: Hawaiian Fruit Cup, Grenadine, Crab Cakes, Chopped Spinach with Eggs, Creamed Potatoes, Apple Pie, Hot Tea. He takes it to the kitchen and returns with a heaping bowl of the B&O's famous "Help Yourself" salad topped with Roquefort cheese. You fill a plate with the colorful assortment of greens and vegetables, add red Catalina dressing, and prepare for a real treat. The meal is served on the B&O's attractive Blue China highlighting scenic locations and historic locomotives associated with the railroad. It ends with the arrival of a silver finger bowl with water and lemon for cleansing. The food was delicious and the service top notch.

Mr. Felmar invites you to extend your stay a while with an after-dinner liqueur. But you're intent on adjourning to your favorite Capitol Limited spot—the club car up toward the locomotives—for an evening cigar and drink, so you settle your account with the steward and head forward, reflecting on the meal you've just enjoyed. What is it that makes dining on the B&O so very appealing? Perhaps it is the basic, down-home food with a distinctively Southern accent. Other roads may feature more extensive and sophisticated menu selections or fancier dining cars, but you conclude it must be the unrivaled mix of well-prepared meals showcasing foods and recipes of the Chesapeake Bay area and the genuine Southern hospitality and courtesy of the crews.

Finally, the head-end club car is reached. A feature of most of the B&O's top trains, this car historically combined a baggage compartment, a crew dormitory, and a somberly lit lounge that often assumed the character of a smoke-filled men's club. It is within earshot of the locomotives, whether they are whistling for grade crossings while racing across the flatlands or struggling up a mountain grade. It's a great place to spend an evening with a brandy and good Cuban cigar, listening to the car's radio. You hear a rumor that a Hollywood starlet is aboard the Los Angeles–Washington sleeper *Pine Dale,* which arrived in Chicago this afternoon on the Santa Fe's Super Chief.

Later, Number 6 is braking for its stop at Willard, where you step down to the station platform to stretch your legs with a walk back along the train while it is being serviced and the operating crew changed. You board again at the *Tygart* as the new conductor gives the highball to depart on time at 10:25, and you decide to call it a night. Preliminaries completed, you fold down the bed, nearly filling the room in the process. The last thing you remember is hearing a grade crossing signal sounding far in the distance ahead.

The porter's buzzer and "good morning!" awaken you. It's 6:00 a.m. Entering the diner at 6:45 for breakfast, you are seated by Steward Felmar and promptly greeted by a demitasse seated on a paper doily proclaiming "Good Morning—This Is on the House." Nice touch! From a wide selection of menu choices, you settle on Half a Grapefruit and Grilled Ham with Scrambled Eggs, accompanied by Corn Muffins with Apple Butter. And, of course, one of your favorite breakfast beverages on the B&O, an individual pot of Hot Chocolate.

The stop at Martinsburg, West Virginia, affords a brief look at railroad facilities dating back to before and just after the Civil War. After breakfast, you make your way once again to the dome, now nearly full as the train traverses the picturesque Blue Ridge Mountains, an area rich in Civil War lore, including the town of Harpers Ferry, where the states of West Virginia, Virginia, and Maryland meet. This morning, a light fog hangs over the confluence of the Shenandoah and Potomac rivers.

Suburban commuter stations—Dickerson . . . Barnesville . . . Gaithersburg . . . Rockville . . . Kensington—are passed at a 75 mph clip, with the train finally easing to a stop at a modern depot in the fast-growing suburb of Silver Spring, Maryland.

You head for the observation car to watch the train begin its backup move through the maze of tracks leading into Union Station, with the U.S. Capitol standing behind it. Before arrival, you make your way back to your room through vestibules accumulating luggage and people. The porter comes to collect your bag. You accept his offer to brush off your coat and you tip him, with thanks for an excellent trip.

As you step off the *Tygart,* you spot the beautiful Italian actress Sophia Loren accompanied by friends, photographers, and Stewardess-Nurse Ivelic moving quickly down the platform. So that's who was aboard the transcontinental sleeper!

The porter hails a redcap for your luggage and you follow him through the iron gates into the cavernous concourse of Union Station, refreshed and ready for the day ahead.

WILLIAM F. HOWES, JR.
The B&O's last Director of Passenger Services

PREFACE

The Baltimore and Ohio Railroad has been the subject of a host of books dealing with weighty topics ranging from its history as the Rail Road University of the United States (Hungerford 1928, p. 112) to the philosophy and practice of management by its leaders. So why would we come before you with a book about—of all things—the Baltimore and Ohio's *food*? Is this the only facet of the B&O that *hasn't* been covered in print?

We do this because the food served aboard its dining cars demonstrated the B&O's attitude toward its passengers. Readers who love to cook—or to be fed well—will understand this concept. Think of the energy and anticipation you feel in preparing a special meal for friends or family. Then think of the bond that develops or strengthens as a result of your efforts, even more so if the product is of consistently excellent quality. The Baltimore and Ohio viewed its passengers as friends and family and did what any good host would do: strove to make them feel welcome aboard its trains.

Our interest in B&O dining car food grew from a similar basis: a lifelong love of the B&O. From that point we trod widely divergent paths to arrive at our joint authorship of this book. As a youngster, Karl spent hours with his father, John Spence, at the Silver Spring station watching the parade of the B&O's finest trains in the late afternoon and evening. John helped Karl decide that the B&O would definitely be his favorite railroad from then on. Both his parents taught him to appreciate fine dining, excellent service, and "things done right." Part of the curriculum was regular travel on the Baltimore and Ohio and meals in its dining cars. The lesson "took," and Karl's interest drew him to investigate the road's cuisine further, while it could still be done first-hand. Karl and his then-future wife, Carolyn, visited the Dining Car and Commissary Department in Baltimore in 1964 to purchase B&O Colonial China for their dinner table and became friends with Mr. William H. Bond, the assistant manager of the department. Bill made it possible for Karl and Carolyn to photograph many of the passenger cars on the scrap tracks a few blocks from Camden Station, and the two made many buying trips through the huge warehouse where the B&O china was stored. Bill waited patiently while they dug through stacks of china and picked out free pieces from the cracked china barrel. He made them feel like Camden Station was a second home.

Karl and Carolyn were married in December 1964 and, after a few years in California (Carolyn) and Vietnam (Karl), they returned home to Washington in 1968. Bill Bond was at Union Station by that time, and he and his assistant, Jim Hart, were stocking the Capitol Limited and the few trains that the B&O and C&O were still running. Bill retired a few years later, and Karl and Carolyn were invited to his retirement party. Bill and his fellow department staffers exemplified the B&O—its professionalism and especially its old-fashioned kindness and hospitality. Bill was a true gentleman and will long be remembered fondly. He went far beyond the "call of duty" to befriend a young couple.

Tom, on the other hand, was propelled into this journey at age fifty-five by that most primal of human instincts—an empty stomach. Home alone one evening with no leftovers to be had, he opened that seminal volume *Dinner in the Diner,* by Will Hollister, which he had bought as a teenager. That response to desperation was successful in more ways than one; it quelled the hunger pangs and kindled an interest in cooking that developed by turns into an interest in railroad dining car food, then focused on recipes of the B&O, Tom's favorite railroad from an early age. There were precious few recipes to be had, but Tom was still hungry and began the research that led to what you now hold in your hands.

So why go to the trouble of writing a book? Why not just stay at home collecting menus and china or "cooking B&O"? Because we want to preserve and perpetuate one remarkable facet of the way in which the Baltimore and Ohio made friends and grew its business. The preservation part of the equation begins with discovering and recording the recipes used by B&O

chefs. But there is much more to it than that. Save for a few specialties of the house, most of these dishes could be had in any number of good restaurants throughout the territory served by the company. What made them shine was the atmosphere, the style, and the attitude with which they were served. All of this is what we are looking to convey.

We as authors aim to perpetuate the B&O's cuisine by making it possible for you the reader to *cook* it. Or, at the very least, to appreciate what went into serving this food to trainloads of guests day in and day out for decades. Modern cooking owes much to tradition and longstanding practice. But tools and techniques have changed, as has the "anthropology" of cooking and the way in which knowledge of cooking is transmitted. Cooking was once the province of two professions: cooks and housewives, both of whom usually learned their craft on the job starting at a young age.

A B&O chef of 1925, let us say, would be amazed to find that his life's labor has become a passion and recreation for many, far beyond simply a means of providing sustenance or a paycheck. We've taken recipes written years ago for professionals and rendered them usable for readers with a wider spectrum of experience and ability. This is what we mean by perpetuation.

If you finish this book with a greater understanding of how the Baltimore and Ohio Railroad built its reputation for the best dining car cuisine in America—or if a year or two from now you find its pages stained with grease, splattered with sauce, or scribbled with notes from your own efforts in the kitchen—we will have accomplished our goals.

HOW OFTEN we've each read books in which the author feels humbled by the need to thank those who have made the book possible. Now we are faced with the same daunting task! When it came time to think about publishing this mass of information, we received the enthusiastic help of a number of people.

Bob Brugger, acquisitions editor at the Johns Hopkins University Press, responded positively to a "cold call" and almost immediately took the project in hand. He articulated a vision that transformed the work from a somewhat disjointed collection of information to a culinary history of the B&O. And that biblical stalwart Job could take lessons in patience from Bob.

Nick Fry, archivist for the Baltimore and Ohio Railroad Historical Society, not only steered us toward valuable material in the Society's "World Headquarters" but sat with us late into the evening, encouraging us to talk about our dreams for this book, not merely the limited possibilities we saw for it. A "possibility thinker," that man.

Dennis Fulton, of the B&O Historical Society, provided what may be the heart, if not the soul, of this book in the form of copies of *Old Standard B&O Recipes* and *B&O Chef's Notes*. These documents were unknown to us before Dennis brought them to our attention, and they were the first indication that a significant body of B&O recipes could be assembled.

The late Jim Hart, who proudly claimed to be the last surviving employee of the B&O's Dining Car and Commissary Department in Baltimore, wisely collected artifacts and memorabilia from the department during the 1960s and made this treasure trove available to us. Among many other things, we can thank Jim for the beautiful color photographs of B&O food, which were used to illustrate menus in the early 1950s.

The late Reverend Jimmy Kearse worked as a waiter and waiter-in-charge for the B&O from 1944 to 1962.

He spent hours helping us understand what life on a dining car was like and what had to be done to offer guests the finest food available. When we were uncertain of our qualifications for writing about the work of several generations of the B&O's African American dining car employees, Jimmy summoned his best homiletic style, telling us *Write your story!*

Jim Mischke, dear friend and B&O historian *sans pareil*, lent encouragement and offered to check our manuscript for historical accuracy.

Mick Weis, who spent years in the food service business and has a love for the B&O, was a natural for checking the technical details of the recipes in this book.

Courtney Wilson, John Maranto, and Janelle Rider of the Baltimore and Ohio Railroad Museum in Baltimore greeted two strangers warmly and embraced the project wholeheartedly. Courtney's positive energy helped us really believe this could happen.

TOM GRECO *would specifically like to acknowledge the following:*

I would be deeply remiss (and perhaps at some risk!) in failing to thank my beautiful wife, Helen Beggane. Many years ago I crowned Helen "The World's Best Cook" and will gladly add to that "World's Best Wife," as well. On April 19, 1975, Helen married a railroader (I was with the Missouri Pacific Railroad from 1971 until 1984), and on May 13 of that year, home for scant days from our honeymoon, she surprised me with a dinner of B&O Corn Bread Pie in honor of the Capitol Limited's fifty-second birthday. I knew then that Helen would be "a keeper."

I'd also like to recognize the late Robert McGoings, who made a career as a waiter in the Baltimore and Ohio's dining car service. His random gesture of kindness to an overwhelmed newlywed will never be forgotten.

The best I can do is to brand Helen's lifelong friend Cathy Quiñones with that tired appellation "gourmet cook." Fortunately for me, Cathy's enduring friendship was one of the loveliest wedding presents I received on that spring day in 1975. Having traveled the world, learning from cooks all the way, Cathy taught me the art of describing the provenance and history of each dish as it is served.

Far from sneering at a newby, Helen and Cathy have joyously supported my struggle to learn how to cook. They are truly two of my culinary heroes.

During the spring of 2004, it seemed clear that I needed something more if I were to really learn how to cook B&O food. That something turned out to be the Food and Hospitality Institute at El Centro College in Dallas, Texas, home to some excellent professors whose primary goal is the education of those who would enter the country's burgeoning food service industry. Nevertheless, these fine folks have embraced my goal of learning to "cook B&O."

Chef Alison Hodges taught me the fundamentals of baking and how to make breads and rolls. Her good humor and patience have been infinite, as attested to by her allowing me to model the B&O's Brentwood, Maryland, station in gingerbread for my class project just before Christmas 2005.

Chef Tom Nixon's help exceeds my ability to acknowledge. Tom possesses that rare gift of having become a dear friend even while serving as my mentor and requiring my very best work. Many are the out-of-class hours Tom has spent introducing me privately to the wonders of good food and the joys of its preparation and presentation. And how Tom's eyes lit up when I served a final exam on B&O Capitol China on a sheet pan covered with a B&O tablecloth and accentuated by B&O napkins, silver, and glassware! He is another of my culinary heroes.

Chef Jeff Robinson took me "off the street" with not a minute's kitchen experience since spending my twenty-first birthday on KP duty at Fort Riley, Kansas, on July 4, 1968. He taught me the basics of food preparation before the truth came out: Jeff is himself a railfan, having cut his teeth riding the New York subway system as a young boy.

Chef Beth Sonnier, who accepted the writing of this book for academic credit in a co-op course at El Centro, was the first to suggest that I should put my collection of B&O recipes into the form of a book. She has given most generously of her own experience as a culinary author. Her energy for this project has kept me going at times when my own energy flagged.

KARL SPENCE *would specifically like to acknowledge:*
My wife, Carolyn, who has enjoyed our B&O hobby for over forty years.

My father, John M. Spence, who would have enjoyed this book and would fondly remember all those afternoons long ago watching B&O trains.

My friend Mr. William H. Bond, who introduced Carolyn and me to the operation of the Baltimore and Ohio's Dining Car and Commissary Department and shared his enthusiasm for his railroad and his job. He also taught us all about B&O china, and the pieces we purchased are still in our china cabinet except when used for a "B&O meal."

Dining on the B&O

CAR 1026. Built in 1912, the Class F-3 represented the first all-steel dining cars operated by the B&O. They would also be some of the last cars to feature the beautiful stained glass Gothic transoms above the windows. Lee Street Tower in Baltimore stands behind the car. Baltimore and Ohio Railroad Historical Society

Cooking the B&O Way

———

The Baltimore and Ohio Railroad was noted for its dining car cuisine and service. The Dining Car and Commissary Department rarely turned a profit, but the railroad believed that if it provided superior dining and impeccable courtesy, it would attract passengers, shippers, and investors. The company had plenty of time to refine its service: it began operating its first dining car in 1881, after having prepared and served the first onboard meals on November 5, 1842, just twelve years after inaugurating the country's pioneer rail passenger service, and it continued operations until 1971.

Nowadays on Amtrak, most dining car food is prepared off-site and simply heated or microwaved onboard. Airlines have done this for years and modern "TV dinners" taste very good, but this type of food did not exist during most of the years that the B&O operated dining cars. The B&O and other rail passenger carriers believed that food prepared on board would provide the freshest and finest cuisine for its passengers. Entrées were prepared from scratch in a kitchen that occupied a space about 16 feet long and only 7½ feet wide. A passageway around the kitchen led to the 40-foot-long dining section.

Lawrence Sagle, of the B&O's Public Relations Department, described a typical full-size 80-foot dining car and associated service in his article "Meals en Route," published in the January 1941 issue of *Trains* magazine. The kitchen was a marvel of efficiency, with only a few feet between the oven, broiler, charcoal grill, and steam table on one side and the icebox, sinks, and vegetable storage on the other. No space was wasted: lockers or cupboards occupied every extra square inch. Fresh meats, fish, crabmeat, oysters, and shrimp were kept in a large refrigerator. Under the table were iced lockers for vegetables. A supply of coal or coke fueled the range and broiler. Immense overhead tanks and double sinks provided ample water facilities, while salt, flour, and spices were found in bins above the work areas. Rolls, muffins, and pies were baked onboard the car and then placed in warming ovens above the range, where plates were also kept warm for service. There were racks for pots, pans, and dishes as well as lockers for towels and dishcloths. Over 50 cooking utensils along with more than 700 plates, cups, saucers, and miscellaneous pieces of china and crockery, 300 pieces of glassware, and 600 pieces of silverware could be found in the kitchen of a full-length dining car.

Waiters prepared salads, fruits, ice cream, and other foods in a pantry between the kitchen and dining room

A B&O CHEF IN HIS KITCHEN. This photo exemplifies the pride B&O employees took in the food offered on the road's dining cars. Here the chef cuts individual-portion-sized servings from a glorious roast turkey. Baltimore and Ohio Railroad Museum

within easy reach of cupboards for canned goods, cereals, and condiments and still more dish racks. It was the waiter, not the cook, who added the final touch to the dishes he served and who, afterwards, washed his own dirty dishes and replaced them in the racks. There were 145 pieces of equipment in the pantry.

Outside the pantry, on the kitchen side of the passageway, was another iced locker for fruits and vegetables. Across the aisle was the linen locker where more than 1100 items such as tablecloths and napkins were stored. A similar space was reserved for dirty linen being returned to Baltimore for laundering. A walk to the opposite end of the car would find a locker and a refrigerator in which the steward kept cigarettes and cigars, beer, liquors, mineral waters, and other beverages. There was even room here for the machinery that kept the car comfortably cool during the warmer months and made dining a pleasure throughout the year.

The staff of a full dining car worked under the supervision of a steward and consisted of as many as six waiters and three cooks. Cars with fewer than twenty-four seats were supervised by a waiter-in-charge. Heavily traveled trains such as the Capitol Limited were assigned up to eight waiters and four cooks. Long before dinner was served, the crew would be busy with preliminary preparations. The steward, chef, and pantry man would check the menu, plan the club plate dinner, and write inserts for the menus. The chef and his assistants would start cooking the soups, baking rolls and muffins, and preparing anything else that could be made up in advance of orders. The pantry man would organize ingredients and dishes for salads and desserts so that everything would go smoothly when service began.

Duties on the car were assigned to the waiters in seniority order, the pantry man holding highest honors. One of the waiters was assigned as assistant pantry man, one had charge of the linen, another the silver and glassware, and another was responsible for the cleanliness of the car.

On popular trains such as the Capitol and National Limiteds, one waiter did no serving at all but made himself generally useful by changing linen, filling water glasses, bringing extra butter, and clearing away dishes. This "upstairs man" or "swing man" would not be seen the next morning, as he detrained at a division point after the last dinner guest had been served.

New menus were planned and printed in Baltimore and sent to stewards monthly. A menu typically offered two forms of meal service—à la carte and table d'hôte. A la carte allowed one to choose any dish available, paying a separate price for each item. Table d'hôte service (called "tab" by the crews) came into its own during the 1930s as a way of enticing the more budget-minded travelers into the dining car. Here a complete meal was provided for a fixed price. Portions were smaller, but then, so was the bill.

A table d'hôte dinner—costing $1.25 in 1941—might feature Fresh Shrimp Cocktail, Chilled Celery, or Melon Mangoes as an appetizer, followed by a choice of two kinds of soup. Entrées consisted of Panned Fresh Fish with Parsley Butter, an Imperial Crab with Coleslaw, Sauté of Calf Sweetbreads with Canadian Bacon, Half a Fried Chicken Southern Style, Roast Leg of Lamb with Mint Jelly, or Assorted Cold Cuts with Potato Salad. For a Broiled Sirloin Steak, the cost of the dinner skyrocketed to $1.75.

Then there was a choice of two or three vegetables— perhaps Potatoes au Gratin, Fresh Garden Peas with Parsley Butter, or Green Corn on the Cob. The salad for the day was Hearts of Lettuce with Thousand Island dressing, and a small plate off to the left held hot Potato Rolls, Ginger Muffins, or sliced bread. For the

guest who could still eat by this time, dessert options included Green Apple Pie, Ice Cream with Wafers, or cheese and crackers. Beverages were tea, coffee, Sanka, Kaffee Hag, Instant Postum, cocoa, milk, malted milk, and buttermilk. And, of course, water from the B&O's Boiling Spring at Deer Park, Maryland, was used exclusively on the road's diners.

To provide such variety required considerable planning. Unlike chefs in a restaurant, the dining car steward or waiter-in-charge could not send out a rush order to the nearest grocery store when there was a run on a particular menu item. Experience taught him just how much would have to be ordered in advance to avoid the embarrassment of telling a guest that he or she could not have something that was on the menu.

Sagle described the B&O's system of commissaries, beginning with the main facility at Camden Station in Baltimore. Branches were located in Cincinnati, Chicago, Pittsburgh, and Washington, D.C. The Pittsburgh commissary was closed during the Depression while Washington closed in 1958 and reopened in the late 1960s, near the end of B&O passenger service. Dining cars assigned to the National Limited and the Diplomat, for instance, ran straight through from New York to St. Louis and back. Passing through Baltimore on the way to New York, the steward would submit a requisition for supplies to be picked up there as he passed through on the westbound run. He would also wire a requisition to Cincinnati for the supplies needed for the round trip from there to St. Louis. In determining what was required, the steward would sit down with the chef and pantry man, inventory the supplies on hand, and make requisitions accordingly.

Each morning at 5:00, the storekeeper in the Baltimore commissary took all of the requisitions received during the night and went over them carefully, abstracting the various items into total pounds of meat, fish, vegetables, etc. Each month, approved dealers submitted bids for supplying certain foodstuffs, the monthly contract being let to the bidder who could provide the highest quality at the lowest cost. When the storekeeper determined just what was needed, he contacted the suppliers and in short order had sufficient goods to fill the requisitions.

For cars operating from or through Baltimore, orders were made up in cases and hampers to be put aboard at Camden Station. For cars not serving Baltimore, supplies were rushed by the first passenger train to points on the system where the cars could be stocked. Special watertight hampers, properly iced, ensured the safety of perishable food during transit; canned and dry goods were shipped in the same hampers, minus the ice.

Cars running through Pittsburgh, Buffalo, Rochester, Wheeling, Columbus, Parkersburg, and other remote locations ordered from the nearest commissary. If necessary, the steward had authority to buy emergency supplies at terminals such as St. Louis or Jersey City. When tours or other special movements were scheduled, the Dining Car and Commissary Department would be notified sufficiently in advance so that regular cars could be stocked or extra cars added to take care of the anticipated demand.

The amount of perishables consumed was staggering. Sagle describes a month during which the B&O purchased 3,712 pounds of bacon, 22,316 pounds of beef, 11,253 pounds of fowl, 5,432 dozen eggs, 15,167 pounds of fish, 8,900 pounds of ham, 1,326 pounds of lamb, 1,024 pounds of shrimp, and 2,226 pounds of turkey. The last item would lead one to think the month was November or December, but it was June. Fresh-water fish from the Great Lakes were served aboard eastbound B&O trains; westbound the diners offered salt-water fish from Chesapeake Bay as well as crab and oysters in season. The average monthly cost of foodstuffs purchased for B&O dining cars in 1941 was about $50,000. To put this in perspective, the price tag on a new 1941 Pontiac read $874.

The B&O was then operating a total of 102 cars on which food and drink could be purchased. These required a total of 45 stewards, 194 cooks, and 332 waiters—all of whom required sleeping quarters and meals as well. On some of the longer runs, sleeping quarters for the crew were provided in the baggage section of the combination car forward. On trains such as the Capitol and National Limiteds, there were beds for 12 men as well as washroom and toilet facilities. At the away-from-home terminal the company provided hotel accommodations.

It took an amazing variety of equipment to support food and beverage service across the system. In 1957, for instance, there were 43 full dining cars, 8 café-club cars, 6 café-parlor cars, 2 lounge-snack cars, and 9 observation cars serving snacks and drinks. The railroad also operated 23 baggage-lounge and coffee shop cars and 17 coaches with lunch counters. An additional 19 cars with buffets, bars, or lounges catered to Pullman passengers, and there were even Rail Diesel Cars with a dining section, which operated as the Daylight Speedliner between Philadelphia and Pittsburgh.

The F-4B-class dining cars built between 1923 and 1930 had beautiful colonial interiors, and one, the *Martha Washington*, became the first air-conditioned dining car in 1930. In short order the ever-innovative B&O could boast that all diners in regular service were air-conditioned. Many cars were modernized during the 1940s, and 1957 saw the acquisition of twin-unit cars from the New York Central to equip the Capitol Limited.

A dinner on the Capitol or National Limited was a memorable experience. Tables were covered with

COME AND SIT FOR A SPELL. "Dining car and train crews will not be fed," stated the B&O's *Book of Rules for Dining Car Department Employees*, "until guests who have come at the last call have practically finished their meals. If guests linger longer than necessary, the Steward or Waiter-in-Charge will ask if they mind having the crew eat at tables farthest from them." Here, two crew members take their meal break. They were allowed to choose from any item on the regular menu at reduced rates but were required to sign their meal checks to keep peace with the accountants in Baltimore. Baltimore and Ohio Railroad Museum

heavy silver-plated cutlery and hollowware. Water was served in Deer Park Spring bottles with acrylic holders. Food was served on beautiful Centenary pattern blue and white china featuring pictures of scenery along the B&O as well as historic and modern locomotives. Some trains employed the Black and Gold pattern china also known as Capitol—elegant plates in white with black and gold borders and top-marked with a gold B&O logo. Sample pieces of Centenary were stored on the diners for sale to patrons. Pieces could also be ordered by mail from the Dining Car and Commissary Department in Baltimore or, in later years, from the B&O Railroad Museum in Mt. Clare Station, from which the first passenger train in the United States departed in 1830. The demand for this china was so great that it was eventually reproduced especially for the museum.

At the conclusion of each meal, a silver finger bowl was provided. Service was impeccable. The waiters and stewards were true gentlemen, and right up until the end of passenger service, with the advent of Amtrak in 1971, the B&O never stinted in providing the finest personal service possible.

The company understandably took pride in its oft-cited reputation for offering the best dining car service in the country. In March 1946, Virginia Tanner, assistant editor of *Baltimore and Ohio* magazine, was basking in the glow of plaudits from the redoubtable Lucius Beebe, author, railfan, and all-around raconteur.

snow-white—or in later years, ivory—linen. In 1939, anticipating the shortages that impending war might cause, the B&O stockpiled scores of tablecloths from Irish linen suppliers; in 1964 the railroad sold surplus tablecloths—still in their original wrappers—for one dollar each out of the Camden warehouse.

Tables were set with sparkling crystal and polished

For the facts, go to an authority! Recently a real orchid was handed the B&O's meals by no less an authority on the subject of food than the widely read magazine "Gourmet." In an article written by Lucius Beebe . . . the B&O's dining car fare was rated as good as the best in the country, and high praise for its continued high quality throughout the war was given. In this much-appreciated tribute, Manager of Dining Car & Commissary Department H. O. McAbee and his staff may take justifiable pride.

Writing in his monthly column "Along the Boulevards," Beebe had criticized the poor quality of food on "many railroads, and to name names, the Pennsy in exaggerated particular," which, he moaned, "indulged their virulent hatred of the demon passenger to a degree of insolence and starvation combined." He heaped praise on railroads and trains "which have kept the faith and provided comfort and good food throughout a period of general abuse and imposition: the Baltimore & Ohio, the New Haven, the Twentieth Century Limited and the City of San Francisco." Beebe had honed his opinion to the point of naming specific trains whose cuisine was noteworthy. But there was only one railroad besides the B&O that rated a blanket endorsement for its dining service as a whole.

Although there was no formal policy regarding the racial makeup of dining car crews, the B&O adhered to the tradition of employing African Americans as cooks, chefs, waiters, and waiters-in-charge, while Caucasians were hired as stewards. By the '60s, the B&O had not hired new dining car personnel for years, owing to the precipitous decline in rail passenger traffic. Once equal employment laws were passed and Amtrak assumed operation of most U.S. passenger trains (May 1, 1971), all racial and ethnic groups served in all capacities aboard dining cars. Although Amtrak contracted for the operation of passenger trains over B&O and C&O rails, the B&O/C&O Dining Car Department still operated the diners for several years after 1971.

Management and supervisory personnel in the Dining Car and Commissary Department typically came up through the ranks as stewards and cooks, and all

fully understood the problems faced in day-to-day operations. They were deeply disappointed at the rapid disappearance of passenger trains during the 1960s and the substitution of Food-Bar Coaches for many dining cars. They did the best they could with dwindling resources and constant change. In the mid-1960s the B&O merged with the Chesapeake and Ohio Railway, and C&O dining car management personnel transferred to Baltimore. A tiny commissary was reincarnated in Washington's Union Station, lasting right up until the end of passenger service. The railroad still ran the Capitol Limited in style after virtually all other long-distance trains had been downgraded or discontinued entirely. It was not the all-Pullman streamliner it had been in the 1950s and earlier, but it still operated a full sleeping car as well as a diner-lounge and a five double-bedroom sleeper-lounge-observation car.

The B&O dining car operations Lawrence Sagle had described in the early 1940s remained essentially stable for nearly another twenty years—diminished only when intercity passengers began traveling by car and air and dining car service was reduced along with the number of long-distance trains. The B&O's legendary service, however, was never compromised. Unlike some railroad companies, the B&O took great pains to provide food service on as many trains as possible, and even on the most basic coach snack bar, the old standard of B&O service endured right up to the end. It was a long ride from 1842 to 1971, and it is hoped that through this book, readers can once more have "dinner on the Capitol Limited" and thoroughly enjoy their trip.

SOURCES OF B&O RECIPES

As far as we know, the Baltimore and Ohio Railroad never published an official book of recipes or preparation instructions for its cooks. The company used existing recipes from a variety of sources, some published, others internal to the railroad. Although research has uncovered much valuable information, there is just as much that may never be known. What we do know is that there were at least two collections of recipes used by B&O cooks: *Old Standard B&O Recipes* and what we've called *B&O Chef's Notes.* Their unknown authors or editors, it seems, gathered the recipes from numerous sources of the day and perhaps added their own original creations. A third source, called *What's Cooking on the B&O?* was less an institutional cookbook and more of a promotional tool for families and friends who wanted to "cook B&O." A series of pamphlets entitled *Echoes from Colonial Days,* issued to commemorate the twenty individual Colonial dining cars, each contained a recipe, but these functioned more as souvenirs for travelers. Nonetheless, these marketing materials, too, provide a window into the B&O kitchen. But it would be best to begin our story at the beginning.

Early in the twentieth century, the concept of good institutional cooking was synonymous with French cooking. Auguste Escoffier, "emperor of the world's kitchens," had been setting standards that would remain virtually unchanged for decades. But one Charles Fellows was about to challenge France's hegemony in the culinary world. Arriving in Chicago about the time of the 1893 World's Columbian Exposition, this Australian native found himself in a chef's paradise. Within easy reach lay America's bounty of meat, grain, and vegetables; close at hand were straightforward, no-frills midwestern cooking methods.

Fellows had grown weary of French influence in the kitchen. Here's his introduction to *The Culinary Handbook* in 1904:

It is believed that of the culinary writers for the catering profession acknowledged by the intelligent and cultivated to be great, none, whether Foreign or American have heretofore written the dishes in plain English without the foreign affectation 'A LA', an affectation when appearing on the Bill of Fare causing the guest to expect much, and disappointing him by receiving little.

Charles Fellows minced no words.

This first purely American institutional cookbook apparently provided many of the recipes that found their way into *Old Standard B&O Recipes.* There, the entry for Ox Joint Sauté reads simply "Same as shown in Culinary Handbook." A copy of Fellows's volume reveals the secrets of the B&O's culinary world of the early 1900s.

In 1991, prolific writers Jeff Smith and Craig Wollam released an updated and annotated version of Fellows's *Culinary Handbook.* This aptly titled edition, *The Frugal Gourmet's Culinary Handbook: An Updated Version of an American Classic on Food and Cooking,* provided all of Fellows's recipes in their original language, with helpful explanations of some of the now-archaic or obsolete terminology.

Dozens of B&O menu items of the time are described in the concise paragraphs of *The Culinary Handbook.* Later, the unknown author of *Old Standard B&O Recipes* would recount a number of Fellows's recipes, some word-for-word, others with variations that turned them into B&O specialties.

The Culinary Handbook was still in print in 1926, and perhaps as late as 1930, but a study of B&O menus shows that Fellows's influence had begun to wane by 1940. Perhaps it was the austerity prompted by the Second World War or a general trend toward less ostentatious dining that spelled the end for menus of the 1930s that could trumpet, "If you desire some particular dish not listed the Steward will provide the service if available." Quite likely there was a desire by the B&O to modernize its cuisine and to present dishes that would better showcase its enviable culinary reputation. Even so, there were still menu items from the 1960s that could be prepared using the *Handbook*.

Charles Fellows died in Covington, Kentucky, in 1921, at only 55 years of age. He was by then America's best-known culinary author and champion of its developing foodways. His work benefited the Baltimore and Ohio and its patrons for over forty years.

The serendipitous discovery of a copy of Adolphe Meyer's *Eggs in a Thousand Ways,* stamped throughout "Property of Baltimore and Ohio R. R. Co.," provided us with an understanding of how B&O chefs cooked the egg dishes featured not only on breakfast menus but for lunch and dinner as well. Like *The Culinary Handbook, Eggs in a Thousand Ways* was published by John Willy, Inc., owner of the Hotel Monthly Press in Chicago. A catalogue in the back of both books lists dozens of fascinating titles for American restaurateurs, as well as subscriptions to *Hotel Monthly* magazine, from which the firm took its name.

The Hotel Monthly Press was among America's greatest culinary publishing houses. Its offerings ranged from large, beautifully illustrated texts such as its 1894 edition of *The Epicurean* by Charles Ranhofer (1836-1899), the first internationally renowned chef of an American restaurant (Delmonico's in New York), to numerous smaller manuals on various aspects of cooking, baking, training, and food service. The firm of John Willy, Inc., was sold to the American Hotel Register Company in 1971 after eighty years of producing books and forms.

Around 1920, the B&O offered thirteen choices from a Special Egg Menu, which also listed the ingredients of each dish. Names and ingredients for nearly all of these were the same as shown in *Eggs in a Thousand Ways,* and the menu was arranged in the same fashion as the book, classifying selections as scrambled eggs, poached eggs, shirred eggs, and omelets. The recipe for Poached Eggs Washington given in *Old Standard B&O Recipes* was transcribed almost verbatim from Adolphe Meyer's 152-page vest-pocket book, which further verifies its use by B&O chefs of the period.

Old Standard B&O Recipes and *B&O Chef's Notes* are two remarkable manuscripts that apparently came from different employees. They offer a fascinating insight into a time when the B&O was venturing away from institutional cookbooks toward a cuisine and specialties of its own. Far from being publications, these were the private "cheat sheets" of the writers.

The title *Old Standard B&O Recipes* appears on the first of 48 typewritten pages measuring approximately 6 by 8 inches. The last three pages are titled the "Terms from the French in general use in cooking," which are used as a glossary in this book. It is notable for its breadth of coverage; everything from breakfast dishes to meats, salads, appetizers, and desserts appear in its pages.

One of the mysteries of *Old Standard B&O Recipes* is a unique recipe numbering system. Under the heading "Recipe Number 1," for instance, are listed ingredients and directions for preparing Baked Roast Beef Hash, Ginger Bread Pudding, and Coffee Sauce. The sauce was indeed served over the pudding, but what relationship did these have to the hash? "Recipe Number 4" consists of Brown Betty Pudding, Croutons, Rhubarb Pie, Rhubarb Jelly, and Individual Clam Pie, while "Recipe Number 11" includes only Clam Juice Cocktail. Altogether, there are fifty such recipe number headings, and probably nobody alive can explain their significance.

The title of the other document, *B&O Chef's Notes,* is a generic description we have given to the 14 pages

CASUAL DINING. Many daylight trains or those less often traveled on offered a more economical food service option than a full dining car. Lunch counters such as the one seen here often occupied part of a day coach. Absent were the starched tablecloths and napery and the large cadre of waiters and kitchen personnel. Interesting elements in this circa-1940 shot include a glassware cabinet at left with its stout latching mechanism. Below the counter is storage space for silver and paper items. And, as demonstrated by the woman on the right, this was decades before smokers would be segregated from nonsmokers or prohibited altogether from smoking in a public place. Baltimore and Ohio Railroad Museum

assembled in a three-ring binder measuring 4½ by 7¼ inches. This seems more a personal collection of recipes than *Old Standard B&O Recipes*. It is unlikely, for instance, that Dandelion Wine would ever be found on a B&O menu, and it absolutely boggles the imagination to picture the Capitol Limited waiting as its dining car crew scours a trackside cow pasture for the "two quarts of dandelion blossoms, free from stems" called for in the recipe. Still, there is no doubting the primary purpose of these notes, as many well-known B&O dishes are detailed, along with instructions for such kitchen basics as Espagnole and Creole sauces and several types of salad dressing. These were indeed a B&O chef's notes.

On the surface, it may seem unfortunate that no dates are associated with either of these documents. But when one considers that these were most likely compilations done during the course of a career, the omission is less bothersome. The manuscripts themselves provide some clues. *Old Standard B&O Recipes* lifted a number of recipes neat from the pages of *The Culinary Handbook* and *Eggs in a Thousand Ways* and showcased a range of dishes that would not be seen again after America's entry into World War II. It is safe to say that the list was compiled during the 1930s or perhaps as late as 1940, given that the use of the word *Old* could have meant that the recipes were obsolete or no longer in regular use.

One is on firmer ground in dating *B&O Chef's Notes* at around 1950. Most of the recipes were typewritten, but several were in longhand, including three written on a sheet of B&O stationery, "Form 300 Ruled." The form's latest revision was then shown as January 29, 1947.

A third source of B&O recipes is a B&O classic, something that nearly everyone who has tried to "cook B&O" has used. For over fifty years *What's Cooking on the B&O?* has been the most frequently cited source of B&O recipes. The original version of *What's Cooking?* went to press around 1950 and was "Published for the women in B&O families—and for friends of the B&O—by the Dining Car and Safety Departments of the Baltimore and Ohio Railroad," to quote the book's opening remarks. Its 32 pages contained a dozen detailed recipes and tips for cooking seven breakfast dishes. These were interspersed with lessons in kitchen safety for the woman supposedly doing the cooking.

Nowadays, the safety lessons and patter surrounding the recipes would be tolerated as corny and old-fashioned at best. They might be considered condescending and somewhat sexist by many. Illustrations show an attractively dressed and coiffed wife reminiscent of Blondie of comic-strip fame. On one page she smiles lovingly from the stove at her husband and two children, who smile back from the table with eating

utensils pointing skyward in clenched fists. On the previous page, she had been blown through the roof by an explosion resulting from carelessness with cleaning compounds. Still elsewhere, she tends the stove in a seductive kimono meant to charm her husband; the loose sleeves catch fire from a gas burner as her angry spouse rushes in wielding a fire extinguisher.

The great gift of *What's Cooking on the B&O?* was its accurate quantification of ingredients for the home chef. Where earlier recipes might prescribe "a lump of butter the size of an egg," *What's Cooking?* called for 3 tablespoons of butter in the preparation of Egg Plant Creole. It did not assume that the reader was a chef with years of experience on the road—or a trainload of passengers to feed.

The B&O Museum produced a new edition of *What's Cooking on the B&O?* in 1990 "as a result," it said, "of widespread interest in B&O dining car operations." The homey introductions remained, but depictions of the shocking results of unsafe practices were eliminated in favor of reproductions of B&O menus dating from 1904 and 1937, a pair of 1930-era photos, and an advertisement reminding travelers that "B&O is famous for good meals reasonably priced." Will Hollister took all the recipes and tips verbatim from *What's Cooking on the B&O?* for use in his *Dinner in the Diner: Great Railroad Recipes of All Time* (1965). And in 1993, Jim Porterfield borrowed six of those recipes, thankfully minus the by-now stale repartee, for his magnificent *Dining by Rail: The History and Recipes of America's Golden Age of Railroad Cuisine*. His research also turned up several "new" recipes to whet the B&O fan's appetite.

Menus were revised monthly on the B&O, and by 1943 the Dining Car and Commissary Department was including what was later termed a "General Notice" with each menu change, a practice that continued until the end of service in 1971. The notices were addressed to "All Stewards, Waiters-in-Charge, Cooks and Waiters" and were distributed systemwide several days before a new menu was to take effect.

Recipe format in the "General Notice" ran the gamut from a well-detailed and quantified set of instructions for Supreme Sauce (June 2, 1960, for menus effective that date) to this for Golden Omelet with Fried Tomatoes: "Tomatoes on this item are to be more or less of home grown variety. Partly green as well as ripe tomatoes can be used" (June 3, 1964, for menus effective June 11, 1964). A chef could be forgiven for wondering where to find tomatoes that were "more or less home grown."

Still, one wonders whether there was some repository from which these recipes were selected. Lines like "Recipe for this item is again quoted for ready reference" ("General Notice," August 11, 1959, for menus effective August 13, 1959) would beg that question. It would seem that a likely source of recipe ideas would be adaptations of local and regional favorites, as well as the knowledge, traditions, and tricks of the trade brought to the job by the crews themselves. It is known, for example, that some chefs served their own concoctions or adaptations of standard recipes; Capitol Limited Barbecue Sauce *(see* Sauces*)* and Chef George Fulton's variation on the B&O's famous crab cake recipe *(see* Fish and Seafood Dishes*)* are two examples. The explanation may be as simple as realizing that dining car cooks were professionals with long experience cooking the same items day in and day out. No doubt the preparation of these dishes became intuitive as years passed. Indeed some of the instructions in the "General Notices" seem more like gentle reminders of something that might have been overlooked: "One teaspoon of Sherry Wine over each portion" ("General Notice," October 8, 1959,

for menus effective that date) was the only instruction given for Mixed Fresh Fruit in Sherry.

All in all, the "General Notices" depict a more orchestrated approach to cooking, with a greater emphasis on systemwide uniformity, cost, and portion control. Such considerations were less evident in the days when dining car service functioned as an advertisement for superior quality and was not expected to show a profit. They also reveal "B&O food" at the high point of its individuality, when a railroad could become famous for its crab cakes and corn bread pie.

Another classic compendium of recipes, *Eat, Drink, and Be Merry in Maryland,* was originally published in 1932. The cover of a 1998 paperback reissue describes its author, Frederick Philip Stieff, as "scion of an old piano-making Baltimore family, [who] was a celebrated amateur chef and a sort of menu historian. He made a personal crusade of collecting . . . old Maryland recipes." Among the pages of Stieff's classic are found nine recipes credited to the "Dining Car Service, B & O R.R." Several of these are right from the pages of *Old Standard B&O Recipes,* but others are not to be found elsewhere. It is clear that Stieff viewed the B&O with affection and the respect due an old-line Maryland institution. An appendix gives the Bill of Fare for the grand soirée thrown by the B&O in Cincinnati to celebrate the opening of a through route from Baltimore to St. Louis in 1857 (p. 312).

Indeed, *Eat, Drink, and Be Merry* is not a book about B&O cookery, but it is a touching reminder of how well loved the road was in its home state. Pressed by Stieff for recipe contributions, author Christopher Morley responded in part:

But if you really want a recipe from the heart, it would go like this:—On a fine spring or autumn day . . . take one B&O bus from any of several convenient Depots in N.Y. City. Mix with this a North River ferryboat to Jersey City and a comfortable uncrowded ride on a B&O express (4½ hrs. approx.).—Let stand for 2 minutes to cool in Mount Royal Station, the world's most agreeable Railroad halt. (p. 18)

That by itself is worth the price of admission.

What was surely one of the B&O's earlier efforts to publish recipes took the form of a series of pamphlets entitled *Echoes from Colonial Days*. A pamphlet was printed for each of the twenty dining cars in the F-4B series. These were the famous Colonial cars, each bearing the name of a well-known female figure from early American history. The cover featured a picture of the car's namesake and stated the pamphlet's purpose as "Being a little souvenir issued from time to time for the benefit of the guests of The Baltimore and Ohio Railroad Company as a reminder of pleasant memories spent in travelling [sic] in the Dining Car 'Betty Zane'" (in the case of Car 1035).

Included in each pamphlet was a biographical sketch of each colonial heroine along with a period recipe. Several of these recipes were attributed to Martha Washington, after whom Car 1036 was named. They were said to have come from her "manuscript book," *A Book of Cookery*. Several were drawn from another manuscript entitled *Catherine Taylor Her Book 1743*, while others were provided by that consummate party animal Dolley Madison, whose name graced the sides of Car 1044. Renaissance man Thomas Jefferson held forth in the pamphlet for Car 1067, sharing with diners aboard the *Catharine Greene* his method for making Mulled Grape Juice. It is unclear how many of these recipes were actually served aboard B&O dining cars, although at least two—Potato Rolls and Sally Lunn Muffins—made the transition nearly verbatim from *Echoes from Colonial Days* (Cars 1045, the *Betsy Ross*, and 1046, the *Betsy Patterson*, respectively) to the pages of *Old Standard B&O Recipes*.

The B&O's Dining Car and Commissary Department issued a booklet called *Standard à La Carte Prices*, which listed menu items individually, as opposed to table d'hôte, or "tab," service, in which a complete meal

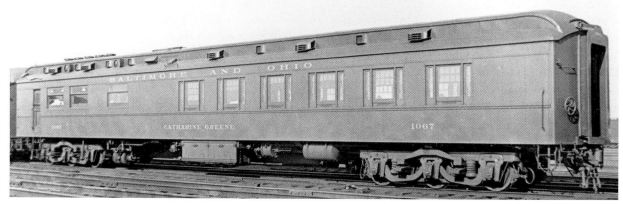

CAR 1067. The last heavyweight steel dining cars built for the B&O were four of the F-4B class, including Car 1067, the *Catharine Greene*, built by the Pullman Company in 1930. Baltimore and Ohio Railroad Historical Society

was offered for one price. This manual was revised on a regular basis, and dishes were arranged in broad categories, beginning with Preserves and Jellies and ending with Beverages. Among the items listed under Salads in the April 15, 1929, edition were "Salads, from The Edgewater Salad Book," which turns out to be *The Edgewater Beach Hotel Salad Book*, yet another publication of the Hotel Monthly Press of Chicago, which was also home to the book's namesake hotel. Author Arnold Shircliffe was caterer at the Edgewater Beach, a title that placed him in charge of all food service at the fabled institution. Writing in the preface to the book's third printing in 1929, publisher John Willy positioned its contents as "suited for people on a diet" and he had "suggested to Mr. Shircliffe that he publish these salads, in particular, as a promoter of the habit of eating for health" (p. vii). He could just as easily have been addressing the concerns of health-conscious eaters eighty years later. A copy of *The Edgewater Beach Hotel Salad Book* in the Baltimore and Ohio Railroad Historical Society archives bears the same rubber stamp, "Property of Baltimore and Ohio R.R. Co.," found in *Eggs in a Thousand Ways*. But its association with actual B&O menu items is sometimes a bit problematical. The B&O was given to naming salads based on their ingredients: "Breast of Chicken Salad, Mayonnaise," "Lettuce, Pimento, and Pineapple Salad," "Head Lettuce Salad." Shircliffe, on the other hand, waxed eloquent with salads named "Beach Walk," "Guillaum," and "Irene Bordoni." Still, that citation in *Standard à la Carte Prices* indicates that B&O chefs could and would serve salads from this book.

Relatively few salad and dressing recipes appear in *Old Standard B&O Recipes* and *B&O Chef's Notes* and those that do vary significantly from the ones in *The Edgewater Salad Book*. Perhaps the B&O wasn't much of a "salad road," at least until the introduction of the

famed "Help Yourself" salad bowl of the 1950s and 1960s at the suggestion of Roy B. White, president of the company. But the fact that research has found three books published by the Hotel Monthly Press that can be associated with the B&O makes one wonder how many more of this firm's volumes might have been found in the Dining Car and Commissary Department's office in Room 214 of Baltimore's Camden Station.

During most of the 1960s Jim Hart worked in the B&O's Dining Car and Commissary Department. At one point he was secretary to Manager James B. Martin. Fortunately Hart kept a number of mementoes from his career on the B&O. Among them was a fragile copy of *Potato Cookery* by Alfred Suzanne and C. Herman Senn, subtitled *300 Ways of Preparing and Cooking Potatoes*. What makes this copy remarkable is the owner's signature on the flyleaf: "E. R. Baugh, Baltimore, Md. Balto. & Ohio R.R." The much-beloved Mr. Baugh—known as Ernie or "The Baughss" to his people—was manager of the Dining Car and Commissary Department at least as early as 1900 and until 1929.

The book opens with a 9-page treatise on "the Cultivation and Cooking of the Potato," which is followed by 103 pages of clearly written recipes that look just as appetizing today as they must have in 1907 when the book was published by the Food & Cookery Publishing Agency in London. Recipes for about a dozen B&O menu items from the early twentieth century have been found in this book, ranging from the mundane—Browned Potatoes—to the exotic—Pommes Soufflé. If a wider sampling of menus from the 1900–1925 period were available, one would doubtless find many other B&O dishes here as well.

Let no one think that in using *Potato Cookery* the B&O had forsaken the Hotel Monthly Press. The title page of this volume is stamped "From John Willy, 443

So. Dearborn Street Chicago." Willy was, of course, owner of the Hotel Monthly Press, and apparently had a bookstore less than a quarter-mile from B&O's Grand Central Station. One can easily imagine Ernie Baugh strolling there to browse after arriving in town on the Capitol Limited.

A WORD ABOUT THE RECIPES IN THIS BOOK

The original sources provide today's culinarian with some wonderful recipes. They were, however, primarily written for restaurant chefs. Charles Fellows is quite literally upfront about this in the preface to *The Culinary Handbook*: "The work is not a cookbook, and does not pretend to teach cookery, yet to those who have already received the fundamental ideas of cookery, it will be found to be the best theoretical teacher obtainable . . ."

Recipes in the *Handbook* are generally confined to a single paragraph, giving only the most basic information about ingredients and preparation. For example, take this entry for Lyonnaise Potatoes: "Cold boiled potatoes, either minced or sliced thinly, seasoned with salt and pepper, mixed with a little chopped parsley and minced fried onions; fried with butter in the form of an omelet" (p. 142). The ingredients are there, the process is there, but no more. A novice cook might well ask, "How much of each ingredient should I use?" While the judgment of the Capitol Limited's chef might be trusted, a small variation in seasoning or preparation can easily transform a dish from delectable to inedible. The same was true of two of the other institutional cookbooks used by the B&O, *Eggs in a Thousand Ways* and *The Edgewater Beach Hotel Salad Book*. These were written for professionals, not for casual or home chefs.

Old Standard B&O Recipes, *B&O Chef's Notes*, and the "General Notices" do a better job of explaining how much of each ingredient is required, but recipes from all of these sources often require a bit of interpretation and interpolation to be of use to the uninitiated. The originals are rife with jargon, some of which is obsolete or different in its current meaning. To an experienced cook, certain terms clearly describe a multi-step process, but a rookie might be left baffled or overwhelmed.

Since this is by its very nature a historical work as well as a cookbook, we begin by showing each recipe in its original form, including nonstandard capitalization, punctuation, usage, and spelling. Where the terse prose of the originals might be unclear or lacking in detail, the authors have added "Chef's Comments" that describe exactly what has to be done in order to cook something that will be palatable. When our own experience or the B&O recipes offered no clue as to amounts or procedures, guidance was sought from similar recipes elsewhere, preferably those from other railroads. Never to the extent, however, that any of the recipes in this book are other than "genuine B&O."

Most of the dishes in this book came from those blissful days before calorie counts, body-mass indices, and life expectancies beyond the age of seventy. Transfats were not an issue. Yet there are options for those who are rightfully concerned about nutrition. Try substituting ingredients or processes. Use canola oil for cooking instead of butter, shortening, or lard. Go easy on the salt. Pan-fry items instead of deep-frying. Sauté instead of pan-frying. Bake instead of sauté. Rest assured the B&O would have done all these things if its dining cars had to cater to the health-conscious patrons of today. Remember the dictum of "moderation, balance, and variety." Select a wide variety of food from these pages and exercise portion control, although this may prove difficult after having tried some of these recipes.

Now turn the page and start cooking the B&O way!

RECIPES

TABLE FOR ONE *(previous page)*. The maitre d' of most brick-and-mortar restaurants would look askance at the use of a four-top table for a solitary dinner guest, but dining car stewards sometimes had no choice. However, they also had no qualms about seating strangers together. Such opportunities to meet interesting people were one of the attractions of rail travel. Here a man begins dinner with a lettuce salad, to be followed by a steak, an oven-browned potato, vegetables, rolls, and gravy. The meal check has been left on the table should he wish to have dessert or an after-dinner drink. The handwriting on the check shows the car number as 1083 on Train 5. This would date the photo between 1954 and 1957, when this car was assigned to the Capitol Limited between Washington and Chicago. Baltimore and Ohio Railroad Museum

APPETIZERS, SNACKS, DRINKS, FRITTERS, AND SANDWICHES

APPETIZERS AND SNACKS

Antipasto

Apple Sauce

Assorted Cold Cuts with Deviled Egg

Assorted Cold Cuts with Hard-Boiled Egg

Clam Juice Cocktail Recipes

Cocktail Sausages

Crab Flake Cocktail

Deviled Smithfield Ham

Salmon and Lemon Jell-o

Sardine Canapés

Sea Foam Candy

Tomato Juice Cocktail

DRINKS

Christmas Cocktail

Frosted Chocolate

FRITTERS

Corn Fritters

Hush Puppies

Pineapple Fritters

SANDWICHES

B&O Egg Sandwich

Club Sandwich

Cold Baked Ham and Swiss Cheese Sandwich on Rye Bread

ANTIPASTO

From *Old Standard B&O Recipes*

A B&O APPETIZER PLATE

Cover flat part of bread plate with tender lettuce leaves, one slice of tomatoes, cut in quarters, placed in center of plate on top of lettuce. Dash of mayonnaise in center of tomatoes with paprika on mayonnaise. Place around the following: 2 Sardines, 1 Bay Mackerel, 2 rolled fillets of anchovies with capers, garnish with two thin strips of pimentoes and two strips of green peppers, a thin slice of lemon.

Chef's Comments

INGREDIENTS FOR 1 SERVING

Lettuce Leaves, as needed
1 slice Tomato
1 tablespoon Mayonnaise
Dash Paprika
2 Sardines
1 Bay Mackerel
2 Anchovy Fillets
Capers, as needed
2 Pimento Strips
2 Green Pepper Strips
1 thin slice Lemon

APPLE SAUCE

From *Old Standard B&O Recipes*

Use green apples and cook with peeling on, when finished cooking, put through a chinese cap, then add sugar to taste. If red apples are used they should be peeled before using.

Chef's Comments

INGREDIENTS FOR 4–6 SERVINGS

6 Green Apples
1 cup Water
2 tablespoons Sugar

Core the apples and chop roughly. Place apples and water in a saucepan, cover and simmer for 30–40 minutes. Apples should be soft and most of the water evaporated.

Then place the apples in a blender or food processor, add the sugar, and process to the desired texture. If a blender or food processor is not handy, the apples can be mashed with a potato masher or by pushing them through a strainer (as B&O chefs did). A "chinese cap" is a large conical strainer.

ASSORTED COLD CUTS WITH DEVILED EGG

From *"B&O General Notice,"* July 5, 1960, for menus effective July 7, 1960

Use sliced cold baked ham (not boiled ham), boiled tongue, breast of turkey, roast beef and slice of cheese. This item is to be attractively garnished. Recipe for deviled egg is as follows: Hard boil six eggs, cool, peel off shell, cut in half lengthwise and remove yolk. Mix yolk with a teaspoon of finely chopped parsley and one-quarter teaspoon salt. Add a dash of Worcestershire Sauce and mix thoroughly. Refill egg whites with mixture. Two halves of egg with each order.

Chef's Comments

INGREDIENTS FOR 6 SERVINGS

6 hard-boiled Eggs
1 teaspoon Parsley, chopped fine
¼ teaspoon Salt
Dash Worcestershire Sauce

AS NEEDED

Baked Ham, sliced
Boiled Tongue, sliced
Breast of Turkey, sliced
Roast Beef, sliced
Cheese, sliced

This recipe does not specify how the plate should be garnished, but a good start would be to line the plate with lettuce or colorful cabbage leaves. Add thin strips of carrots, green, yellow, or red bell peppers, thin slices of onion, etc.

There is more to hard boiling eggs than simply plopping them in boiling water. Fresh eggs can be difficult to peel when hard boiled. For the best results, select eggs that are 5–10 days old and allow them to come to room temperature. Boil plain tap water and use a spoon to lower each egg quickly but gently into the pan. Set a timer for no more than 14 minutes, then plunge the eggs into very cold water. Change the water often until the eggs are completely cool.

ASSORTED COLD CUTS WITH HARD-BOILED EGG

From "B&O General Notice," July 2, 1964, for menus effective July 9, 1964

Use sliced cold baked ham (order imperial ham and bake, slice as needed), breast of turkey, roast beef and slice of American cheese. Slice hard-boiled egg in quarters, lengthwise, two quarters with each order. This item to be attractively garnished.

Chef's Comments

INGREDIENTS, QUANTITIES AS NEEDED

Ham, sliced
Turkey Breast, sliced
Roast Beef, sliced
American Cheese, sliced
Eggs, hard-boiled, sliced

To "attractively garnish" this dish, serve the items listed above on a bed of lettuce leaves.

CLAM JUICE COCKTAIL RECIPES

From *Old Standard B&O Recipes*

RECIPE NUMBER II

To one quart of clam broth add
1 demi tasse Catsup
2 dashes Tabasco Sauce
1 tablespoon Worcestershire Sauce

Dissolve one teaspoon sugar in juice of one lemon,

mix and strain through a fine strainer. Shake with ice, strain into glass, celery salt on top and serve cold.

RECIPE NUMBER 16

⅔ cup Clam Juice
1 tablespoon Lemon Juice
1 tablespoon Tomato Juice
Dash Tabasco Sauce
1 teaspoon Lea & Perrin's Sauce

Add crushed ice and shake well after which a dash of celery salt.

Chef's Comments

The ingredients listed for Recipe Number 11 will make a quart of cocktail, while those shown for Recipe Number 16 make only one drink.

Readers may wonder about the size of a "demi tasse" cup. A genuine B&O demitasse cup in author Tom Greco's collection holds 6 tablespoons of liquid, which is ⅜ cup.

COCKTAIL SAUSAGES
From *Old Standard B&O Recipes*

Wrap with part sliced bacon, season with pepper and salt, dredge with flour, fry until bacon is crisp. Serve on trenched toast.

Chef's Comments

INGREDIENTS, QUANTITIES AS NEEDED

Cocktail Sausages
Bacon Strips, cut in half crosswise
Salt and Pepper
Flour

As each sausage is wrapped with bacon it can be secured with a toothpick.

Sardine Canapés, Deviled Smithfield Ham, and Cocktail Sausages were shown under the heading of "Recipe Number 27." These were "to be placed on a platter and passed to the guest for selection."

One can only wonder about the "trenched toast" mentioned here. It is tempting to call this a typographical error meant to read "frenched toast" until one considers the other components of "Recipe Number 27." Then it is hard to conceive of French toast, that beloved breakfast concoction, being part of what is obviously meant to be a snack tray. More likely the Cocktail Sausages were placed on pieces of toast with crusts removed, perhaps cut into rounds.

No less a light than Auguste Escoffier emphasizes the need to butter all toast used for hors d'oeuvres. This prevents the top side of the toast from drying out, becoming soggy, or curling up in an unattractive fashion.

CRAB FLAKE COCKTAIL
From *B&O Chef's Notes*

Use back fin in lump, chill thoroughly and serve with this cocktail sauce.

1 cup catsup, 2 tablespoons tarragon vinegar, ⅛ teaspoon Tabasco sauce, 1 teaspoon Worcestershire sauce, 1 tablespoon horseradish, 1 tablespoon finely minced celery, 1 tablespoon finely minced onion salt.

DEVILED SMITHFIELD HAM

From *Old Standard B&O Recipes*

Spread on thin triangular toast, garnish border with mashed hard-boiled eggs, white and yolks.

Chef's Comments

INGREDIENTS FOR 16 CANAPÉS

1 can Deviled Ham
4 pieces Toast, crusts trimmed off
Hard-Boiled Eggs, mashed, as needed

Spread the deviled ham onto the toast, then cut each piece of toast into 4 triangles.

SALMON AND LEMON JELL-O

From *Old Standard B&O Recipes*

Boil Salmon, cut into pieces large enough for the Jell-o to surround the fish when placed in a small dish or mould. Place chopped parsley at the bottom of the dish, with slices of lemon at each end of this dish. Put the pieces of fish in the dish. Dissolve plain Jell-o, flavored with lemon juice, pour over the fish and set in a cold place to jell. Serve on lettuce leaves.

Chef's Comments

INGREDIENTS

Salmon Filets, as needed
Parsley, chopped, as needed
Lemon Segments, peeled, 2 per serving
Jell-o, unflavored or lemon, as needed
Lemon Juice (optional), as needed
Lettuce Leaves, as needed for garnish

When the gelatin has set, turn it out onto lettuce leaves arranged on a plate.

It appears that when this recipe was written there was no such thing as lemon-flavored gelatin.

SARDINE CANAPÉS

From *Old Standard B&O Recipes*

RECIPE NUMBER 27

Mash sardines to a paste, spread on thin triangular toast, garnish with sliced stuffed olives.

Chef's Comments

INGREDIENTS FOR 8 CANAPÉS

1 can Sardines
2 pieces Toast, crusts trimmed off
Stuffed Olives, sliced, as needed

In spreading the sardine paste onto the toast, first trim the crusts off a whole slice, then spread the paste; finally cut the toast diagonally into four triangles. Some of the oil from the sardines may be needed to make a spreadable paste. Be sure the bread is well toasted and as thick as possible. Try not to make these up too long before service, or else lightly butter the toast. Otherwise it can become soggy.

Sardine Canapés, Deviled Smithfield Ham, and Cocktail Sausages were shown under the heading of "Recipe Number 27." These were "to be placed on a platter and passed to the guest for selection."

SEA FOAM CANDY
From *B&O Chef's Notes*

Boil 2 cups of sugar, ½ cup of corn syrup and ½ cup of water together until a small ball forms when dropped in cold water. Pour slowly into the beaten whites of 2 eggs and beat constantly with a rotary egg beater until the candy begins to stiffen. Add a cup of broken walnut meats and ¾ of a teaspoon of vanilla. Drop onto an oiled paper and allow to cool and dry somewhat before attempting to remove.

Chef's Comments

INGREDIENTS FOR APPROXIMATELY 25 PIECES

2 cups Sugar
½ cup Corn Syrup
½ cup Water
2 Egg Whites, beaten

A COLONIAL DINING CAR. Pride of the B&O's dining car fleet were the twenty Class F-4B cars built by Pullman between 1923 and 1930. Each was named for a female figure in American colonial history and had its own menu. The photo shows one of the cars in its as-built condition; the menus are visible on each table. Baltimore and Ohio Railroad Museum

APPETIZERS, SNACKS, AND SANDWICHES

1 cup Walnut Meats, broken
¾ teaspoon Vanilla

"Boil 2 cups of sugar, ½ cup of corn syrup and ½ cup of water together until a small ball forms when dropped in cold water," or until the temperature on a candy thermometer reaches 260 degrees, about 10 minutes.

Meanwhile, beat two egg whites in the bowl of a mixer on high speed. When fluffy, "add a cup of broken walnut meats and ¾ of a teaspoon of vanilla."

With the mixer still on high speed, pour the sugar/syrup/water mixture slowly into the egg white/walnut/vanilla mixture "until the candy begins to stiffen," 5–10 minutes.

When finished mixing, work quickly while the mixture is hot and soft. The trick is to do this without getting burned. "Drop onto an oiled paper and allow to cool and dry somewhat before attempting to remove." As the mixture cools, it stiffens and becomes unworkable. On the other hand, some cooks find that on a very humid day the mixture may not stiffen at all.

Use a "No. 40" cookie scoop, which dispenses 1 ⅝ tablespoons onto a cookie sheet covered with baker's parchment paper or waxed paper. A short time in the refrigerator makes the candy easy to remove and serve.

Make only one batch at a time unless an industrial-strength mixer is available that will not overheat as the candy thickens.

A Sweet Subterfuge

Baltimore—January 30, 1947
Memorandum for Mr. Van Horn

Before the war we used to buy our sugar in wrapped tablets with Baltimore and Ohio advertising thereon. During the war it was impossible to get it in this manner but in the past several months the American Sugar Refinery has again started to furnish the wrapped article. Sugar, of course, is still rationed and we are able to draw only what O.P.A. allows us, consequently the Sugar Company is unable to let us have all the sugar they have wrapped with our advertising thereon because the quantity that they have is in excess of our quota.

Apparently they have been disbursing some of our Baltimore and Ohio wrapped sugar to local restaurants because several of our friends have noticed it and mentioned it to me.

This morning I received an inquiry from Mr. J. F. Finnegan, General Superintendent Dining Car Service, Pennsylvania Railroad, sending me a lump of this sugar which one of their local employees picked up in one of the Oriole Cafeterias in Baltimore. He passed it on to headquarters at Philadelphia and they are apparently concerned as to how this came about.

It is good advertising for us and evidently the Pennsylvania Railroad are under the impression that we engineered it that way. *(signed) H. O. McAbee*

NOTE: This was undoubtedly the source of a good laugh on the Pennsylvania Railroad, who apparently didn't put it past the B&O to convince local restaurants to advertise its passenger service. It's interesting to see how the tactics of a relatively weak competitor could interest—and somewhat irritate—the mighty Pennsylvania. This letter was found in the archives of the Baltimore and Ohio Railroad Historical Society, along with the original wrapped sugar cube in a PRR envelope. (Howard O. McAbee was manager of the B&O's Dining Car and Commissary Department; Charles W. Van Horn was vice president of operations and maintenance.)

TOMATO JUICE COCKTAIL

From *Old Standard B&O Recipes* and *B&O Chef's Notes*

1 quart canned Tomatoes
1½ teaspoons (heaping) Sugar
1½ teaspoons Worcestershire Sauce
½ Onion, small, chopped fine
Pinch Red Pepper
¼ teaspoon Salt

Wash the tomatoes through a colander and strain, add ingredients. Let stand until ready to serve and then strain again to eliminate pieces of onion.

Chef's Comments

MAKES 1 QUART

Nowadays all the ingredients can be pureed in a blender to save straining them. If the final product seems too thick, it can be thinned with water or tomato juice. Some may also wish to add more salt.

NOTE: Also listed as Virginia Tomato Juice Cocktail.

CHRISTMAS COCKTAIL

From *Old Standard B&O Recipes*

5 parts Cranberry Juice
1 part Orange Juice
Dash Lemon Juice

Chill and serve in orange juice glass, with mint leaf on top.

Chef's Comments

Add sugar to taste if a sweetened juice is desired.

FROSTED CHOCOLATE

From *Old Standard B&O Recipes*

Cook two squares of chocolate, three tablespoons sugar, one quarter cup boiling water until smooth, stir in one teaspoon of cornstarch, mixed with two tablespoons cold milk. Add the chocolate mixture gradually to four cups of scalded milk, cook fifteen minutes in a double boiler. Two teaspoons vanilla, beat well until foamy.

The chocolate mixture, before adding the four cups of milk, may be allowed to cool and used as needed by adding the necessary quantity of scalded milk and cooking.

Hot frosted chocolate—serve in cup, topped with whipped cream.

Cold frosted chocolate—serve in Ice Tea Glass, line the inside of the glass with whipped cream, and top with the whipped cream when the glass is filled.

(Chill the chocolate before putting in the glass.)

Chef's Comments

INGREDIENTS FOR 1 QUART

4 cups (1 quart) Milk, scalded
¼ cup Water, boiling
2 squares Chocolate
3 tablespoons Sugar
2 teaspoons Milk, cold
1 teaspoon Cornstarch
2 teaspoons Vanilla extract
Whipped Cream, as desired

In a double boiler or a 2-quart saucepan, heat the milk almost to the boiling point. Stir regularly as it warms to prevent it from scorching and sticking to the pan.

In a smaller saucepan, bring the water to a boil and add the chocolate and sugar. Stir until smooth.

In a cup, combine the cornstarch and cold milk and add to the chocolate mixture. Stir to combine thoroughly.

CORN FRITTERS

From *The Culinary Handbook* (Fellows)

Canned corn or cooked corn cut off the cob, pounded, mixed with a little flour, beaten eggs, salt, pepper and a little butter, dropped by spoonfuls into hot fat and fried brown; served as a garniture to chicken, Maryland style, or as a vegetable.

Chef's Comments

INGREDIENTS

15 ounces Corn, frozen, canned, or fresh
1½ tablespoons Butter
2 Eggs, beaten
3 tablespoons Milk
⅜ cup Flour

In *The Frugal Gourmet's Culinary Handbook,* Jeff Smith and Craig Wollam suggest that "[i]f the fritters break apart when frying, you may need to add a bit more flour to the batter." They go on to note that "[t]hese fritters can be deep-fried, but they are better pan-fried with just a little oil" (p. 187). The latter bit of advice provides an easier method for cooking the larger fritters served with some B&O dishes, including Chicken Maryland. For these, one would portion the batter with a ladle instead of a spoon. Ideal temperature for the cooking fat would be 375 degrees. Also be sure not to overload the cooking vessel in order to keep the oil hot enough to cook the fritters quickly without allowing them to become greasy.

HUSH PUPPIES

From *What's Cooking on the B&O?* (circa 1950)

2 cups Cornmeal
1 cup Flour
2 Eggs
1 tablespoon Baking Powder
1 Onion, chopped fine
1 teaspoon Salt
Milk, as needed

Mix all these ingredients, drop in the eggs, then add enough milk to make a medium batter and stir well. Drop the mixture into hot deep fat a spoonful at a time. Remove when outside is crisp and golden.

Chef's Comments

Approximately ¾ cup of milk will yield the desired consistency.

What's Cooking on the B&O? did not see fit to define "a spoonful," and if one uses a tablespoon, this recipe will yield something on the order of 60 fritters. We suggest cutting the amounts shown in half and using a "#40 scoop," which is 1⅝ tablespoons, to measure the batter into the fat. This should yield a more manageable quantity of 20 fritters.

PINEAPPLE FRITTERS

From B&O Southwestern Menu, Thanksgiving, 1904

Two cups of sifted flour, one and one-half teaspoons of baking powder, half teaspoonful of salt, three eggs, whites and yolks beaten separately, three tablespoons sugar, half teaspoon butter, half cup of milk. Pare one large pineapple, cut in slices quarter of an inch thick, then cut each slice in halves. Stir the butter and sugar to a cream, add the yolks of the eggs, then the flour and milk, and last of all the whites of the eggs beaten to a stiff froth. Dip the pieces of pineapple in the batter and drop into boiling fat. When done, dust with powdered sugar and serve.

Chef's Comments

INGREDIENTS FOR 40–50 FRITTERS

1 Pineapple
½ teaspoon Butter
3 tablespoons Sugar
3 Eggs, separated
2 cups Flour, sifted
½ cup Milk
1½ teaspoons Baking Powder
½ teaspoon Salt
Powdered Sugar, as needed

Charles Fellows's *Culinary Handbook* lists much the same recipe using canned pineapple sliced but not cut in half.

This menu states that these were served with wine sauce, which *The Culinary Handbook* describes as a "wine syrup glace sauce." That would indicate wine simmered until reduced to a syrup-like consistency.

NOTE: The Baltimore and Ohio Southwestern Railway and Cincinnati, Hamilton and Dayton Railway were B&O subsidiaries that issued festive holiday menus in 1904 including recipes for several of the dishes listed.

B&O EGG SANDWICH

A B&O RAILROADER'S FAVORITE

This sandwich recipe comes from Grafton, West Virginia. A visit to a signal tower led to a conversation about the railroader's favorite food, an egg sandwich, which he had every day for lunch. An easy and delicious sandwich, popular with everyone, for any occasion!

ITEMS NEEDED

1 or 2 Eggs
2 slices Toast
1–2 tablespoons Butter
Kraft Miracle Whip, as needed
Salt and Pepper, to taste

Melt 1 or 2 tablespoons of butter in an 8-inch non-stick omelet pan or skillet over medium heat. Break open eggs into pan and immediately reduce heat to low. Cook slowly until the whites are completely set and the yolks begins to thicken, but are not hard. Break open yolks and flip over for 15 seconds until cooked.

Do not salt eggs before or during cooking. Salt can cause the eggs to become tough during cooking, so for best results salt eggs (if desired) only after cooking.

Toast bread, place eggs on toast, and spread Kraft Miracle Whip Salad Dressing on one slice of the toast. Salt and pepper to taste and enjoy!

Chef's Comments

Not "technically" a B&O dining car recipe, this recipe must be close to the Fried Egg Sandwich listed on the Capitol Limited's dinner menu dated March 17, 1960.

CLUB SANDWICH

From *Old Standard B&O Recipes*

RECIPE NUMBER 44

In making a club sandwich, use a nice piece white meat breast of chicken, put a lettuce leaf on a piece of toast, then a small portion of mayonnaise on the lettuce, 3 slices of medium bacon, approximately 7½ inches long, cut in half on top of the chicken, then a piece of toast. Place chicken on the lettuce leaf, then duplicate the second layer as you did the first layer, on top of the second layer a slice of tomato, with a small portion of mayonnaise and then top with a piece of toast. The sandwich to be put together with skewers and served.

Chef's Comments

INGREDIENTS FOR 1 SANDWICH

3 slices of Toast
2 Lettuce Leaves
Mayonnaise, as needed
2 slices Chicken Breast, cooked
3 slices Bacon, cooked
1 slice Tomato

To prevent bread used in sandwiches from becoming soggy, consider lightly buttering the inside of each slice before building the sandwich.

COLD BAKED HAM AND SWISS CHEESE SANDWICH ON RYE BREAD

From "B&O General Notice," July 5, 1960, for menus effective July 7, 1960

Serve open face with a slice of ham on one piece of rye bread and a slice of cheese on the other. Serve potato salad on one side of sandwich and two or three slices of tomato on the other. Chefs will exercise care in garnishing, using pickle chips and parsley bouquet to make plate appetizing and appealing. Serve mustard with same.

Chef's Comments

INGREDIENTS FOR 1 SANDWICH

2 slices Rye Bread
1 slice Ham, baked, cold
1 slice Swiss Cheese
½ cup Potato Salad
2–3 slices Tomato
Pickle Chips, as needed
Parsley, fresh, as needed
Mustard, as needed

There was no indication as to whether this was served on one plate or several. One could make a nice presentation by using a large platter, placing the potato salad and tomato slices on a leaf of lettuce next to the sandwich. The mustard would have been served in a small bowl on the side.

B&O CUISINE ON DISPLAY. The Baltimore and Ohio was a much-loved institution. Other notable institutions, such as Gimbel's Department Store, profited by association with the B&O and the excellent quality of its food and service. There is much to see in this photo, which menus help date to the mid-1930s. The banner reads "Gimbel's Pure Food Department presents the Head Chef of the Baltimore and Ohio Railroad making delicious salads as served on the B&O." Taking center stage in the display is the road's famed Blue China, introduced in 1927 for the B&O's centennial. Clovelly silver and a fine selection of B&O glassware complete the setting. In the foreground is a stack of the pamphlet *Echoes from Colonial Days,* free for the taking. Of special note is the Capitol Limited armband on the left sleeve of Chef Joe Press's jacket. Baltimore and Ohio Railroad Historical Society

SALADS AND DRESSINGS

SALADS	SALAD DRESSINGS
Chicken Salad	*Baltimore and Ohio Cream Dressing for Fruit Salad*
Chicken Salad in Quartered Tomato	
Cole Slaw Dressing	*French Dressing*
Crab Flake Salad	*French Dressing, Baltimore and Ohio Style*
Fruit Salad	*Marshmallow Mayonnaise*
Princess Salad	*Nectar Dressing*
Victory Salad	*Russian Dressing*
	Thousand Island Dressing
	Croutons

CHICKEN SALAD

From *Old Standard B&O Recipes*

Use white meat of chicken only, cut in cubes one quarter of an inch thick, and use one part of celery to three parts of chicken diced, bean pot used for measure.

Place chicken and celery in mixing bowl, season with salt and pepper, sugar, half teaspoon vinegar, heaping teaspoon mayonnaise, mix these ingredients thoroughly, mould in bean pot on leaf of lettuce in oatmeal bowl, garnish with quarters of hard-boiled eggs, strips of green peppers, strips of pimentos, top with a teaspoon of mayonnaise and capers.

Chef's Comments

INGREDIENTS FOR I SALAD

FOR THE SALAD

3 ounces Chicken, white meat, ¼-inch dice
1 ounce Celery, ¼-inch dice
1 tablespoon Sugar
½ teaspoon Vinegar
2 teaspoons Mayonnaise
Salt and Pepper, to taste

FOR THE GARNISH

Lettuce Leaves
Hard-Boiled Eggs
Strips of Green Peppers
Strips of Pimentos
Mayonnaise
Capers

The B&O and the Milwaukee Road, among others, gave instructions and even measurements in terms of "bean pots," whatever those were. A coffee cup yields excellent results.

Raw celery can, at times, have a bitter aftertaste. This can be prevented by using a vegetable peeler to remove the dark green outside layer of the celery before dicing.

NOTE: Perhaps a bit unsettling to Americans, the use of the word "mould" in the instructions is a chiefly British variant of the word "mold," and is found this way in many older sources.

WATCHING THE WORLD GO BY. Enjoying a breakfast of toast and coffee on the Capitol Limited, this B&O passenger contemplates the passing countryside. It appears to be a drizzly or rainy morning in northern Indiana or central Maryland, where "the Cap" would be at that early hour. Baltimore and Ohio Railroad Museum

CHICKEN SALAD IN QUARTERED TOMATO

From "B&O General Notice," September 1, 1960

On a bed or nest of lettuce place a whole ripe tomato slit four times from top to stem, but base left intact. Fold back quarters of tomatoes and place therein chicken salad so that it is between petal on lettuce. Garnish with two very thin strips of green pepper across the top. Use two level demi-tasse cups of chicken salad to the order.

Chef's Comments

INGREDIENTS FOR 1 SERVING

Lettuce, as needed to line a salad plate
1 fresh Tomato
¾ cup Chicken Salad
2 strips Green Pepper

COLE SLAW DRESSING

From *B&O Chef's Notes* and *Old Standard B&O Recipes*

2 cups Vinegar
4 Whole Raw Eggs
1 tablespoon Dry Mustard
2 cups Sugar
Pinch Salt

Mix dry ingredients together well. Stir in the eggs thoroughly. Place in a double boiler, and add vinegar, whipping it until the dressing assumes a jelly-like consistency. The cabbage should be shaved thinly in one direction, and these sections cut in fine pieces.

Chef's Comments

INGREDIENTS FOR 6–8 SERVINGS

¾ teaspoon Dry Mustard
½ cup Sugar
Pinch Salt
½ cup Vinegar
1 Egg, beaten
1 pound Cabbage

Combine the cabbage and dressing; chill and serve.

It is a safe bet that most B&O diners were not (and many homes are not) equipped with a double boiler. One can be "made," however, by placing a smaller diameter pot or bowl within a larger pot. Bring the large pot of water to a boil. Combine the dressing ingredients in the smaller saucepan or a stainless steel bowl. With one hand, hold the pot or bowl just above the water. With the other hand whip the ingredients as specified. This is a handy method in that one can remove the dressing from the heat at any time to check its consistency and return it easily if necessary.

CRAB FLAKE SALAD

From *The Edgewater Beach Hotel Salad Book* (Shircliffe)

Line a bowl with white inner leaves of lettuce. Place an equal amount of large crab meat flakes and small diced hearts of celery. Pour over a creamy mayonnaise made with lemon juice instead of vinegar. Garnish with quartered hard-boiled eggs. Season crab meat before adding mayonnaise.

Chef's Comments

One can indeed make mayonnaise "from scratch," but it is a tedious process. Try adding a bit of lemon juice to ready-made mayonnaise to get the same effect.

FRUIT SALAD

From *The Edgewater Beach Hotel Salad Book* (Shircliffe)

Line a bowl with lettuce. Place cubed pineapple, pear and apple on bottom. Alternate on top of apple and pineapple, two slices of orange and two of grapefruit. Garnish with hot-house grapes, fresh cherries or strawberries, or any small fruit in season. Maiden Blush, French or mayonnaise dressing.

The term "excellent customer service" is overused these days and has almost become meaningless. Here is how the B&O did it in 1951, although one could suspect an ulterior motive, given that Manager Howard O. McAbee was writing to a member of the road's board of directors. Even so, this is a remarkable offer to a passenger who had enjoyed what he had eaten on the B&O.

———————

May 4, 1951

Mr. J. D. Biggers, President
Libbey-Owens-Ford Glass Co.
Toledo, Ohio

Dear Mr. Biggers:
I have your letter of May 2 about fresh crabmeat.
We have just started to carry crabmeat on our May menus and are glad to know that you like it. The season opens legally in Maryland in April but we shy away from it on the April menus because it is not always up to top quality in the beginning. Crabmeat can be had all year round in Virginia waters but the crabs have to be dug from the mud where they hibernate for the winter. For this reason you will very often find streaks of mud with the meat in off season.

We purchase our crabmeat from Charles W. Howeth & Bro., Crisfield, Md., which is the center of the crab industry. We get a shipment daily by Express which arrives Washington early in the morning, representing the catch of the previous day. We buy exclusively what is termed "Back Fin Lump" which at present is selling for $1.50 per pound.

I shall be very happy to send in care of the Steward on the "AMBASSADOR" any quantity you might wish at any time. He could put it off at Toledo at 6:30 A.M. (E.S.T.) in care of the Station Master, or perhaps you might have some other plan of picking it up.

As an alternate arrangement, we could send it from Cincinnati on Train 54 which is due Toledo 5:15 P.M. (E.S.T.). The shipment from Cincinnati would be just as fresh as that which you would get from Washington for the reason that we ship daily to Cincinnati on Train 1 arriving there 7:15 A.M. This would give ample opportunity to have the meat transferred to Train 54 which does not depart until 12:50 P.M.

Please let me know your wishes as we will be very happy to accommodate you.

Sincerely,
H. O. McAbee

No doubt, you know about our B&O "Help Yourself" salad bowl, where before dinner the kitchen and the steward made sure it was presented graciously as a work of art. The bowl would be passed from one table to the next with the tongs, the guest would take the amount of salad he or she wanted and return the tongs to the bowl, where it would then be delivered to the next table by the waiter.

The guest at that table placed his salad on his plate, but after taking a bite or two, he started chewing on the first guest's used chewing gum, much to his chagrin. The "Help-Yourself" Salad Bowl has disappeared from the dining car scene with a boost from the U.S. Public Health Service!

Chef's Comments

INGREDIENTS AS NEEDED FOR I SALAD

Lettuce
Pineapple, cubed
Pear, peeled, cubed
Apple, peeled, cubed
2 Orange Sections
2 Grapefruit Sections
Grapes, Cherries, or Strawberries, as needed for
 garnish

In an "Author's Note" to this recipe, Shircliffe adds, "A fruit salad can be made out of any combination of fruits and can be cubed, shredded or sectioned; the cubes are preferable. Fruits are blood, bone and nerve builders." Wise words even today.

PRINCESS SALAD

From *The Edgewater Beach Hotel Salad Book* (Shircliffe)

On a bed of lettuce, place a peeled slice of ripe tomato; on top of tomato place five spears of asparagus tips.

Band tips with two strips of julienned pimentos and one green pepper.

Chef's Comments

INGREDIENTS FOR I SALAD

Lettuce, as needed
1 Tomato, ½-inch slice
5 spears Asparagus Tips, cooked
2 Pimentos, ¼-inch slices
1 Green Pepper, ¼-inch slice

Place several lettuce leaves on the plate and the slice of tomato in the center.

The asparagus tips (about the same length as the circumference of the tomato) are then "stacked" in two layers on top of the tomato, three spears on the bottom, two on top.

When slicing the green pepper, do so horizontally, in order to get a curved band. Place this around the center of the stack of asparagus tips and place the sliced pimentos between the center and ends of the tips. This should give the appearance that the bundle of asparagus tips is "tied" with strips of green pepper and pimento.

Fortunately, *The Edgewater Salad Book* had a number of illustrations, one of which showed how this attractive salad went together.

To peel a tomato, take a sharp knife and cut a large X in the skin centered on the bottom of the tomato. Place the tomato in boiling water for 30–45 seconds, then place in ice water until completely cooled. The skin will peel right off.

VICTORY SALAD
From *The Edgewater Beach Hotel Salad Book* (Shircliffe)

In a nest of lettuce, place a slice of pineapple. Cover the pineapple with cream cheese mixed with ground nuts, chopped celery, red and green peppers. Make a rosette of cheese in the center and insert a small American flag. Garnish border with sprigs of cress.

Chef's Comments

INGREDIENTS FOR 1 SALAD

Lettuce, as needed
1 slice of Pineapple
Cream Cheese
Watercress
Nuts, ground, any kind
Celery, chopped fine
Red Bell Pepper, chopped fine
Green Bell Pepper, chopped fine

Author Arnold Shircliffe calls this "A Fourth of July salad—a novelty salad—a salad to be used for any victory dinner or luncheon."

The B&O offered Victory Salad on a "Cold Dishes and Salads" menu during the 1920s, served with French dressing and/or mayonnaise. There is no documentation of the use of an American flag on the B&O's salads.

BALTIMORE AND OHIO CREAM DRESSING FOR FRUIT SALAD
From *Old Standard B&O Recipes* and *B&O Chef's Notes*

RECIPE NUMBER 9

1½ Individual Cakes Cream Cheese. Sweet Cream of sufficient amount to make these two ingredients of the consistency of heavy cream. Pinch of salt. 1 teaspoon sugar, 1 tablespoon mayonnaise.

Dissolve the cream cheese and sweet cream thoroughly to avoid lumps, then add the balance of the ingredients. Serve in a gravy boat with an order of fruit salad.

Chef's Comments

INGREDIENTS FOR 1 SERVING

3 ounces of Cream Cheese
Sweet Cream, as needed
Pinch of Salt
1 teaspoon Sugar
1 tablespoon Mayonnaise

FRENCH DRESSING
From *B&O Chef's Notes*

1 pint olive oil, 1 pint malt vinegar, 2 teaspoonful of sugar, 2 teaspoonful of paprika, 1 kernel of garlic, juice

of 1 orange. Put in bottle and shake and remove garlic after 1 hour. Shake well before using.

Chef's Comments

INGREDIENTS FOR 2 CUPS

1 cup Olive Oil
1 cup Malt Vinegar
2 teaspoons Sugar
2 teaspoons Paprika
1 clove Garlic
¼ cup Orange Juice (juice of one orange)

FRENCH DRESSING, BALTIMORE AND OHIO STYLE

From *Old Standard B&O Recipes*

3 cups Olive Oil, 1 cup Vinegar, Juice of one orange, 1 Tablespoon Catsup, 1 Tablespoon Sugar, 1 Teaspoon Worcestershire Sauce, 1 Teaspoon Dry Mustard, 1 Teaspoon Salt, ¼ Teaspoon Pepper (white), dash paprika.

Drop in one small onion for seasoning, only allow same to remain in contents for 15 minutes. Mix dry ingredients, then add the orange juice, then beat oil and vinegar together in dry mixture until properly mulsified, or you can whip this with an egg whip. Shake well before using.

Chef's Comments

INGREDIENTS FOR 2 CUPS

1 cup Olive Oil
⅓ cup Vinegar
¼ cup Orange Juice (juice of one orange)

1 teaspoon Catsup
1 teaspoon Sugar
¼ teaspoon Worcestershire Sauce
¼ teaspoon Dry Mustard
¼ teaspoon Salt
Dash of White Pepper
Dash of Paprika
½ Onion

This is the "original" type of French dressing, more of a vinegar-and-oil concoction than the thick stuff found in most grocery stores.

When the writer of this recipe typed "mulsified" he meant "emulsified," which is the complete combination of two ingredients that do not normally mix. In this case those ingredients are the vinegar and olive oil.

MARSHMALLOW MAYONNAISE

From *Old Standard B&O Recipes*

Boil one pint of Cream to six ounces of Marshmallow, adding yolks of four eggs, ¼ teaspoon mustard, ¼ teaspoon of salt. Boil together in oatmeal steamer. Afterward chill.

Whip one quart XX cream mixing with above, slowly adding juice of one lemon and serve over fruit salad.

Chef's Comments

INGREDIENTS FOR 2 CUPS

½ cup Cream
1½ ounces Marshmallows
1 Egg Yolk

Dash of Mustard
Dash of Salt
1 cup Whipping Cream
¾ teaspoon Lemon Juice

Any pan will substitute for an oatmeal steamer.

NECTAR DRESSING

From *Old Standard B&O Recipes*

3 ounces Cream Cheese
2 tablespoons Honey
¾ cup Olive Oil
1½ tablespoons Lemon Juice
1 Lemon Rind, grated
¾ teaspoon Salt
Dash of Cayenne Pepper

Beat the cheese, honey, lemon juice and seasoning until smooth, add oil slowly, beat well until blended, chill.

Chef's Comments

MAKES 8–10 SERVINGS

This is an example of an "emulsion," in which ingredients are combined that normally do not mix (think of oil and water).

RUSSIAN DRESSING

From *Old Standard B&O Recipes*

¼ cup Mayonnaise, ¼ cup Chili Sauce, 2 Tablespoons

Catsup. Mix these ingredients thoroughly and serve with hearts of lettuce or with other salad vegetables.

THOUSAND ISLAND DRESSING

From *Old Standard B&O Recipes*

½ cup Mayonnaise, 1 Tablespoon Tarragon Vinegar, ½ cup of whipping cream, 1 chopped hard-cooked egg, 1 tablespoon chopped green pepper, 1 tablespoon chopped onion, ½ teaspoon minced parsley, 2 tablespoons chili Sauce. Mix the ingredients in the order given and serve with lettuce and other salad vegetables.

Chef's Comments

INGREDIENTS FOR 1½ CUPS

½ cup Mayonnaise
1 tablespoon Tarragon Vinegar
½ cup Whipping Cream
1 Hard-Boiled Egg, chopped
1 tablespoon Green Bell Pepper, chopped fine
1 tablespoon Onion, chopped fine
½ teaspoon Parsley, minced
2 tablespoons Chili Sauce

CROUTONS

From *Old Standard B&O Recipes*

Cut bread into dices about ¼-inch square. Brown in frying pan in butter. Keep hot until served.

SOUPS

Baltimore and Ohio Clam Chowder

Consommé Recipes

Fish Chowder, Baltimore and Ohio Style

Leek Soup

Cream of Leek Soup

Lentil Soup

Old-Fashioned Navy Bean Soup

Onion Soup au Gratin

Old-Fashioned Vegetable Soup

BALTIMORE AND OHIO CLAM CHOWDER

From *Old Standard B&O Recipes*

1 gallon Clear Stock
2 quarts Clams, chopped, with liquor
1 pound Tomatoes
2 Onions
4 ounces Salt Pork, sautéed in butter
1 stalk Celery, cut fine
6 Cloves
6 Bay Leaves
1 basting spoon Chili Sauce
1 teaspoon Worcestershire Sauce
6 Raw Potatoes cut in small dice

Make a roux, 2 basting spoons flour, add 6 ounces butter, cook until crumbled, then add the above ingredients, and cook one hour.

Chef's Comments

INGREDIENTS FOR 1 GALLON

2 tablespoons Butter
2 tablespoons Flour
2 quarts Fish Stock
1 quart Clams, chopped, with liquor
¼ pound Tomatoes, peeled, ¼-inch dice
½ Onion, ¼-inch dice
2 ounces Salt Pork
½ stalk Celery, ¼-inch dice
3 Cloves
3 Bay Leaves
½ tablespoon Chili Sauce
½ teaspoon Worcestershire Sauce
3 Potatoes, raw, peeled, ¼-inch dice

Canned chopped clams can be bought at most grocery stores. The "liquor" is simply the juice in which the clams are packed.

To peel tomatoes, take a sharp knife and make a large X-shaped cut on the bottom through the skin only. Be sure that these cuts wrap around the sides of the tomato. Place each tomato in boiling water for 30–45 seconds, then drop in an ice-water bath until cooled. The skin will then peel right off.

When the writer of this recipe instructed that the roux be cooked "until crumbled," he was recognizing that a roux made of equal amounts of flour and water will, if left mostly undisturbed during cooking, form a surface texture that appears crumbly. This indicates that the roux is ready to use after a brief stir. For a "white" soup such as this, the roux would not be browned but would be cooked just long enough to eliminate the taste of the flour, about 5–10 minutes.

CONSOMMÉ RECIPES

From *The Culinary Handbook* (Fellows)

Consommé—name applied in cookery to a strong clarified soup, the different consommés seen on bills of fare, called Consommé à la this and à la that, simply terrorizes the guests as well as the young cook, and are mere significant of the different garnitures that are placed in the soup or plate before being served, or else the flavor of the principal meat of which the consommé was made. The ingredients for a good general everyday consommé is given here.

Consommé Ingredients—To make five gallons (which quantity should serve 100 guests) take fifteen pounds of LEAN beef trimmings, six medium-sized peeled carrots, same of onions, twelve leeks, two heads of celery, a bunch of parsley and a gallon of tomatoes all chopped fine, mix with them after chopping, one tablespoon of whole peppers, twelve cloves, six bay leaves, eighteen beaten whites of eggs and their shells, a little salt, then add stirring all the time, eight gallons of good stock free from fat, COLD, or if hot, place a chunk of ice in the saucepan before pouring in the stock. Next, place saucepan on the range, add three hens (they can be used as salads after), fetch to a slow simmer and reduce to about five gallons in four hours, then strain through a consommé towel (double cheese cloth).

Chef's Comments

Fellows's opening remarks illustrate his disdain for the pervasive French influence in the culinary arts at the turn of the twentieth century. Still he finds himself unable to avoid French terms entirely, including the word consommé itself. And although he does not specify the stock from which consommé is to be made, it is invariably started with beef stock minus the addition of "three hens."

Fellows's emphasis on starting with cold stock is well advised. Cold liquid gives up its impurities more readily, whereas hot liquid coagulates the impurities, clouding the consommé. The ingredients added to the stock are called *clearmeat* or *clarification,* and they rise to the top of the pot to form a *raft;* the albumen in the egg whites serves as a glue to hold the raft together and collect bits of debris in the stock, provided that the cooking temperature does not exceed a gentle simmer. In the traditional process, one clears a hole in the raft to allow the liquid to bubble through and help maintain clarity.

Nowadays, consommé is usually purchased in canned or powdered form, and the home chef can obtain a much smaller quantity than that required to "serve 100 guests." No doubt the B&O made consommé "from scratch" in the Baltimore commissary, but one can be equally certain that the road switched to the ready-made variety when it became available.

Below is a sampling of some of the many types of consommé served aboard B&O dining cars.

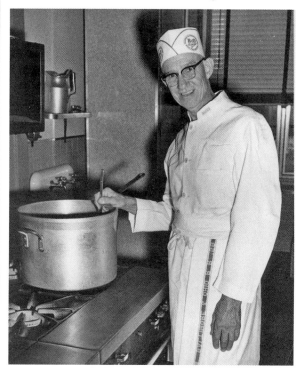

COMMISSARY CHEF. Rather little information is available regarding the range of work done at the B&O's online commissaries, but this photo, labeled "B&O commissary employee," was clearly not taken on a train. If correct, this would indicate that prep work was done here for the dining cars. This smiling chef might be cooking soup or preparing a sauce. The side towel tucked into his apron dates this photo circa 1958. Baltimore and Ohio Railroad Historical Society

CONSOMMÉ PRINCESSE

From "B&O General Notice," January 6, 1961

Add a small amount of finely diced (cooked) chicken and green peas to regular consommé.

CONSOMMÉ ROYALE

From "B&O General Notice," November 5, 1963

Hot consommé with bits of custard dropped in same before serving.

CONSOMMÉ VERMICELLI

From "B&O General Notice," July 8, 1963

Consommé with vermicelli, a type of macaroni.

FISH CHOWDER, BALTIMORE AND OHIO STYLE

From *Old Standard B&O Recipes*

Can be made with either fresh or salted fish, if the salt, soak it overnight. Blanche it twice so as to extract the salt, fry some small pieces of salt pork, with some onion minced fine, when of a light brown color, remove from the fire, add the fish in flakes (freed from bones), some raw peeled potatoes cut in squares, a seasoning of thyme, marjoram and pepper, and a small can of tomatoes. Fill the saucepan half full of fish broth, put on the lid and let it simmer for an hour. Take out and work in without breaking the potatoes an equal quantity of cream sauce, add a little chopped parsley and serve.

After the cream sauce is put in, it must not be allowed to boil again or it will curdle.

Chef's Comments

INGREDIENTS FOR 1¼ QUARTS

1 tablespoon Butter or Cooking Oil
4 ounces Salt Pork, ½-inch slices
1 Medium Onion, ¼-inch dice
2 Fish fillets, flaked
2 Small Potatoes, raw, peeled, ½-inch dice
1 14½ ounce can Tomatoes
1 quart Fish Stock
⅔ teaspoon Thyme
⅔ teaspoon Marjoram
⅔ teaspoon Black Pepper
1 pint Cream Sauce
3 teaspoons Parsley, minced

To blanch salted fish, place it in a pot of boiling water for 2–3 minutes and drain. Start again with fresh water and repeat the procedure.

LEEK SOUP

From *Old Standard B&O Recipes*

Into a quart of mutton or chicken stock add six leeks and simmer for an hour, rub through a chinese cap. Return to the fire and thicken with two tablespoons flour. Rub to a paste with two tablespoons butter. Bring a pint of milk to the boiling point, and stir into the soup. Season with salt, white pepper, and a tablespoon of minced parsley.

Chef's Comments

INGREDIENTS FOR 1¼ QUARTS

1 quart Chicken or Mutton Stock
6 Leeks, sliced (white part only)
2 tablespoons Flour
2 tablespoons Butter
1 pint Milk
Salt and White Pepper, to taste
1 tablespoon Parsley, minced

Simmer the leeks in the stock for 1 hour, then gradually stir in the flour and add the butter. Bring the milk to the boiling point and stir it into the soup.

Purée in a blender or food processor and season with salt and white pepper. Ladle into a bowl and add the minced parsley.

Clearly this recipe was written long before the advent of blenders and food processors. Anyone who tries rubbing ingredients through a chinese cap (a conical strainer) or a colander will develop a tremendous amount of respect for those old-time B&O chefs.

Takeout on the B&O?

From *Baltimore and Ohio* magazine, November 1927

(B&O dining car Steward) "Dashing Dick" Dasch declares that the opportunity given to passengers to purchase the new colonial chinaware makes it possible for our guests to order a meal as before, but places them in a quandary as to whether to eat it in the dining car or carry off the entire service, dishes and all, and eat it at home.

CREAM OF LEEK SOUP

From *Old Standard B&O Recipes*

Use veal or chicken stock, have mixture ready when leeks are soft. Strain in stock and put in half as much boiling milk. Season with salt, pepper and catsup.

Chef's Comments

INGREDIENTS FOR 1¼ QUARTS

6 Leeks, sliced (white part only)
2 tablespoons Butter
1 quart Chicken or Veal Stock
1 pint Milk
Catsup, to taste
Salt and Pepper, to taste

In a 2-quart pot (or larger), sauté the leeks in the butter until soft.

Meanwhile, in separate pans, bring the stock and the milk to a boil.

Stir the stock into the leeks, followed by the milk. Simmer for 5–10 minutes and "season with salt, pepper and catsup."

LENTIL SOUP

From *Old Standard B&O Recipes*

Lentils boiled until tender in white stock with leeks, celery, parsley and a piece of salt pork, when done, pork removed and soup lightly thickened, then run through the tamis, served with frankfurters, cut in small pieces, served the same as you would croutons.

INGREDIENTS FOR 2 QUARTS

2 cups Lentils
2–2½ quarts Chicken or Beef Stock
1 Leek, ¼-inch dice
2 spears Celery, ¼-inch dice
1 tablespoon Fresh Parsley, minced (or ½ tablespoon Dried Parsley)
1 piece Salt Pork
4 Frankfurters, cooked, ¼-inch dice

Place all ingredients except frankfurters in a pot and simmer for 1½–2 hours.

Remove salt pork and purée the soup in a blender or food processor until smooth, and add frankfurters.

A tamis is a large drum sieve, most often used today for sifting large amounts of ingredients. The B&O's kitchen crews would most certainly have applauded modern blenders and food processors, which can do the same thing in a matter of seconds.

Old-Fashioned Navy Bean Soup

From *Old Standard B&O Recipes*

Soak Navy Beans overnight in lukewarm water, boil until done with a ham shank, or smoked bacon, leeks, a few cloves, salt and pepper for flavoring. Brown two spoonsful of flour and butter (almost burn) add some of the bean stock and mix with the beans. Before serving add boiled diced potatoes.

INGREDIENTS FOR 3–4 QUARTS

1 pound Navy Beans
5 quarts Water
1 Ham Shank or Hock
1 Potato, large, ½-inch dice
1 Leek, ¼-inch slices
6 tablespoons Butter
6 Cloves, whole
6 tablespoons Flour
Salt and Pepper, to taste

Soak the Navy Beans overnight in lukewarm water and drain, placing them in a large pot with a ham shank, or smoked bacon, leeks, a few cloves, salt, and pepper.

Add the water and simmer until the vegetables are tender, 1½–2 hours.

As the soup begins to simmer, make a roux by melting the butter in a saucepan over medium-low heat and adding the flour, stirring until completely blended and smooth. Brown the roux by leaving it over medium-low heat, stirring occasionally. This should prevent the roux from burning, but keep a close eye on it.

About 15 minutes before removing the soup from the stove, add the diced potatoes and continue to simmer until they are tender.

Take about ½ cup of the soup from the pot and gradually add it to the roux until thoroughly combined. Then stir this into the soup to thicken it. Remove the ham shank and serve the soup.

When the ham bone is removed from the soup, any meat left on the bone can be pulled and returned to the pot. If bacon is used instead, cut it into small pieces before adding it to the other ingredients, and double the amount of butter and flour to thicken the soup.

Although most recipes like this one will advise soaking the beans overnight, this step can be eliminated. Count on using a little more water (which can be added as the soup simmers), as well as 20–30 minutes more simmering time.

Onion Soup au Gratin
From *Old Standard B&O Recipes*

3 tablespoons Butter
10 ounces Onions, shredded thin
1 quart Consommé

Sauté the onions in butter slowly until a rich brown, add the consommé and cook for five minutes. Sprinkle a quarter slice of toast, cut diamond shaped, with parmesan cheese, place in the oven a minute to slightly melt. Put the pieces of toast as prepared above in the bottom of the soup cup before putting in the soup.

Chef's Comments

MAKES 1 QUART

This may sound simple, but read that first sentence again: "Sauté the onions in butter slowly. . . ." This means over a very low flame, in order to avoid burning them. Allow at least 90 minutes for this step, more if possible. The longer the onions cook, the better the taste will be.

The onions will "shrink" to a rather small volume as they cook; the amount shown can be doubled for a very hearty and onion-filled soup.

Notice too that no seasonings are listed. It is our opinion that this dish fairly cries out for salt, which can be added to taste.

Old-Fashioned Vegetable Soup
From *Old Standard B&O Recipes*

1 Meat Bone, full of meat
1 can Tomatoes
1 teacup Okra
1 stalk Celery
2 Carrots
½ Onion
1 cup Cabbage
Salt and Pepper, to taste

Add about three or more quarts of water to the ingredients. Boil slowly 1½ hours, add salt and pepper, about twenty minutes before taking off of the stove, add rice or a few tablespoons of oatmeal if thickening is desired.

Chef's Comments

INGREDIENTS FOR 3 QUARTS

4 quarts Water
1 Meat Bone, "full of meat"
1 24-oz can Tomatoes, sliced
4 ounces Okra, ½-inch slices
1 stalk Celery, ½-inch dice
2 Carrots, peeled, ½-inch dice
½ Onion, ½-inch dice
1 cup Cabbage, shredded fine
1 cup Rice or Oatmeal

To improve the color and taste of the soup, use a meat bone that has been cooked in some manner. This would be an excellent use for a leftover.

MENU AS POSTCARD. On December 3, 1951, a B&O passenger not only addressed this menu and sealed it shut with small pieces of tape but also affixed a railroad-themed postage stamp and mailed it from the Railway Post Office car of Train 10, the Washington Express, between Chicago and Pittsburgh. Tom Greco collection

BAKED GOODS

Corn Muffins

Ginger Muffins

Maryland Spoon Bread

Maryland Spoon Bread (Cincinnatian)

Potato Rolls

Sally Lunn Muffins

Shortcake Biscuits

CORN MUFFINS
From Old Standard B&O Recipes

2 cups Corn Meal
2 cups White Flour
1 teaspoon Salt
2 cups Milk
3 Eggs, beaten
1 tablespoon Sugar
2 tablespoons Butter, melted
1 tablespoon Baking Powder

Mix the above ingredients gradually to avoid lumps in the batter, add the baking powder last and beat up well. Place in muffin rings. Bake 20 minutes in a hot oven.

Chef's Comments

Notwithstanding the above instructions, mix the batter only until the dry ingredients are just moistened, as over-mixing muffin batter results in toughness.
Preheat the oven to 450 degrees. This recipe makes 30 muffins.

GINGER MUFFINS
From Old Standard B&O Recipes

MAKES 40 MUFFINS

1 cup Butter
1 cup Sugar
4 cups Flour
1 teaspoon Salt
1 teaspoon Baking Soda
1 teaspoon Baking Powder

2 tablespoon Ginger
1 tablespoon Cinnamon
1 cup Molasses
4 Eggs
1 cup Sour Cream
¼ cup Raisins

Mix all the ingredients together, beat until light, grease muffin rings; fill them half full of batter. Set for five minutes before baking. Bake 20 minutes in moderate oven.

Chef's Comments

Preheat oven to 375 degrees.
Individual tastes may prefer more raisins for this recipe.

MARYLAND SPOON BREAD
From What's Cooking on the B&O? (circa 1950)

½ cup Yellow Cornmeal
1 teaspoon Bacon Drippings
1 teaspoon Sugar
½ teaspoon Salt
½ cup Water, boiling
1 Egg, beaten
1 cup Sour Milk or Buttermilk
1 teaspoon Water, cold
¼ teaspoon Baking Soda

Put the cornmeal, bacon drippings, sugar and salt into a baking dish. Pour the boiling water over them gradually and beat well. When the mixture is cool, add the egg (beaten) and the milk and the soda and one teaspoon of cold water. Beat the whole mixture well. Bake in a deep dish for 20 minutes in a medium oven at 350 degrees.

If you wish to use sweet milk, add one teaspoon of baking powder instead of soda. This recipe will serve about eight hearty eaters.

Chef's Comments

The texture of spoon bread should be rather like a pudding or custard.

In order to obtain the full rising power of the baking powder or soda, combine with the other ingredients and beat immediately before placing the dish in the oven.

And . . . don't believe that line about feeding "eight hearty eaters." We have been lucky to get three or four decent servings out of this recipe.

MARYLAND SPOON BREAD (CINCINNATIAN)
From *Eat, Drink, and Be Merry in Maryland* (Stieff)

Two cups of grits or small hominy or rice boiled, one teaspoonful of salt, thin while hot, put in a piece of butter the size of an egg. Four eggs. Beat the yolks and whites of the eggs separately, thin the grits and milk until it is like thick cream, stir in the yolks of the eggs and half a pint of cornmeal.* Fold in the whites of the eggs last and bake in a deep buttered dish about three-quarters of an hour. Cover if it browns too fast.

*The cornmeal used by the B&O is ground by water in one of the historic old mills of Maryland.

Chef's Comments

INGREDIENTS FOR 2 SERVINGS

1 cup Grits, Hominy, or Rice, cooked
½ teaspoon Salt
½ tablespoon Butter
¼ cup Milk
2 Eggs, separated
½ cup Cornmeal

Place the cooked grits, hominy, or rice in a casserole or baking dish and, while still hot, mix in the salt and butter. Add the milk gradually until the grits are thinned to the consistency of cream. (The entire amount shown may not be needed.)

Separate the eggs, beat the yolks, and add them and the cornmeal to the grits. Beat the egg whites until stiff but not dry and fold them into the mixture. Bake at 350 degrees for 45 minutes, covering if the spoon bread browns too quickly.

Forty-five minutes in the oven yields a "solid" bread. For a custard or pudding-like consistency more characteristic of spoon bread, bake for 20–30 minutes.

This recipe was given to dining car guests on the Cincinnatian, most likely between 1947 and 1950, when that train ran between Baltimore and Cincinnati. The reverse of the 5 by 7-inch card plugged the B&O's reputation for "good eating."

Judging from other recipe sources, the ingredients and procedure shown here (aside from the baking time) seem more typical of spoon bread than the recipe given in the booklet *What's Cooking on the B&O?* published around 1950. Doubtless the constraints of time, space, and heavy demand prompted the railroad to develop the simpler method listed in *What's Cooking*. Either way, the results are well worth the effort.

Frederick Stieff secured this recipe from Mrs. Charles Sterett Grason, Cornwalys Cross Manor, Beechville, St. Mary's County. Cornwalys Cross Manor, the oldest house in Maryland, was built in 1642 by Sir Thomas Cornwalys, lieutenant governor of the province under Leonard Calvert, Lord Baltimore. It was named Cornwalys Cross because of the planting of a cross in memory of a friend who was killed by accident by Sir Thomas Cornwalys. Mrs. Grason is a direct descendant of the builder.

POTATO ROLLS

From *Old Standard B&O Recipes*

One cup of yeast, one cup of flour, one cup of mashed potatoes. Set these to rise. When light add two eggs, cup of sugar, one cup of lard, some salt, make up stiff. Let stand until light. Roll out until one half inch thick, then cut with a round cutter. Butter. Let stand until very light. Bake in a hot oven ten minutes. These are the old Maryland Potato Rolls.

Chef's Comments

INGREDIENTS FOR 24 ROLLS

½ cup Mashed Potatoes*
¼ cup Potato Water
½ cup Lard or Shortening
1½ teaspoon Salt
1½ teaspoon Yeast, active dry
¼ cup Water, warm
1 Egg, beaten

4 cups Flour, sifted
½ cup Sugar

*A 4-ounce potato will yield the ½ cup required.

Combine the hot fresh mashed potatoes, water in which the potatoes were boiled, lard or shortening, and salt. Mix until the hot potatoes and water have melted the lard or shortening.

When cooled to lukewarm, add the yeast, egg, and 2 cups of the flour, and mix well. Gradually add more flour, saving ½ cup to sprinkle on the countertop or to add to the dough if it needs to be stiffer.

Sprinkle flour on the work surface and knead the dough by hand 5–8 minutes until smooth. Then place the dough in a lightly greased bowl and cover with a damp dishtowel for 1½–2 hours.

Divide the dough into 1½-ounce pieces, rolling each into a ball. Place on a lightly greased baking sheet and cover again with the damp towel for 60 minutes. Preheat oven to 400 degrees.

Bake for 10–12 minutes.

The B&O's twenty F-4B-class dining cars were built between 1923 and 1930. These Colonial cars were each named for a famous woman in America's early history. The series of pamphlets produced for each car, entitled *Echoes from Colonial Days,* included a picture and biographical sketch of the woman for whom the car was named, along with a recipe, often one connected with the car's namesake. Although the Potato Roll recipe is shown in *Old Standard B&O Recipes*, it is duplicated nearly verbatim in the pamphlet written for Car Number 1045, the *Betsy Ross.*

SALLY LUNN MUFFINS

From Old Standard B&O Recipes

Rub three ounces of butter into a pound of flour, then add three eggs beaten light, a little salt, one tablespoon baking powder, and as much milk as will make it into a soft dough. Knead it well. Put in a buttered pan, cover it and place it in a warm place to rise. Bake in a moderate oven.

Chef's Comments

INGREDIENTS FOR 18 MUFFINS

3 ounces Butter
1 pound Flour
3 Eggs, beaten lightly
½ teaspoon Salt
1 tablespoon Baking Powder
1 cup Milk

Preheat the oven to 400 degrees.
Combine the butter and flour by hand or with two forks. Add the eggs, salt, and baking powder.
Gradually add the milk until you have a soft dough (this may not require the entire cup of milk shown). Mix only until the dry ingredients are completely moistened.
Place in well-buttered muffin pans and cover with plastic wrap or a damp cloth until ready to bake.
Bake for 18–20 minutes.

SHORTCAKE BISCUITS

From Old Standard B&O Recipes and *Eat, Drink, and Be Merry in Maryland* (Stieff)

RECIPE NUMBER 5

Sift the flour, salt and baking powder together, then add the Crisco, and last add the milk gradually, the dough should be as soft as can be handled, without sticking; then turn it out onto a moulding board and knead lightly, then roll to one inch thick, and cut with a three and one half inch round cutter and lay them in a baking pan not touching each other, and bake in a hot oven for fifteen or twenty minutes.

Chef's Comments

INGREDIENTS FOR 4 BISCUITS

5¼ ounces (1 cup) Flour
¼ teaspoon Salt
1 teaspoon Baking Powder
2 tablespoons Crisco
½ cup Milk

Preheat oven to 400 degrees.
An alternative to the rolling and cutting process is to divide the dough into four pieces of equal weight. Roll each piece into a ball and flatten until one inch thick.
Pay particular attention to two instructions: add the milk gradually, so the dry ingredients can absorb it, and knead the dough lightly. Although the ingredients must be thoroughly combined, less mixing and kneading will yield flakier biscuits.
Like other B&O recipes, this specifies Crisco by name, but any shortening will do, including lard, which while not as healthful, often improves the biscuits' flavor.

A TRIP TO NEW YORK. The young man seated at dinner on the Royal Blue does not appear pleased that the camera has caught his Dad cutting his food, something he would have done himself at home. But this is "polite company" and the folks are taking measures to avoid the chance of public embarrassment. Menus such as the one propped against the window were used between 1950 and the end of B&O passenger service between Baltimore and New York in April of 1958. Dinner was served eastbound on the Royal Blue, which would have left Philadelphia around 5:00 p.m. The bemused steward is armed with an abundance of pencils, as guests were required to write their own meal selections. Baltimore and Ohio Railroad Museum

BEEF DISHES

Boiled Brisket of Beef, Horseradish Sauce	German Pot Roast with Noodles
Casserole of Beef with Mashed Potato Topping	Braised Short Ribs of Beef
Corn Bread Pie	Roulade of Beef
Hungarian Goulash	Sour Beef
Baked Roast Beef Hash	Prime Beef Stew
Hash with Egg Recipes	Braised Swiss Steak
Mock Chop Suey	Beef Steak, Swiss Style
Ox Joint Sauté	Braised Sirloin Tips of Beef
Philadelphia Pepper Pot	Yorkshire Pudding with Roast Meats

BOILED BRISKET OF BEEF, HORSERADISH SAUCE

From "B&O General Notice," August 11, 1959,
for menus effective August 13, 1959

Fresh brisket (not corned) to be used. Put brisket into boiling salt water, with peeled onion, carrots and outside stalks of celery. Skim and cook until done and tender. Strain broth for further use.

Chef's Comments

INGREDIENTS FOR 10 SERVINGS

8 pounds Beef Brisket
8 ounces Onion, peeled and chopped
4 ounces Carrots, peeled and chopped
4 ounces Celery, chopped
2 cups Horseradish Sauce

This dish and its sauce are an excellent example of classic French techniques that have informed cooking throughout the western world. The vegetables listed here comprise a standard mirepoix, which is used to flavor many meat dishes, stocks, and sauces.

As this recipe suggests, the brisket can be boiled until done. If simmered, however, the final product will be more tender and less stringy. An 8-pound brisket will take approximately 3 hours of simmering.

The meat is done when it becomes nice and tender. Test by inserting a large kitchen fork; the meat should slide right off.

The last sentence advises saving the cooking liquid, which will have become beef broth after 3 hours of cooking. This in turn is the basis for many sauces and soups, including the Horseradish Sauce with which the B&O served its brisket.

CASSEROLE OF BEEF WITH MASHED POTATO TOPPING

From "B&O General Notice," January 7, 1964,
for menus effective January 9, 1964

In preparing this dish, use ¼ lb. of ground beef to each order, browning same in frying pan, stirring constantly with a fork to keep it separated. Place this beef in the bottom of a chicken pie dish. Over this place stewed tomatoes which have been seasoned and slightly thickened. Cover this with a layer of mashed potatoes, placing the pie dish in the oven until the potatoes are nicely browned. In serving, place on a tea plate with an additional tea plate for service. Use bakers for vegetables.

Chef's Comments

INGREDIENTS FOR 4 SERVINGS

1 pound Ground Beef
28 ounces Stewed Tomatoes
Mashed Potatoes (from 3 large Potatoes)

Preheat oven and bake at 350 degrees. At this writing no B&O recipe for stewed tomatoes has been discovered. In the absence of a favorite recipe, canned tomatoes can be used, seasoned to taste.

This is real B&O "comfort food."

CORN BREAD PIE

From *Baltimore and Ohio* magazine, May 1961, and *What's Cooking on the B&O?* (circa 1950)

1 pound Ground Beef
1 Onion, chopped

1 can (10½ ounces) Tomato Soup
1½–2 cups Water
1 teaspoon Salt
¾ teaspoon Pepper
1 tablespoon Chili Powder
½ cup Green Peppers, chopped
1 cup Whole Kernel Corn

Brown the beef and onion in a skillet. Add the soup, water, seasonings, corn, and green pepper. Mix well and allow to simmer for 15 minutes. Then fill a greased pie dish or casserole ¾ full, leaving room for the corn bread topping. To make the corn bread top, sift together the following:

¾ cup Cornmeal
1 tablespoon Sugar
1 tablespoon Flour
½ teaspoon Salt
1½ teaspoon Baking Powder

After they are sifted together, add one beaten egg and ½ cup of milk. Stir lightly and fold in 1 tablespoon of melted fat. Cover the meat mixture with this topping and bake in a medium oven at 350 degrees for 18 to 20 minutes. Don't be surprised when the topping disappears into the meat mixture. It will rise during the baking and form a good layer of corn bread. Don't be surprised when the whole dish disappears after you put it on the table, because it's one of the most popular items—with both men and women—that the B&O serves.

Chef's Comments

This recipe as shown in *What's Cooking on the B&O?* called for 2 cups of water, which yields a "soupy" filling.

The more recent version, quoted in *Baltimore and Ohio* magazine, gave the amount as 1½ cups, which seems preferable to most tastes.

The "fat" in the topping could be butter, bacon grease, or anything else that will melt to a liquid state. Either version will make six servings.

Among B&O fans, Corn Bread Pie is the dish that seems most emblematic of the road's cuisine, yet it appeared on rather few B&O menus. Still, it was published not only in *What's Cooking on the B&O?* and *Baltimore & Ohio* magazine, but also in *True Story* magazine and on a little card offered to dining car guests.

In a conversation in August 2007, Jimmy Kearse, a waiter for the B&O between 1944 and 1962, told us, "I only knew one man who could cook [Corn Bread Pie]—(B&O Chef) Joseph Roddy. He came from Asheville, North Carolina." So this dish does indeed have real Southern roots.

HUNGARIAN GOULASH

From *What's Cooking on the B&O?* (circa 1950)

1 pound Beef, cut into ½-inch cubes
1½ ounce Ham Fat, chopped fine
1 Onion, large, chopped
Flour, as needed
1 Potato, large, cubed
Paprika, to taste

Brown the onions lightly in a frying pan with the chopped ham fat, and add the paprika. Stir for a few minutes, letting meat simmer until it's brown. Then add enough flour to make a medium-thick gravy. Continue cooking until the gravy has thickened, then add enough water to cover the concoction. Cook for 60 minutes; then add the cubed potatoes. Season with salt and pepper and cook for 15 more minutes. When you call "come and get it," stand aside or you'll be trampled in the rush.

Chef's Comments

It is implied that the cubed beef is added just after the paprika is stirred into the browned onions. A nearly identical version in *Old Standard B&O Recipes* confirms this and further advises that the potatoes be cubed the same size as the beef.

The finished product should be a thick spicy stew. Our experience suggests using about ¼ cup of flour and ½ tablespoon of paprika. Water may be added during the cooking process to maintain this consistency. Covering the pot also helps. Be sure to check the potatoes to ensure that they are adequately cooked before serving.

This recipe makes 3–4 servings.

BAKED ROAST BEEF HASH
From Old Standard B&O Recipes

RECIPE NUMBER I

5 pounds Minced Beef
3 pounds Minced Potatoes
½ dozen Green Peppers
1 tablespoon Thyme
2 Eggs
1 bunch Parsley
½ pound Celery
4 Onions
1 tablespoon Salt

1 teaspoon Nutmeg
1 cup Bread Crumbs

Salt and pepper to taste. Cover with crumbs, mix and bake for half an hour until brown. Gravy served with essence of meat already cooked.

Chef's Comments

INGREDIENTS FOR 6 SERVINGS

1 pound Beef
9 ounces Potatoes
1 Green Bell Pepper
¾ teaspoon Thyme
1 Egg
2 ounces Parsley
1½ ounce Celery
1 Onion
¾ teaspoon Salt
¼ teaspoon Nutmeg
¼ cup Bread Crumbs
Pepper, to taste

Preheat the oven to 350 degrees.

For the beef, use the leftovers from a roast or boiled meat dish. Mix all ingredients thoroughly and place in a baking dish or pan. Note that not only must the beef and potatoes be minced, but the green peppers, parsley, celery, and onions should be as well.

Although the recipe advises 30 minutes baking time, more time in the oven may be necessary to cook the potatoes and brown the hash. Alternately, the potatoes could be chopped into 1-inch dice and boiled for five minutes or so before being minced and added to the mixture. This recipe will yield a fairly dry finished product. For a moister hash, add a bit of beef stock, butter, or water.

As that cryptic last sentence indicates, this dish is excellent with a rich brown gravy.

HASH WITH EGG RECIPES

From *The Culinary Handbook* (Fellows)

BROWNED BEEF HASH WITH FRIED EGGS

Minced onion lightly fried in butter added to finely cut roast beef two parts, and minced cold potatoes one part, mixed together, seasoned with salt, pepper and powdered marjoram with a very little roast beef gravy; the whole then tossed together, placed in a pan and baked; or kept in a saucepan over a slow fire till thoroughly heated; or portions put into a frying pan, browned on both sides, then formed into the shape of an omelet; served either with or without a poached egg, and with a crouton at ends of dish.

CORNED BEEF HASH, POACHED EGG

Prepared (onion optional), cooked, and served the same way as "roast beef hash" above, but omitting the herb, and using corned beef instead of roast beef.

Chef's Comments

INGREDIENTS FOR 4 SERVINGS

1 Onion, ¼-inch dice
1 tablespoon Butter
1 pound Roast or Corned Beef, ¼-inch dice
8 ounces Potatoes, boiled, minced
Salt and Pepper, to taste
Marjoram, to taste

Roast Beef Gravy, as needed
4 Eggs, fried or poached

If baking the hash, preheat the oven to 350 degrees, browning as desired.

The recipe calls for "a very little roast beef gravy"; start with ½ cup, adding until the desired consistency and moisture is achieved.

Was the B&O asserting a bit of "independence" by listing the Browned Beef Hash on its menus with a fried egg versus the poached egg specified by Fellows?

MOCK CHOP SUEY

From *B&O Chef's Notes*

One pound lean beef; ¼ pound fresh pork; 2 tablespoons shortening; 1 pint stock; 1 cup chopped celery; 1 cup thinly sliced onion; 1 cup mushrooms; 2 teaspoons salt; ½ teaspoon pepper; 1 teaspoon brown sugar. Cut the meat up into small pieces. Brown the meat in the hot fat. Add the stock, cover the pan and simmer for 30 minutes. Add celery, onions, mushrooms and seasonings. Cover and simmer for half hour longer. Serve with boiled rice.

Chef's Comments

INGREDIENTS FOR 3–4 SERVINGS

1 pound Beef, lean
¼ pound Pork, fresh
2 tablespoons Shortening
2 cups Beef Stock
1 cup Celery, chopped
1 cup Onion, sliced thin

1 cup Mushrooms
2 teaspoons Salt
½ teaspoon Pepper
1 teaspoon Brown Sugar

Serve ½ cup of boiled rice with each portion.

OX JOINT SAUTÉ

From *The Culinary Handbook* (Fellows)

Tails separated in their natural joints, the large end split, seasoned with powdered mixed herbs, rolled in flour, sautéed a light brown with butter, taken up into a sautoir, covered with sauce Robert, simmered till tender; served garnished with a braised jardinière of vegetables.

Chef's Comments

INGREDIENTS FOR THE OXTAILS

1–1¼ pound Oxtails
½ tablespoon Basil, powdered
½ tablespoon Parsley, powdered
½ tablespoon Oregano, powdered
½ tablespoon Rosemary, powdered
½ tablespoon Thyme, powdered
½ cup Flour
3 tablespoons Butter
2 cups Robert Sauce *(See* Sauces *Section)*

INGREDIENTS FOR THE GARNISH

3 Carrots
12 ounces String Beans
2 stalks Celery

Combine the herbs and cover oxtails with these, then roll each oxtail in flour. In a large saucepan (sautoir), sauté the oxtails in butter until light brown. Cover with Robert Sauce and simmer until tender, 2–3 hours.

Chop the vegetables fine and simmer in water or beef stock until tender, then drain. Serve the oxtails on the gravy and garnish with the vegetables.

A "jardinière of vegetables" could include a wide variety of root vegetables, beans, peas, cauliflower, etc. The selection given here is taken from a different B&O recipe of 1964, which called for "carrots, string beans, celery, etc."

It was this recipe that provided a clue to the B&O's use of *The Culinary Handbook. Old Standard B&O Recipes*, under the heading "Ox Joint Sauté," reads "Same as shown in *Culinary Hand Book*."

PHILADELPHIA PEPPER POT

From *Old Standard B&O Recipes*

RECIPE NUMBER 40

First use a strong veal stock, made from veal bones, thickened lightly with roux, then strained through a sieve, to this add some shredded onions and shredded green peppers and tripe cut in half inch strips, season with salt, pepper and thyme.

Chef's Comments

INGREDIENTS FOR 1½ QUARTS

1 pound Beef Tripe
2–3 teaspoons Salt
6 tablespoons Butter
6 tablespoons Flour

1 quart Veal or Beef Stock
1 Green Bell Pepper, shredded
1 Onion, shredded
1 tablespoon Thyme
Salt and Pepper, to taste

Rinse the tripe well in cool water and sprinkle with 2–3 teaspoons of salt. Allow to stand for 30 minutes; then rinse the salt off.

Simmer (do not boil) for 1½–2 hours; then drain and cut into ½-inch strips.

Melt the butter over low heat and add the flour, stirring constantly until smooth. Add the stock, bring to a boil and reduce to a simmer, stirring until thickened.

Add the remaining ingredients and simmer for 30 minutes. Season to taste with salt and pepper.

Some people do not care for the texture or appearance of tripe. These concerns can be addressed by cutting the meat into very small pieces and/or by simmering it for up to 2½ hours. Another issue that folks may find disconcerting is the "aroma" of the simmering tripe. Rest assured that the hearty taste of this dish is nothing at all like its hearty "bouquet."

The consistency of this dish should be thicker than that of a soup or stew.

GERMAN POT ROAST WITH NOODLES
From *Old Standard B&O Recipes*

Use short hip, taking out the best part of this for the pot roast, place in a saucepan and place on top of the range to brown. Then put in an oven, cover, you will add a cup of stock to this, and after this is cooked, a few minutes, you can then put in a sufficient amount of vegetables to give it the proper flavor. When making the gravy, this should be strained and all the grease removed before being served. The small piece of tenderloin that you get from the short hip can be listed as small tenderloin steak, the flank of the short hip not used for pot roast could be cut up and used in many other ways on the Diner, such as beef stew with vegetables or Hungarian Goulash.

SERVICE ON POT ROAST

Serve on platter with brown gravy, in a gravy boat and not over the pot roast.

NOODLES

Use the wide noodles, boil and put away in a jar in the ice box. When an order is served, take the noodles out, put in a pan with melted butter, and brown both sides.

Chef's Comments

INGREDIENTS FOR 6–8 SERVINGS

4–5 pounds Beef Pot Roast
3 cups Beef Stock
8 ounces Onions, ¼-inch dice
4 ounces Carrots, ¼-inch dice
4 ounces Celery, ¼-inch dice
¾ cup Flour
Salt and Pepper, to taste
Wide Noodles, 2 ounces per serving
2–3 tablespoons Butter

Preheat oven to 350 degrees.

On the stovetop bring a very small amount of oil or butter to high heat in a pot or roasting pan. Put the roast in the pot and brown nicely on all sides. Add

1 cup of the beef stock, place in the oven, and cover. Dice the vegetables and add them to the roast.

Roast for approximately 1 hour, or until the beef is done as desired. (It is "well done" when the internal temperature reaches 170 degrees.)

When the meat is done, remove it from the pan, strain the cooking juice into a saucepan, and remove grease. Add beef stock and flour as needed to make gravy. (Add the flour gradually, stirring constantly to avoid lumps.)

Bring the gravy to a boil, reduce to a simmer, and cook over medium-low heat for 10 minutes or so. If too thick, thin with warm beef stock or water. Season to taste.

Any type of flat pasta can be used for the noodles.

THE BEST BEEF. The westbound Chicago Express is shown arriving in Brunswick, Maryland, in 1962. In the left background is the B&O Railroad YMCA, which burned in 1980. The wonderful restaurant at the "Y" served great meals at inexpensive prices. A favorite of author Karl Spence was the Roast Beef Sandwich with gravy for 50 cents. Karl Spence collection

BRAISED SHORT RIBS OF BEEF

Two methods from *Old Standard B&O Recipes*

Put shortribs in saucepan with one quart of nice stock, with one onion cut fine, steam until nice and tender. Place in roasting pan and put in oven until they are nice and brown. Then make a brown gravy or sauce and serve in gravy boat.

RECIPE NUMBER 14

Simmer beef in saucepan, covered, until tender. Use about four inches of water, carrots, celery, spices, salt, pepper and onions. When tender remove short ribs, dust with flour, place in oven to brown, strain liquor remaining in saucepan, brown and thicken with gravy served with beef.

Chef's Comments

INGREDIENTS FOR 3–4 SERVINGS (RECIPE NUMBER 14)

3 pounds Beef Ribs
3 Carrots, ½-inch dice
3 ribs Celery, ½-inch dice
1 Onion, ½-inch dice
6 Black Peppercorns
6 Parsley Stems
1 Bay Leaf
¼ teaspoon Thyme
¼ teaspoon Cloves or Garlic
Salt and Pepper, to taste
Flour, as needed to thicken gravy

It was fascinating to find two recipes for this dish in the same document. The unnumbered first version is simpler but will not yield the complex flavor of Recipe Number 14 with all of its added vegetables and spices.

Although the spices were unspecified, the vegetables form the standard mirepoix of French cuisine. Thus it seemed reasonable that the spices would have been those of a standard sachet.

Regardless of which version of this recipe is used, it will take 1½–2 hours of simmering for the ribs to become tender.

The instruction to "dust with flour" means to go very lightly on the flour, so that it will brown properly. Setting the oven to 450 degrees will also help in this regard.

To make the gravy, strain the "liquor" into a saucepan and heat. Sprinkle in flour very gradually, stirring constantly to avoid lumps, until the desired thickness is reached. Then bring to a boil, reduce to a simmer, and cook for 10 minutes or so to remove the flour taste. If the gravy is too thick, simply stir in hot water. Check for flavor and season with salt and pepper to taste.

ROULADE OF BEEF

From *Old Standard B&O Recipes*

Slice beef from the butt about four inches wide, six inches long, one half inch thick. Cut dill pickles in quarters, place one quarter and a slice of bacon, piece of celery on the slice of beef, roll and fasten with a skewer. Braise, make thick brown gravy from the drippings, serve one to the order.

Chef's Comments

INGREDIENTS FOR 1 SERVING

1 slice Beef Butt
Dill Pickles, ¼ per serving
1 slice Bacon

1 rib Celery
Flour, as needed
Salt and Pepper, to taste

Preheat oven to 350 degrees.

Braising is a combination method of cooking in which the assembled roulade will first be browned in oil or butter in a frying pan, then placed in a baking dish in the oven for about 45 minutes.

To make the "thick brown gravy" called for in the recipe, drain the cooking juices into a saucepan and very gradually stir in a small amount of flour. Bring to a boil and reduce to a simmer for 5–10 minutes. Season to taste with salt and pepper; stir in a little hot water if gravy is too thick.

Sour Beef

From *Old Standard B&O Recipes*

RECIPE NUMBER 23

Place beef in crock, cover with water and vinegar (one cup of vinegar to two pounds of beef) bay leaves and whole cloves; allow meat to pickle 48 hours.

Drain meat, dredge with flour, salt, pepper and ground allspice, brown in drippings, add carrots and onions, and a part of the pickling liquid, cook slowly until tender.

Thicken the liquid the meat has been cooked in with crumbled ginger snaps; sugar to taste.

Chef's Comments

INGREDIENTS FOR 4 SERVINGS

1 pound Beef

FOR THE MARINADE

2 cups Water
1 cup Vinegar
10 Cloves, whole
5 Bay Leaves

FOR COOKING

Salt and Pepper, to taste
Allspice, ground, to taste
½ cup Flour
4 tablespoons Beef Fat or Cooking Oil
1 Onion, ½-inch dice
2 Carrots, ¼-inch dice

FOR THE SAUCE

Sugar, to taste
Ginger Snaps, crumbled, as needed

Place the beef in a covered container, add all the marinade ingredients and marinate for 48 hours. Drain the meat, reserving the marinade. Roll the meat in flour mixed with salt, pepper, and ground allspice.

In a very hot pot or pan, brown the meat in beef fat or oil, then add the carrots, onions, and enough of the marinade to cover meat if possible. Add beef stock or water if more liquid is needed. Cover the pot and simmer until the beef is tender, about 3 hours.

Remove the beef, strain the cooking liquid and discard the vegetables and seasonings. To thicken the liquid, add ginger snaps that have been put through a blender or food processor. In the absence of ginger snaps, use ¾ teaspoon of powdered ginger and 2 tablespoons flour to thicken the sauce. Add sugar to taste, and simmer for 5 minutes or so to combine flavors.

NOTE: James Oseland, in the September/October 1999 issue of *Saveur* magazine, mentions that "sour beef [is] Baltimorese for sauerbraten" ("Lady Baltimore Eats," pp. 102–16), so it is only fitting that it was known by this name on the B&O.

PRIME BEEF STEW

From *B&O Chef's Notes*

Cut beef one inch thick, place in oven until tender, cut carrots ½ inch thick, cut potatoes ½ inch thick, use onions, use canned tomatoes, use salt pepper and paprika to taste, use brown sauce for thickening.

Place beef in oven until brown and tender, then put in sauce pan, add vegetables, the tomatoes and seasoning to taste, then thickening, cook until done, sprinkle parsley on top when serving.

Chef's Comments

INGREDIENTS FOR 4 SERVINGS

2 pounds Beef, cut in 1-inch cubes
3 Carrots, peeled, ½-inch dice
2 Potatoes, medium, peeled, ½-inch dice
2 Onions, medium, ½-inch dice
1 14½-ounce can Tomatoes
Salt and Pepper, to taste
Paprika, to taste
3 cups Espagnole Sauce *(See* Sauces *Section)*
Parsley, as needed for garnish

Preheat oven to 400 degrees.
Place beef cubes on a cookie sheet in the oven until brown, approximately 30 minutes. Place browned beef in a saucepan or small pot and add the diced vegetables and tomatoes. Season to taste and add the Espagnole sauce.

Cover the pot and simmer on the stovetop until done, approximately 1½ hours.

Sprinkle parsley on top when serving.

The title of this recipe implies that B&O chefs used pieces of prime beef, which is open to debate. Excellent results can be had using less-tender (and less-expensive) cuts, such as beef round or chuck or "beef for stew." The long simmering time will make the meat and vegetables nice and tender.

If no Espagnole sauce is handy, heat three cups of beef stock or bouillon and gradually stir in ½ cup of flour. Bring this mixture to a boil, then reduce to a simmer. Make this sauce in the pot in which the stew is to be cooked. Then add the meat and vegetables to the sauce.

BRAISED SWISS STEAK

From *Old Standard B&O Recipes*

Cut steak half inch thick, mix flour with salt and pepper, pound well into the steak. Brown steak in pan on both sides, in fat, but do not cook done. Place the steaks on top of each other in covered roaster. Dice bacon, fry in pan, add in finely chopped onions, celery and green peppers, brown altogether. Add boiling water and tomatoes to the browned mixture over the steaks, and roast slowly in a covered roaster. Serve the pan gravy over the steaks.

Chef's Comments

INGREDIENTS FOR 2 SERVINGS

2 Steaks, ½-inch thick

Flour, as needed
Salt and Pepper, to taste
Fat or Cooking Oil, as needed
4 slices Bacon
1 Onion, ½-inch dice
3 ribs Celery, ½-inch dice
1 Green Pepper, ½-inch dice
1 quart Water, boiling
2 Tomatoes, ½-inch dice

Preheat the oven to 300 degrees and roast until the internal temperature of the steaks reaches 165–170 degrees, about 1 hour.

The cooking juices can be served for the gravy. If thicker gravy is desired, strain the juices into a saucepan and gradually add flour, stirring constantly. Bring to a boil and then reduce to a simmer for 10 minutes or so. Season to taste with salt and pepper.

BEEF STEAK, SWISS STYLE

From *Old Standard B&O Recipes*

RECIPE NUMBER 19

Order steaks from commissary, dip in flour, fry brown, make gravy in same pan steaks were fried in, using onions, celery, mushrooms and apples, regular stock. Salt, pepper and Worcestershire sauce, add steak and let simmer until tender.

Chef's Comments

INGREDIENTS FOR TWO SERVINGS

1½ tablespoons Butter
2 Steaks, small

1 Onion, ½-inch dice
2 ribs Celery, ½-inch dice
4 ounces Mushrooms, ½-inch dice
1 Apple, peeled, cored, ½-inch dice
Flour, as needed
2 cups Beef Stock
1 tablespoon Worcestershire Sauce
Salt and Pepper, to taste

Melt the butter in a large pot.

Dip the steaks in flour and fry in the butter until brown; then remove from pot.

Add the onion, celery, mushrooms, and apple to the pot and cook a few minutes before adding the flour. Stir thoroughly to moisten all the flour, then add the remaining ingredients, mixing thoroughly.

Place the steaks back in the pot and simmer until tender, about 50–60 minutes.

The cooking method for this dish (braising) suggests that the steaks called for need not be a tender or choice cut of meat. Any flat boneless cut from the beef chuck or round would be ideal, as the long simmering time will render the final product tender.

BRAISED SIRLOIN TIPS OF BEEF

From "B&O General Notice," December 6, 1963, for menus effective December 12, 1963

Order sirloin tips from the commissaries by the pound. These will be in pieces 1½ inch by 1 inch. Use 5-lbs. of beef, 2 onions (about size of baseball) finely chopped, 5 tablespoons of flour, 2 8-ounce cans of mushrooms that have been drained, 1 pint tomato purée, 2 cups water and 2-lbs. diced raw potatoes. Braise the meat in shortening and when good and brown add onions, cook 10 minutes and drain off fat. Add the 5 tablespoons of flour, purée and water and when the meat is nearly done, add the diced potatoes which have been previously blanched in deep grease. Cook well and add mushrooms. This is to be served PIPING HOT in a casserole dish to which one ounce of Sherry wine has been added, and garnished with chopped parsley. Cover upon serving. Makes 16 portions.

Chef's Comments

INGREDIENTS FOR 8 SERVINGS

2½ pounds Beef Sirloin Tips
2–3 tablespoons Shortening
1 pound Potatoes, peeled, ½-inch dice
1 Onion, finely chopped
2½ tablespoons Flour
8 ounces Mushrooms, canned
1 cup Tomato Puree
1 cup Water
½ ounce Sherry Wine
Parsley, chopped, as needed for garnish

This is a fairly straightforward recipe requiring minimal explanation. This recipe's use of the word *braise* is a bit ambiguous. Normally that term describes a combination method of cooking in which meat is browned over high heat and then cooked in a liquid. Here the term seems to refer only to browning the meat.

Then there is the reference to "blanching" the diced potatoes in "deep grease," which means simply that they were deep-fat fried for 2–3 minutes until slightly browned, then removed from the fat and drained before being added to the pot. This ensures that the potatoes will retain their shape and still be thoroughly cooked.

To "cover upon serving" means that this dish was served "under glass" beneath a dome-shaped hot food cover.

YORKSHIRE PUDDING WITH ROAST MEATS
From Old Standard B&O Recipes

1½ cups Flour
2 cups Milk
1 cup Roast Beef Drippings
1 ounce Butter, melted
3 Eggs
Salt, to taste
½ teaspoon Baking Powder

Mix the flour, milk and essence of roast beef carefully, not to have it full of lumps, add the melted butter, salt, the eggs well beaten, and then beat together thoroughly. Butter a small baking pan and warm in the oven, pour the batter in, only about a half inch deep, and bake 15 or 20 minutes. Cut squares and serve with roast beef and gravy.

Chef's Comments

Preheat the oven to 450 degrees and do not open the oven door while the pudding is cooking. Although baking powder is called for, the recipe fails to mention that it should be mixed with the other ingredients at the start of the procedure.

During baking, the pudding will rise to form a puffy irregularly shaped mass. Allow it to stand for several minutes and it will settle fairly evenly with a golden outer crust and a custard-like center. Use of a cupcake pan makes for very nice individual servings. Preheat the pan as noted above.

..A la Carte..

CRAB LUMP COCKTAIL .90

SOUP OF THE DAY . . . . CUP .35; TUREEN	.50
JELLIED CONSOMME, CUP	.35
CHILLED ORANGE JUICE	.35
CHILLED TOMATO, PRUNE OR GRAPEFRUIT JUICE	.30
FRESH FRUIT CUP	.60

Salads

CRAB LUMP, MAYONNAISE	1.75
TUNA FISH, MAYONNAISE	1.25
CHICKEN, MAYONNAISE	1.50
B&O SALAD BOWL	1.00
LETTUCE AND TOMATO	.75
SPECIAL SALAD BOWL WITH JULIENNE HAM AND CHICKEN	1.75
(FRENCH OR MAYONNAISE DRESSING)	

Sandwiches

SLICED CHICKEN	1.00
COLD SLICED HAM	.60
LETTUCE AND TOMATO WITH BACON	.75
HAM AND EGG	.90
CLUB	1.75
AMERICAN CHEESE ON TOAST	.40
HOT ROAST LAMB, POTATOES AND PICKLE CHIPS	1.60
TUNA FISH	.75

Beverages

COFFEE (HOT OR ICED), POT	.35
TEA (HOT OR ICED), POT	.30
SANKA, POT	.35
POSTUM, POT	.35
INDIVIDUAL MILK OR BUTTERMILK	.25

Desserts

OLD FASHIONED STRAWBERRY SHORTCAKE	.50
FRESHLY BAKED PIE .35, A LA MODE	.60
ICE CREAM	.30
CHILLED MELON	.40
CHEESE WITH SALTINES	.40
GRAPEFRUIT SEGMENTS	.35

May we Suggest
A Half Bottle of
TAVEL
ROSÉ
WINE
$1.85

..Dinner..

MANHATTAN, MARTINI OR OLD FASHIONED COCKTAIL 75c

TOMATO JUICE COCKTAIL · CHILLED ORANGE JUICE

SOUP OF THE DAY · FRESH FRUIT CUP · JELLIED CONSOMME

DE LUXE MARYLAND CRAB CAKES, Tartar Sauce—3.35

BROILED CHESAPEAKE BAY ROCK FISH, Lemon Butter—3.10

ASSORTED COLD CUTS, Sliced Tomatoes—3.50

BRAISED LEG OF SPRING LAMB, Mint Jelly—3.50

FRIED HALF SPRING CHICKEN, Country Style—3.35

BROILED SELECTED SIRLOIN STEAK—4.75

NEW POTATOES, PERSILLADE · FRENCH FRIED POTATOES
SAUTE CORN AND GREEN PEPPERS · BUTTERED ASPARAGUS TIPS

BALTIMORE AND OHIO "HELP YOURSELF" SALAD BOWL

ICE CREAM OR SHERBET · CHILLED MELON
OLD FASHIONED STRAWBERRY SHORTCAKE
GRAPEFRUIT SEGMENTS · CHEESE WITH SALTINES
FRESHLY BAKED PIE

COFFEE (HOT OR ICED) · SANKA · POSTUM · TEA (HOT OR ICED)
MILK OR BUTTERMILK

*A charge of 50c per person will be made
for food service outside of dining car*

CAR IN CHARGE OF

J. B. Martin
Manager, Dining Car and
Commissary Department
Baltimore & Ohio R.R.
Baltimore 1, Maryland
92-04-F-12-8

AMAZING SELECTION. Any fine restaurant would be proud of the variety of offerings shown on this B&O dinner menu of June 12, 1958. A five-course dinner featuring the road's legendary Maryland Crab Cakes tops the list for what was then a lofty price of $3.35. An entirely different selection of somewhat lighter dishes could be had à la carte, along with the appetizers, beverages, and desserts offered with the table d'hôte meals. Karl Spence collection

CHICKEN DISHES

Chicken à la Chef

Chicken à la King on Toast

Breast of Chicken on Smithfield Ham, Mushroom Sauce

Southern Style Fried Chicken

Curry of Chicken

Chicken Hash Recipes

Chicken Maryland

Chicken Pie, Individual

Sauce for Chicken Pie

Roast Chicken

Southern-Style Chicken Shortcake

Chicken Tetrazzini

CHICKEN À LA CHEF

From *Old Standard B&O Recipes*

Prepare three-pound chickens the same as for chicken à la Maryland. Wash two cups of Rice thoroughly and boil in salted water. Drain and dry, keep it hot. Fry the chicken, make a roux of flour and butter, reduce with chicken stock, add chopped chicken livers, parboiled, and mushrooms to the roux with the fried chicken, cook slowly until chicken is tender. Serve on bed of rice with some of the roux poured over.

Chef's Comments

INGREDIENTS FOR 2 SERVINGS

1 Egg
2 Chickens, cut in 8 pieces
Bread Crumbs, as needed
8 tablespoons Butter
8 tablespoons Flour
3 cups Chicken Stock
¼ cup Chicken Livers
¼ cup Mushrooms, chopped
1 cup Water
½ cup Rice

Beat the egg into a large bowl, add a little water, and mix well to make an egg wash. Coat each piece of chicken in the egg wash and dredge in bread crumbs to cover thoroughly. Place in refrigerator until needed. Chop the chicken livers and sauté in butter or oil until lightly browned.

To make the sauce, melt the butter and stir in the flour. Add the chicken stock, chicken livers, and mushrooms. Bring to a boil, then reduce to a simmer and leave on the heat until reduced to two-thirds of the original volume.

Fry the chicken in butter or oil until brown. Then place in the sauce, cover the pan, and cook over medium heat until tender, approximately 30–40 minutes.

Meanwhile bring water to a boil and add the rice. Cover the pot and reduce to a simmer for 20 minutes.

Serve the chicken on a bed of rice with the sauce poured over.

CHICKEN À LA KING ON TOAST

From "B&O General Notice," January 7, 1964, for menus effective January 9, 1964

½ pound Chicken, cooked, diced
1 quart Heavy Cream Sauce
¼ cup Green Peppers, diced, sautéed
½ cup Pimentos, diced
3 Egg Yolks
2 tablespoons Sherry Wine
Salt and Pepper, to taste

Method: Beat egg yolks, add to cream sauce and let come to a boil, stirring constantly. Remove from stove and add other ingredients. Serve on a dinner plate on slices of trimmed toast, garnished with small wedges of toast and parsley.

Chef's Comments

FOR TWO SERVINGS

If possible, add the egg yolk while the sauce is fairly cool, and be sure to mind those instructions to stir constantly while it comes to a boil. This will keep the sauce smooth and free of floating bits of cooked yolk.

If these instructions are followed as written, the green pepper will be nearly raw when the dish is served. To avoid this, it can be sautéed or simmered a bit first or simply added to the sauce before the other ingredients and simmered for a few minutes.

BREAST OF CHICKEN ON SMITHFIELD HAM, MUSHROOM SAUCE

From "B&O General Notice," July 2, 1964, for menus effective July 9, 1964

Cover chicken breasts with cold water, add small pieces of celery leaves, onion, parsley and one bay leaf. Season with salt and pepper, cook until done. Remove skin. DO NOT OVERCOOK. On a piece of buttered toast place one slice of warmed Smithfield ham, place chicken breast on top of ham. Heat a can of condensed mushroom soup (DO NOT DILUTE), and pour about 6 tablespoons over breast of chicken. Garnish with chopped parsley and a sprinkle of paprika. *The Smithfield Ham Must Be Warmed To Order. This Dish Should Be Piping Hot When Served.*

Breast of chicken comes to you in 7 oz. portions. The Smithfield Ham will be sliced in the commissaries, 12 portions to the pound. Order condensed mushroom soup in 10½ oz. cans from the commissaries. *Order chicken breasts and Smithfield Ham from Baltimore Commissary.*

Chef's Comments

INGREDIENTS FOR 1 SERVING

1 Chicken Breast
Celery Leaves from 3 ribs
1 Onion, ¼-inch dice
4 sprigs Parsley, fresh
1 Bay Leaf
Salt and Pepper, to taste
1 slice Toast, buttered
1 slice Smithfield Ham
6 tablespoons Mushroom Soup
Parsley, chopped, as needed
Paprika, as needed

We suspected the replacement of homemade sauce with canned mushroom soup was a result of a 1960s-era cutback until reading the December 2006 issue of *Saveur* magazine. According to author Irene Sax, soup and sauce are basically the same concoction, and the Campbell Soup Company promoted the use of its canned soups in this manner as early as 1916. But, says *Saveur*, "It wasn't until the invention of its cream of mushroom soup, in 1934, that the concept really started to take root in the American culinary imagination." The article goes on to cite an author who substituted a homemade sauce for Campbell's Cream of Mushroom, and found that "the experiment was a failure."

So the Baltimore and Ohio was still using the finest ingredients after all.

SOUTHERN STYLE FRIED CHICKEN

From "B&O General Notice," September 1, 1960

Disjoint a half spring chicken, bread and fry to golden brown. Add a teaspoon of consommé, salt and pepper, cover and cook until done.

Chef's Comments

INGREDIENTS FOR 1 SERVING

2 tablespoons Butter or oil
½ Chicken, disjointed
1 Egg, beaten
2 tablespoons Water
Bread Crumbs, as needed
1 teaspoon Consommé
Salt and Pepper, to taste

In a large skillet, heat the butter or oil over medium-low heat.

Mix the water and egg and coat each piece of chicken with this egg wash. Then cover thoroughly with bread crumbs.

Increase the heat under the skillet to medium-high and "fry to golden brown." Reduce heat to medium and add the consommé and salt and pepper. Cover and cook until done, 30–40 minutes.

After the outside of the chicken is browned, it is actually cooked with steam until done. The butter or oil plus juices from the chicken will cook the meat; the teaspoon of consommé (or beef stock) is more for flavor than for added "steam." Just be sure to keep the flame high enough to turn the liquid to steam in the covered skillet, but not so high that the outside of the meat burns.

Chicken pieces can be had at any grocery store; leg quarters work especially well in this recipe.

CURRY OF CHICKEN

From *What's Cooking on the B&O?* (circa 1950)

2 pounds Chicken
2 Onions, small
4 tablespoons Butter (or margarine)
2 teaspoons Curry Powder
1 tablespoon Flour
1 Egg Yolk

Have your butcher cut up the chicken as for fricassee. Wash it well and place it in a stew pan with enough water to cover it. Cover pan and let boil slowly until chicken is tender. Now add a heaping teaspoon of salt and boil a few minutes longer. Remove chicken from pot, but save the liquid. Now cut up the onions and fry them in the butter. When the onions are brown, remove them from the frying pan and put in the chicken. Fry the chicken for 3 or 4 minutes, then sprinkle it with the curry powder, and pour over it the liquid in which the chicken was boiled. Add the brown onions, stir thoroughly and stew for five more minutes. Now mix in a tablespoon of flour which you have thinned with a little water and stir in the beaten egg yolk. Remove from the fire and that's it!

Chef's Comments

MAKES 4 SERVINGS

The recipe in *What's Cooking on the B&O?* begins "Have your butcher cut up the chicken as for fricassee." Usually this means "disassembling" the chicken into breasts, thighs, drumsticks, and wings. Nowadays these pieces can be bought separately.

No specific amount of water is given for simmering the chicken. Thus individual cooks may not wish to add all of the water back to the pan. The more water added, the thinner the sauce will be. Start with a moderate amount of cooking liquid and add more if the sauce is too thick.

The mixture of flour with water is meant to prevent the flour from lumping when added to the heated liquid. However, this can result in an inferior texture and flavor. As an alternative, add the flour gradually, making sure that each bit added is thoroughly moistened and blended with the other ingredients.

One important precaution not mentioned in this recipe concerns the addition of the egg yolk when the dish is on the stove. If the ingredients are over 145 degrees, the yolk will be cooked instantaneously, resulting in bits of yolk suspended in the cooking liquid. To avoid this, remove the pan from the heat and allow it to cool a bit before stirring in the beaten yolk.

Most recipes for this dish call for the chicken and sauce to be served over rice, and the B&O menus featured an item called Curry of Chicken with Rice, which was no doubt the same recipe.

CHICKEN HASH RECIPES

From *Old Standard B&O Recipes*

CHICKEN HASH

Chicken is diced in ¼-inch cubes, moisten with stock, add fine chopped celery and green pepper, season with salt and pepper to taste.

CHICKEN HASH AU GRATIN

Prepare the same as for chicken hash, adding bread crumbs and parmesan cheese, place into individual Pyrex dishes, sprinkle with bread crumbs, brown in oven, serve hot.

Chef's Comments

INGREDIENTS FOR 2 SERVINGS

FOR CHICKEN HASH

9 ounces Chicken, cooked, ¼-inch dice
¼–½ cup Chicken Stock
2 ounces Celery, ¼-inch dice
2 ounces Green Pepper, ¼-inch dice
Salt and Pepper, to taste

FOR CHICKEN HASH AU GRATIN

1½ ounces Bread Crumbs
2 ounces Parmesan Cheese, grated

Preheat oven to 350 degrees. Bake until the ingredients are browned, 25–30 minutes.

If a moister hash is desired, add more chicken stock.

CHICKEN MARYLAND

From *The Culinary Handbook* (Fellows) and "B&O General Notice," May 1, 1963, for menus effective May 9, 1963

FROM 'THE CULINARY HANDBOOK'

Spring chickens singed, split down the back, the breastbone and backbone removed, left in halves for restaurant, and the leg and breast separated for hotel orders, making four portions of each chicken; seasoned with salt and pepper, dipped in beaten eggs, then fresh breadcrumbs, arranged in baking pan with slices of bacon, brushed with melted butter, roasted and basted with the bacon fat till done; served, the chicken resting on a corn fritter, flanked with two slices of the bacon, and a ladle of Béchamel sauce poured around.

FROM "B&O GENERAL NOTICE"

Half of spring chicken will be used, fried to a golden brown. Serve on a small bed of thick cream sauce and garnish with a nice sized corn fritter and a strip of bacon.

Chef's Comments

INGREDIENTS FOR 1 SERVING

Chicken (½ chicken per order, or as needed)
1 Egg, beaten
Salt and Pepper, to taste
Bread Crumbs, as needed
Butter, melted, as needed
Bacon, 2 pieces per serving
Béchamel or Cream Sauce, 2–3 tablespoons
   per serving *(See* Sauces *Section)*
Corn Fritters, 1 per serving *(See* Appetizers *Section)*

It is interesting to note that over the years this classic recipe was offered two ways—baked or fried. Other than the cooking method itself, the procedure and garnish remained nearly the same. For the baked version, preheat the oven to 400 degrees and bake to an internal temperature of 180 degrees, basting with bacon grease regularly until done.

CHICKEN PIE, INDIVIDUAL

From *Old Standard B&O Recipes*

Bone your chicken, cut into small pieces, using an equal amount of white and dark meat, two or three parisienne potatoes, one or two small pearl onions, a small piece of salt pork, several slices of carrots, bake crust separate, sprinkle half teaspoon peas over top of pie. Then put on your crust and put in oven.

Chef's Comments

INGREDIENTS FOR 4 SERVINGS

10 ounces Chicken, cooked, chopped fine
12 Parisienne Potatoes *(See note)*
8 small Pearl Onions
Sauce for Chicken Pie *(See recipe below)*
2 ounces Mushrooms, sliced *(See note)*
1 recipe of Flaky Pie Crust (no sugar) *(See* Desserts
   and Pie Crust *Section)*
1 Carrot, ¼-inch slices
4 small pieces Salt Pork
Salt and Pepper, to taste
4 tablespoons Peas

Preheat the oven to 350 degrees.
Simmer the potatoes and sauté the onions in butter or oil for 5–10 minutes.
Line individual chicken pie dishes with rolled-out pie crust. Bake these bottom crusts for 10–15 minutes.
Add all ingredients except the peas to the sauce; mix well and fill the crusts, then sprinkle peas over the top and add the top crusts. Make several vent holes in each top crust with a knife or fork, and bake until the crusts are golden and the filling bubbles through the vent holes.

This recipe offers instruction for making individual servings of this dish. But the same ingredients can just as easily be placed in a large casserole or pie dish and served family style.

If starting this dish with a raw chicken, cook it by simmering in water for an hour. Remove the chicken and refrigerate the liquid for several hours, after which the fat will solidify on top, with broth below. Both fat and broth can be used to make the sauce required for this dish.

To make Parisienne Potatoes, peel a potato and use a Parisienne cutter or melon baller to cut out small spheres. Alternatively, the potatoes can be cut in ¾-inch dice. The "General Notice" of August 8, 1963, left potatoes out of the recipe entirely, substituting the sliced mushrooms.

For a nice finishing touch, save the egg white from the sauce recipe and mix with a small amount of water. Brush it over the crust just before baking to give it a beautiful golden glaze.

CLASS F-8 DINING CAR NUMBER 1083. Assigned to the Capitol Limited between 1954 and 1957, this car began life in 1924 as F-4C Number 1043. In February 1954 it was rebuilt in the road's Mt. Clare shops in Baltimore, giving it lines and styling that better matched the lightweight streamlined cars coming into service on the B&O. Today, this car is displayed at the Baltimore and Ohio Railroad Museum in Baltimore. Baltimore and Ohio Railroad Historical Society

SAUCE FOR CHICKEN PIE

From *Old Standard B&O Recipes*

1 pint of chicken broth, render fat from chicken, take grease off, half pint of boiling milk, one cup of sweet cream, one kitchen spoonful of chicken butter, one spoonful of flour. Cooked until well mixed and brown, add boiling milk. After boiling, add one cup of cream into which two egg yolks have been well beaten, mix well and do not boil after.

Chef's Comments

INGREDIENTS FOR 4 SERVINGS

3 tablespoons Butter or Chicken Fat
4 tablespoons Flour
1 cup Chicken Broth or stock
1 cup Milk, boiling
½ cup Sweet Cream
1 Egg Yolk

In a large saucepan, melt the fat or butter over low heat. Add the flour, stirring until thoroughly blended. Continue cooking over low heat for 15–20 minutes, stirring occasionally, until the mixture is brown.

Meanwhile, heat the chicken broth and milk separately. Stir the broth and milk into the saucepan, bring to a boil and reduce to a simmer until the mixture thickens.

Add the egg yolk to the cream and mix until blended. Remove the sauce from the heat, let stand for 5 minutes, add the cream and egg yolk and mix thoroughly.

As explained in the Chicken Pie recipe, an easy way to obtain the broth and chicken fat called for in the sauce is to simmer the raw chicken intended for use in the pie. The original recipe used the interesting euphemism "chicken butter" to denote chicken fat.

This sauce is made in the classical French tradition, starting with the butter-and-flour roux and adding the *liaison* of egg yolks and cream as a thickening agent. The sauce must be cooled before adding the *liaison* to avoid cooking the egg yolks, which would result in bits of cooked yolk suspended in the sauce.

ROAST CHICKEN

From *The Culinary Handbook* (Fellows)

Young chickens drawn, singed, washed, trussed with slices of bacon tied over the breast, roasted and basted, and when nearly done, the bacon removed and the breast browned; served with bread sauce at one end of the dish, sautéed mushrooms in sauce as a border, also a garnish of fresh crisp watercress.

Chef's Comments

PROCEDURE FOR ONE CHICKEN

Preheat oven to 350 degrees.

Place the chicken, breast-side-up, on a rack in a roasting pan with the water in the bottom of the pan. Place slices of bacon over the breasts and roast to an internal temperature of 180 degrees (allow 16–20 minutes per pound of chicken).

When the chicken is nearly done, remove the bacon strips and increase the oven temperature to 450 degrees in order to brown the breasts.

The bacon in this recipe will keep the meat from drying out and will provide an excellent starting point for gravy to be served with the chicken.

The bread sauce mentioned is really stuffing, the recipe for which is given on page 87. There is no evidence that the B&O went so far as to serve this dish with "mushrooms in sauce," but photos do exist of whole roasted birds plated with a lush garnish of greens that could indeed be watercress.

SOUTHERN STYLE CHICKEN SHORTCAKE

From "B&O General Notice," February 9, 1960, for menus effective February 11, 1960

Use short biscuits, separating same into two pieces, with one piece of biscuit on a tea plate, sliced chicken with supreme sauce on same and the second piece of biscuit with a little more chicken and sauce.

Chef's Comments

INGREDIENTS FOR 2 SERVINGS

4 Shortcake Biscuits (See Baked Goods Section)
8–12 ounces Chicken, cooked, sliced, hot
2 cups Supreme Sauce (See Sauces Section)

The same recipe was listed as Sliced Turkey Shortcake. Apparently the use of chicken made this dish Southern Style.

CHICKEN TETRAZZINI

From *Old Standard B&O Recipes*

1 Fowl, boiled
2 Green Bell Peppers, boiled, ½-inch dice
2 Pimentos, diced
1 pound Mushrooms, sliced
1 quart Milk, heated
Salt, Pepper, and Paprika, to taste
¼ pound Butter
1 cup Cream
1½ cups Béchamel Sauce (See Sauces Section)
5 tablespoons Sherry Wine
16 ounces Spaghetti, boiled

Dice fowl, sauté in butter with mushrooms, green peppers and pimentos, salt, pepper and milk, Béchamel sauce and cream. Cook until properly thickened, flavor with Sherry, mix thoroughly with the cooked spaghetti, fill shirred egg dish, sprinkle with parmesan cheese and paprika, place in oven to brown.

Chef's Comments

MAKES 12 SERVINGS

Heat the oven to 400 degrees for this dish, which can be prepared as shown in individual ovenproof dishes or in a large casserole dish.

The instructions are deceptively simple; they begin at the point when all of the prep work has been done. Allow plenty of time for making the spaghetti and sauce, as well as for all the heating and chopping tasks that lie hidden in the list of ingredients.

This is also an excellent use for leftover chicken, either light or dark meat.

HONEYMOONERS. A young couple starts the salad course of their dinner on the Capitol Limited circa 1957. Baltimore and Ohio Railroad Museum

OTHER MEAT DISHES AND STUFFINGS

MEAT DISHES

Creamed Ham and Turkey on Toast

Grilled Ham Steak with Pineapple Ring

Butter-Panned Ham Steak with Pineapple Ring

Roast Smoked Ham Demi Glace

Stuffed Ham, Individual, with Bread Sauce

Grilled Double Rib Lamb Chops

Grilled Pork Chops, Fried Apple Ring

Pork Chops Normandie

Stuffed Pork Chop with Tomato Sauce

Pork Tenderloin Sauté—German Style

Grilled Frankfurters with Baked Beans

Baked Lentils and Sausage

Calf's Sweetbreads with Creamed Mushrooms

Turkey à la King on Toast

Turkey Croquettes

Turkey Divan

Roast Young Tom Turkey

Sliced Turkey Shortcake

Shirred Sliced Turkey Supreme with Asparagus

Veal Hearts Sauté

STUFFINGS

Bread Sauce

Chestnut Dressing

Oyster Filling (Stuffing)

CREAMED HAM AND TURKEY ON TOAST

From "B&O General Notice," February 4, 1964,
for menus effective February 13, 1964

Use dark and white meat. Dice turkey and ham and
place it in a rich cream sauce. Serve over half slices of
toast in triangular shape. Garnish with a sprig of parsley. DO NOT CHOP MEAT FINE.

Chef's Comments

INGREDIENTS FOR 4 SERVINGS

8 ounces Ham, cooked, diced
8 ounces Turkey, cooked, diced
2 cups Cream Sauce (See Sauces Section)
2 slices Toast
4 sprigs Parsley, fresh

There is a fine line between dicing the ham and turkey and "not chopping it fine." We suggest dicing the
meat in ½–¾-inch cubes.

GRILLED HAM STEAK WITH PINEAPPLE RING

From "B&O General Notice," May 6, 1964,
for menus effective May 14, 1964

Order dinner ham steaks from commissaries. This is
the ready-to-eat kind. Top the ham steak with a ring of
pineapple, add 1 teaspoon of brown sugar and a small
amount of butter. Broil it until it is good and hot.

Chef's Comments

INGREDIENTS FOR 1 SERVING

1 Ham Steak
1 Pineapple Ring
1 teaspoon Brown Sugar
Butter, as needed

It is interesting to note the difference in preparation
of this dish from one month to the next by comparing
this recipe with that for Butter-Panned Ham Steak,
Pineapple Ring, which was offered on the B&O's June
1964 menus (see below).

BUTTER-PANNED HAM STEAK WITH PINEAPPLE RING

From "B&O General Notice," June 3, 1964,
for menus effective June 11, 1964

Order ham steaks from commissaries. These will be
boneless, ready-to-eat type, in 6-ounce portions. Brown
in butter and garnish top with a ring of sliced pineapple
which has been browned in butter.

Chef's Comments

INGREDIENTS FOR 1 SERVING

1 Ham Steak
Butter, as needed
1 Pineapple Ring

ROAST SMOKED HAM DEMI GLACE

From *Old Standard B&O Recipes*

Boil the ham about three quarters done, about three hours, then take out the ham and remove the skin and place it in a roasting pan, and sprinkle it with brown sugar and a teaspoon vinegar, and to this add one quart of Espagnole sauce, and bake in a medium hot oven for one hour, basting frequently with the substance of the ham and Espagnole sauce.

Chef's Comments

Preheat oven to 350 degrees.

The ham is done when the internal temperature reaches 160–165 degrees, thus "three quarters done" would be an internal temperature of 110–115 degrees. Always depend more on the temperature than on the clock.

"Demi glace" is a reduced and thickened Espagnole sauce *(see* Sauces *Section)*, but do not allow it to reduce to the point of not having enough left to serve with the ham. If necessary, add more Espagnole sauce, hot water, or some of the liquid in which the ham was boiled.

Boiling the ham is necessary to reconstitute the dried meat. A good Virginia ham, for instance, that has been dry-cured could not be baked without boiling first.

If you have the luxury of more time, simmer the ham instead of boiling and roast at a lower temperature for a longer duration in order to keep the meat nice and moist.

STUFFED BAKED HAM, INDIVIDUAL, WITH BREAD SAUCE

From *Old Standard B&O Recipes*

One slice of boiled ham, one quarter inch thick, cut from large horseshoe side of ham. Place one basting spoon of bread dressing on ham and fold, fasten with wire skewer, dust with flour, put in baking pan, with stock that ham was boiled in; bake until brown, make gravy of liquor ham was baked in; serve hot, one to the order.

Chef's Comments

INGREDIENTS FOR 1 SERVING

1 slice Ham, boneless, boiled, ¼-inch thick
2 tablespoons Bread Sauce *(See page 87)*
1 cup Ham Juice
Flour, as needed

Use the smallest baking pan into which all orders will fit.

To make the gravy, pour the juice into a saucepan and add flour gradually, stirring constantly to obtain the desired thickness. Bring to a boil and reduce to a simmer for 10 minutes, stirring occasionally. If the gravy is too thick, thin with hot water.

GRILLED DOUBLE RIB LAMB CHOPS

From "B&O General Notice," August 11, 1959, for menus effective August 13, 1959

Order lamb racks for this item. Racks will be frenched and cut at commissary. Serve two double rib chops to the order. Mint jelly to be served in small ramekin on dinner plate.

Chef's Comments

INGREDIENTS FOR I SERVING

Double-Rib Lamb Chops (2 per serving)
Oil, Olive, Canola, etc., as needed
Salt and Pepper, to taste
Mint Jelly, as needed

Coat both sides of each chop with oil and season with salt and pepper to taste.

Place on a hot grill for 2–4 minutes, then rotate the chop about 90 degrees or so and cook another 2–4 minutes. This will produce those attractive criss-cross grill marks. Turn each chop over and do the same on the other side. (This can also be done a broiler, but cooking time may vary.)

The term *frenched* means that about two inches of the rib bones have been stripped of fat and meat.

GRILLED PORK CHOPS, FRIED APPLE RING

From "B&O General Notice," October 7, 1963, and *The Culinary Handbook* (Fellows)

These will come cut 3 to the pound. Serve two chops to the order. Be sure to serve full apple rings on this item and not just fried apples.

Good firm apples, peeled, cored, cut in slices half an inch thick, then dipped in milk, rolled in flour and fried in very hot lard.

Chef's Comments

INGREDIENTS FOR I SERVING

2 Pork Chops
Salt and Pepper, to taste
Butter, melted, as needed
Bread Crumbs, as needed (optional)
Cooking Oil, as needed
½ Apple
Milk, as needed
Flour, as needed

Trim excess fat from the chops and season with salt and pepper to taste. Roll in butter, then in breadcrumbs, if desired. Broil or grill until well done.

A more healthful version of this recipe would substitute cooking oil (say canola or olive oil) not only for the lard in which the apple rings are fried but also for the butter in which the chops are rolled.

One wonders what prompted James B. Martin, manager of the B&O's Dining Car and Commissary Department, to specifically prohibit the use of "just fried apples." He may have been cautioning against the use of scraps or trimmings in order to improve the dish's presentation.

PORK CHOPS NORMANDIE

From "B&O General Notice," February 9, 1960, for menus effective February 11, 1960

When ordering chops for this item show on requisition number of chops desired. These will be furnished ready cut and four to the pound. To prepare, place in a greased baking dish. Season with salt and pepper. Pour apple cider over chops until juice is even with chops. Pare and slice firm tart apples over the chops. About two apples to six chops. Over the apple sprinkle cinnamon, a little ground clove and ground nutmeg. Add two bay leaves and bake in a moderate oven about 1 hour and 15 minutes.

The apple cider, apples and spice flavor impart a most delicious flavor to these chops and is something different from the average pork chop dinner.

TWO CHOPS ARE TO BE SERVED TO THE ORDER.

Chef's Comments

INGREDIENTS FOR 3 SERVINGS

3 Pork Chops, ¾-inch thick
Salt and Pepper, to taste
2 cups Apple Cider
1 Cooking Apple, sliced
Cloves, ground, to taste
Cinnamon, ground, to taste
Nutmeg, ground, to taste
1 Bay Leaf

Preheat oven to 350 degrees and adjust oven time according to the thickness of the pork chops available. Internal temperature should be 160 degrees after 1 hour 15 minutes in the oven.

Thanks to Jim Porterfield, author of *Dining by Rail,* who generously allowed the use of his ingredient measurements. Interestingly, *What's Cooking on the B&O?* used this recipe ten years before this "General Notice" was issued. That source called for pork chops 1¾-inch thick, but only one chop per order, with which Porterfield concurs.

On February 19, 1950, the Pittsburgh *Sun-Telegraph* published an interview with dining car Steward J. J. "Jerry" Collins. Collins stated, "Pork chops should be cut from the rib, about three to the pound" which, when compared with the "General Notice," explains why two chops were served by 1960.

The article continued, "On his run between Washington and Chicago [Collins] has found that [Pork Chops Normandie] ranks highest with the notables he serves." Collins recommended that this main dish be served with peas *(see recipe in the* Vegetables and Pasta Dishes *Section)* and candied sweet potatoes.

STUFFED PORK CHOP WITH TOMATO SAUCE
From *Old Standard B&O Recipes*

Cut pork chop about one inch thick, cut off chine, leave meat on both sides of rib, lay flat and slit from top to bottom down. Lay open and stuff with filling of bread crumbs, onions and celery, as for poultry stuffing. Braise in oven, take out and dip in egg wash, then cracker meal and fry in deep fat to a golden brown.

Chef's Comments

INGREDIENTS FOR 2 SERVINGS

1 ounce Bread Crumbs
1 ounce Onion, minced
1 ounce Celery, minced
2 Pork Chops, 1-inch thick
1 Egg
2 tablespoons Water
Cracker Meal, as needed
Cooking Oil or Butter, as needed
¼ cup Tomato Sauce

Preheat oven to 350 degrees.

When filled, the chops may need to be held together with toothpicks or kitchen twine to retain the stuffing inside. (Be sure to remove the twine or toothpicks before serving.) Bake until the internal temperature reaches 160 degrees. Baste with butter during baking to keep the chops moist and tender.

Break the egg into a shallow bowl or pan and add the water to make the egg wash.

The full title of this recipe was Stuffed Pork Chop, Braised Apple Ring, Tomato Sauce, but no mention was made of how to cook the apple ring.

PORK TENDERLOIN SAUTÉ—GERMAN STYLE

From *Old Standard B&O Recipes*

Cut tenderloin three inches thick, flatten with cleaver, salt and pepper, and dust with flour; sauté in butter with minced onion until brown. Pour half cup of sour cream for each six pieces, cover pan and cook slowly for one half hour.

Chef's Comments

INGREDIENTS FOR 4-6 SERVINGS

3–4 pounds Pork Tenderloin
Salt and Pepper, to taste
Flour, as needed
Butter, as needed
1 Onion, minced
½ cup Sour Cream

When pounded thin with a cleaver (or meat tenderizer), these make rather large pieces that may need to be sautéed separately or on a griddle.

The secret is to sauté each piece until nearly done, then simmer over low heat to avoid scorching the sour cream.

One-half cup of sour cream may not produce enough sauce; we suggest one cup for every six pieces.

GRILLED FRANKFURTERS WITH BAKED BEANS

From "B&O General Notice," September 1, 1960

To one #10 can of beans add one bottle of catsup, one cup of brown sugar, two tablespoons of prepared mustard and a small grated onion. Dice a half pound of bacon and fry medium. Add to beans, mix well and brown in oven. Place three diagonal cuts in both sides of frankfurter, brush with butter and grill until slightly browned. Serve three (3) frankfurters on a bed of baked beans.

Chef's Comments

INGREDIENTS FOR 2–4 SERVINGS

15 ounces Baked Beans
2 ounces Catsup
1¼ ounces Brown Sugar
¼ teaspoon Mustard, prepared
¾ ounce Onion, grated
1¼ ounces Bacon, diced
Frankfurters, 3 per order
Butter, melted, as needed

Preheat oven to 400 degrees.

BAKED LENTILS AND SAUSAGE

From *Old Standard B&O Recipes*

The lentils are to be soaked overnight and prepared the same as you would bake beans, except that no tomatoes or tomato sauce would be put in them, but you are to use a little pork, for seasoning, same as you do the baked beans. Cut the sausage two slices for this service.

Chef's Comments

INGREDIENTS FOR 8 SERVINGS

1 pound Link Sausage
3 tablespoons Butter or Cooking Oil
¼ Onion, minced fine
1 pound Lentils
3½ cups Chicken or Beef Stock
¼ teaspoon Dry Mustard
⅛ teaspoon Baking Powder

Cut the sausages lengthwise in two slices. Heat oil in a 4-quart pot and sauté the sausage and onions until the sausage is well browned.

Add the remaining ingredients to the pot and mix thoroughly. Cover and simmer for 10 minutes.

Bake at 450 degrees until browned (approximately 20 minutes).

This is one of a number of recipes for which the notes in *Old Standard B&O Recipes* were rather vague. This dish was to be "prepared the same as you would bake beans, except that no tomatoes or tomato sauce" was to be added. There was no word as to what liquid was supposed to replace those items, so we have borrowed advice from some other cookbooks with regard to the use of stock.

As with the Baked Beans recipe, the 12-hour soaking step can be shortened by placing the beans in a pot and covering with 2–3 inches of cold water. Bring the water to a boil and immediately turn off the heat. Cover the pot and allow the lentils to stand for an hour. Drain the lentils in a colander, rinse with cold water, and cook according to the recipe.

CALF'S SWEETBREADS WITH CREAMED MUSHROOMS

From *Old Standard B&O Recipes*

Prepared sweetbreads cut in slices and sautéed in butter, piled on toast, surrounded with sliced mushrooms boiled down in reduced cream.

Chef's Comments

INGREDIENTS FOR 2 SERVINGS

1 pound Sweetbreads
2 tablespoons Butter
2 slices Toast
½ cup Mushrooms, sliced
2 cups Cream

Place the sweetbreads in a bowl of lightly salted water and refrigerate for 3 hours. With a sharp boning knife, remove as much of the outer membrane as possible and still keep the sweetbreads from falling to pieces. Place the sweetbreads in a pan and cover with lightly salted water. Bring slowly to a boil, stirring occasionally. When the boiling point is reached, transfer to a bowl of cold water and place under a faucet of cold running water. Continue until cooled.

Heat the cream over medium heat and add the

mushrooms. Bring to a boil and reduce to a simmer until reduced by a third to a half.

Melt the butter in a frying pan over medium-low heat. Meanwhile, hold each sweetbread on end and slice in half. Increase the heat to high and sauté the sweetbreads in the butter until brown. Drain on paper towels.

Pour the cream through a colander to remove the mushrooms.

Put a piece of toast on a plate; pile the toast with sweetbreads, surround with mushrooms, and add the sauce over the top.

TURKEY À LA KING ON TOAST

From "B&O General Notice," January 7, 1964, for menus effective January 9, 1964

½ pound Turkey, cooked, diced
1 quart Heavy Cream Sauce
¼ cup Green Peppers, diced, sautéed
½ cup Pimentos, diced
3 Egg Yolks
2 tablespoons Sherry Wine
Salt and Pepper, to taste

Method: Beat egg yolks, add to cream sauce and let come to a boil, stirring constantly. Remove from stove and add other ingredients. Serve on a dinner plate on slices of trimmed toast, garnished with small wedges of toast and parsley.

Chef's Comments

YIELDS TWO SERVINGS

If possible, add the egg yolk while the sauce is fairly cool and be sure to mind those instructions to "stir constantly" while it comes to a boil. This will keep the sauce smooth and free of floating bits of cooked yolk.

If these instructions are followed as written, the green pepper will be nearly raw when the dish is served. To avoid this, it can be sautéed or simmered a bit first, or simply added to the sauce before the other ingredients and simmered for a few minutes.

TURKEY CROQUETTES

From "B&O General Notice," October 4, 1960, for menus effective October 6, 1960

7 tablespoons Turkey Fat
1¼ pounds Turkey, Minced
6¼ cups Turkey Stock
1½ cups Milk
1 cup Flour
1 Egg Yolk
4 tablespoons Onion, Minced
2½ tablespoons Salt
1 teaspoon Pepper
1 bunch Parsley, chopped

Sauté onions for 5 minutes. Add flour gradually and blend well. Add turkey stock slowly and stir quickly to prevent lumps forming. When flour is cooked thoroughly, beat egg yolk and combine with milk to the blended flour. Add the turkey and parsley and cook a few minutes. Chill and mold into 2-oz. cones, dip in egg batter, roll in bread crumbs and fry in deep fat. CROQUETTES SHOULD BE FRESH MIXED. THEY DO NOT KEEP WELL IN

ICEBOX. Serve 2 Croquettes to order. Above recipe will make 22 portions. Do not pour sauce over Croquettes. Croquettes should be set upright in sauce.

Chef's Comments

ADDITIONAL INGREDIENTS

4 Eggs
½ cup Water
Bread Crumbs, as needed

The flour will be "cooked thoroughly" after about 10 minutes over low heat.

TURKEY DIVAN

From "B&O General Notice," June 2, 1960,
for menus effective June 2, 1960

Extreme care should be taken in its preparation and recipe quoted below should be followed exactly:

Place a portion of cooked broccoli in a shirred egg dish and pour over it a rich cream sauce to be made as follows:

4 tablespoons butter, 4 tablespoons flour, 2 cups turkey stock. Stir constantly until thick and smooth for approximately 10 minutes. Add one cup of milk, one cup of cream and three tablespoons sherry wine. Over the sauce-covered broccoli arrange 4 thin slices of cooked turkey. Cover lightly with more sauce and sprinkle with Parmesan cheese. Place in oven until sauce bubbles and is slightly brown.

Chef's Comments

When making the cream sauce, melt the butter in a saucepan and stir the flour in before adding the stock.

ROAST YOUNG TOM TURKEY

From *The Culinary Handbook* (Fellows)

Take young plump birds, singe, draw, wash, stuff with a mixture of white bread soaked and squeezed dry, seasoned with salt, pepper, mixed herbs, melted butter and yolks of eggs. Truss with legs well into the body; season the bird with pepper and salt, roast for about two hours, well basting during roasting; serve portions with the stuffing under the meat, and a dish of cranberry sauce of jelly separate.

Chef's Comments

Preheat oven to 400 degrees.

Place the stuffing in the turkey loosely to ensure that it will cook thoroughly. Trussing with twine or skewers will keep the stuffing inside the bird during cooking.

Roast uncovered for 30 minutes to brown the skin, basting with butter every 15 minutes. Then reduce the oven temperature to 325 degrees and continue cooking until the turkey and stuffing reach an internal temperature of 180 degrees. Continue basting with butter every 15 minutes. If the turkey begins to overbrown, cover it lightly with aluminum foil.

When the correct internal temperature is reached, remove the turkey from the oven and allow it to rest for 15–20 minutes. This allows for even distribution of juices. Then, remove the stuffing from the bird. Carve the turkey and serve atop a portion of stuffing.

When planning a meal, allow 15–18 minutes cooking time per pound of turkey.

The turkey and stuffing can be roasted in separate pans, which is safer and quicker, but less traditional. Doing so allows the stuffing to cook thoroughly without making the turkey dry and tough. In this case, a cooking time of 12–15 minutes per pound of turkey should bring the internal temperature to 180 degrees.

Although the stuffing in this recipe sounds good, there is no evidence to support its use on the B&O.

As an alternative to the above procedure, most poultry will benefit from roasting breast-side-down for half of the cooking time, which will allow the fat along the back of the bird to baste the meat. This may, however, damage the breast skin and cause presentation issues.

SLICED TURKEY SHORTCAKE

From "B&O General Notice," June 2, 1960, for menus effective June 2, 1960

Use short biscuits, separating same into two pieces, with one biscuit on tea plate, slice turkey and supreme sauce on same, and the second piece of biscuit with a little more turkey and sauce.

Chef's Comments

INGREDIENTS FOR 2 SERVINGS

4 Shortcake Biscuits (See Baked Goods Section)
8–12 ounces Turkey, cooked, sliced, hot
2 cups Supreme Sauce (See Sauces Section)

SHIRRED SLICED TURKEY SUPREME WITH ASPARAGUS

From "B&O General Notice," October 8, 1959, for menus effective October 8, 1959

Place slices of white and dark meat of turkey over 4 spears of asparagus in a buttered shirred egg dish. Cover with supreme sauce and place in oven until ready. Use tea plate for service, vegetables to be served in bakers.

Chef's Comments

INGREDIENTS FOR 1 SERVING

4 ounces Turkey, cooked, sliced
4 spears Asparagus, cooked
½ cup Supreme Sauce (See Sauces Section)

Place the dish in a 300-degree oven for about 20 minutes.

VEAL HEARTS SAUTÉ

From Old Standard B&O Recipes

Slice the hearts and dredge with flour. Sauté with onions until tender, make brown pan gravy.

Chef's Comments

This is one of those recipes that assumes that the cook knows what he/she is doing. Be that as it may, the directions seem fairly simple. It's finding a veal heart that may prove to be a challenge.

BREAD SAUCE

From *B&O Chef's Notes*

BREAD SAUCE, EATEN WITH PHEASANT, PARTRIDGE, ROAST FOWL, ETC.

Rub through a colander a teacup full of breadcrumbs. Into half pint of cold milk—throw in a peeled onion, cut across, and four all spice berries, and boil eight minutes. Take out the onion and berries, put in the bread and an ounce of butter—beat the sauce well with fork—boil slowly five minutes. Serve hot.

Chef's Comments

INGREDIENTS FOR 2 CUPS OF SAUCE

1 cup Milk
1 Onion, peeled, cut in halves
4 Allspice Berries
2 cups Bread, ¼-inch dice
1 ounce Butter

This Bread "Sauce" is, of course, bread stuffing or dressing. Although most cooks think of placing the stuffing inside the bird, it is cooked separately in this recipe. This has two advantages. The first is that the bird cooks faster without stuffing inside, a decided plus in dining car service. The second "plus" speaks to issues of quality and safety. Achieving a finished turkey that is not dry or tough often means running the risk of under-cooking the stuffing, which can cause food poisoning.

This dish should be made as close to serving time as possible.

CHESTNUT DRESSING

From *Old Standard B&O Recipes*

RECIPE NUMBER 26

1 quart Chestnuts
¼ cup Bread Crumbs
2 tablespoons Butter
2 tablespoons Cream
Salt and Pepper, to taste

Shell and blanche the chestnuts, boil until tender, while still warm rub through colander, add other ingredients, chopped celery or onion may be added if desired.

Chef's Comments

If celery and onion are added, use three ribs of celery and/or one onion, each chopped fine.

These days, "rubbing" any ingredient through a colander is unnecessary, not to mention tedious. In this recipe, put the chestnuts into a food processor or blender and pulse until they are reduced to small pieces.

HOW TO "SHELL AND BLANCHE THE CHESTNUTS"

• With a sharp knife, make long cross cuts in the form of an X on each nut.
• Roll the nuts in oil or melted butter until moistened.
• In a shallow pan, bake at 350 degrees for 30 minutes.
• Peel away the shells, which will have broken at the X-shaped cuts.
• Throw the meat of the nuts into a pot of boiling water for 60 seconds.
• Immediately place in a bowl of ice water until cool enough to handle.
• Remove as much of the skin as possible.
• Boil until tender as shown in the recipe.

Oyster Filling (Stuffing)

From *The Culinary Handbook* (Fellows)

For fish and poultry; oysters blanched and drained, cut in quarters, or if using Standards, leave them whole. Moist stale bread grated one part, rolled oyster crackers one part, the third part of oysters, the whole mixed together and seasoned with salt, pepper and chopped parsley, the liquor brought to the boil with an addition of the butter, poured to the dry mixture, stirred, then ready for use.

Chef's Comments

INGREDIENTS FOR 1¾ POUNDS STUFFING

8 ounces Oysters, shucked
8 ounces Bread Crumbs
8 ounces Oyster Cracker Crumbs
Salt and Pepper, to taste
Parsley, chopped, to taste
Oyster Liquor or Fish Stock, as needed
Butter, as needed

Place the oysters in boiling water for about 60 seconds, drain, and cut in quarters. Thoroughly mix the oysters, bread and cracker crumbs, salt, pepper, and parsley. Bring the liquor or stock to a boil, add the butter and stir gradually into the dry mixture until all ingredients are moistened and dough-like in consistency. Stuff the poultry, or bake separately until nicely browned.

An easy way to make bread or cracker crumbs is to process sliced bread or crackers in a food processor to the desired texture. The use of "stale bread" as called for in the recipe will produce a different flavor from fresh bread and may also require additional liquid to moisten it adequately.

Oyster liquor is simply the juice from inside a shell oyster (or the juice that comes in the container with bottled or canned shucked oysters). If you have insufficient oyster liquor to achieve the proper consistency, add fish stock or bouillon as needed.

This recipe makes enough stuffing for a small turkey (15 pounds). Notice that there are equal parts of oysters, bread crumbs, and cracker crumbs, so the amounts shown can easily be adjusted for the size of the turkey.

FORTIETH BIRTHDAY. May 13, 1963, marked the fortieth anniversary of the Baltimore/Washington–Chicago run of the Capitol Limited. The B&O marked the occasion with a large sheet cake appropriately decorated and lettered, which was "presented" to the train on the platform of Washington's Union Station. It was then displayed in the dining car, where it took up a whole table. Here, a young woman is served a piece of the cake by a waiter wearing his fortieth anniversary badge. Baltimore and Ohio Railroad Museum

**Royal Blue Line
Dining Car Service**

PHILADELPHIA AND
READING R. R.

CENTRAL R. R.
OF NEW JERSEY

Dinner

BROILED SARDINES ON TOAST

BLUE POINT COCKTAIL

CREAM OF ASPARAGUS
CELERY
OLIVES

ESSENCE OF FOWL, COLBERT
SLICED TOMATOES
SALTED ALMONDS

BROILED BLACK BASS, LEMON BUTTER SAUCE
POTATOES, JULIENNE

FILET DE MIGNON, WITH MUSHROOMS

FIG FRITTERS, ALMOND SAUCE

PRIME ROAST BEEF, AU JUS

MASHED POTATOES

STRING BEANS

ROAST TURKEY, OYSTER DRESSING

CAULIFLOWER, IN CREAM

SWEET POTATOES, BRAISED

ROMAN PUNCH

LOBSTER SALAD, AU MAYONNAISE

VANILLA ICE CREAM
PLUM PUDDING, BRANDY SAUCE

ASSORTED CAKE
HOT MINCE PIE

NABISCO SUGAR WAFERS

ROQUEFORT AND EDAM CHEESE

TOASTED WATER CRACKERS

SALTINE WAFERS

BLACK COFFEE

COGNAC

MEALS ONE DOLLAR

IF A SUPPER IS PREFERRED TO THIS TABLE D'HOTE DINNER, THE STEWARD
WILL ARRANGE TO HAVE ONE SERVED AT THE SAME PRICE, TO INCLUDE A STEAK,
CHOPS OR FISH, ETC.

THE DRINKING WATER IS FROM THE SPRING AT DEER PARK, MD.

CAR 1008

FRIDAY, DECEMBER 25, 1908.

CHRISTMAS 1906 MENU. A soon-to-be-roasted boar has scattered cranberries across this dinner menu from the B&O's Royal Blue trains between Washington, D.C., and New York. Tom Greco collection

"THE WILL TO PLEASE." B&O president Daniel Willard made this phrase a byword among B&O employees during the late 1920s. The back cover of the November 1928 issue of *Baltimore and Ohio* magazine illustrates how the Dining Car and Commissary Department envisioned the concept. Tom Greco collection

On our railroad YOU are right

YEARS ago we adopted a suggestion from the head of a great department store who was one of our directors. He said that in his store "the customer is always right."

Unfortunately, we can not refund a passenger's fare if—as sometimes happens—he does not enjoy his trip. The law compels us to collect and account for the fare; we are subject to penalty if we fail to do so.

But in our dining service we can within reason make our own rules. And in our dining car *you* are always right.

If you dislike any dish, it is taken back cheerfully and at once.

If, at the end of the meal, you say you have not enjoyed it, you can not pay for that meal. *You* must be satisfied.

"But," people occasionally exclaim, "aren't you imposed upon?" Sometimes perhaps, but rarely.

We believe that we gain much good-will by treating men and women as though they were guests in our home. And good-will is the very life-blood of a railroad.

Travel with us on your next trip east or west and see if we can prove to you that we really value *your* good-will.

The B&O

STOP OVER IN WASHINGTON AT NO EXTRA CHARGE

Between New York and the West the B & O runs through some of the most interesting historical country in America. Harpers Ferry, the Potomac Valley, and the Blue Ridge Mountains —here is a scenic experience not to be missed. And every ticket carries a free stop-over privilege in Washington.

BALTIMORE & OHIO

"YOU ARE RIGHT." One of a series of award-winning advertisements, this beautiful scene appeared in the May 31, 1930, issue of the *Saturday Evening Post*. Two guests are being served dinner aboard one of the F-4B Colonial diners. Tom Greco collection

The "Royal Blue" Dinner

Selection: A—1.25

FRUIT COCKTAIL

ICED CELERY   SPICED WATERMELON RIND

SOUP, CREAM OF CELERY   BEEF BOUILLON

Choice
- BROILED FRESH FISH, POTATO CHIPS
- SAUTE OF OYSTERS ON TOAST WITH BACON
- GRILLED SPECIAL DOUBLE RIB LAMB CHOPS
- BRAISED CALF SWEETBREADS ON SMITHFIELD HAM
- BROILED PRIME SIRLOIN STEAK

BAKED IDAHO POTATO   CANDIED SWEET POTATOES

NEW FRESH BROCCOLI, BUTTER SAUCE

SALAD, WALDORF
Lettuce, Apple, Celery, Walnuts
Mayonnaise Dressing

POTATO ROLLS   PRUNE MUFFINS

GREEN APPLE PIE WITH CHEESE   ICE CREAM

CHEESE AND CRACKERS

COFFEE   TEA   MILK

Steward of this Car

H. O. McAbee
Manager of Dining Car and
Commissary Department
Baltimore, Maryland
10B39

Selection: B—1.00

QUEEN OLIVES

SOUP, CREAM OF CELERY   BEEF BOUILLON

FRIED OYSTERS, COLE SLAW
OR
PRIME RIB ROAST OF BEEF AU JUS

BROWNED POTATOES   NEW STRING BEANS

(Choice)
APPLE DUMPLING, WINE SAUCE   ICE CREAM
CHEESE AND CRACKERS

COFFEE   TEA   MILK

Selection: C—.90

CROSS CUT PICKLES

CUP OF SOUP OR TOMATO JUICE COCKTAIL

PANNED FRESH FISH, PARSLEY BUTTER
OR
OMELET, CREOLE STYLE

CREAMED POTATOES   NEW CREAMED SPINACH

APPLE COBBLER OR ICE CREAM

COFFEE   TEA   MILK

Half portions of items practical to be divided will be served at half price
to children under 12 years of age

Passengers are respectfully requested to write orders on checks and consult
Steward if service is not entirely to their satisfaction

PALMIER DAYS ON THE ROYAL BLUE. A variety of table d'hôte meals awaited the Washington–New York traveler in October 1939. Back then, diners had more of a taste for organ meats than is the case today; note the Braised Calf Sweetbreads on Smithfield Ham entrée. Karl Spence collection

THE BALTIMORE & OHIO RAILROAD COMPANY

Menu

MIDNIGHT LUNCHEON

Consomme, Hot or Cold

Steak with French Fried Potatoes - - - 1.50

Chicken or Shrimp Salad
with
Saratoga Chips 1.00

Dry or Buttered Toast

Tea   Coffee   Milk

SANDWICHES

Minute Steak	1.00
Club	.75
Junior Club	.50
Ham	.20
Tongue	.30
Chicken	.40
Cheese	.20
Coffee, Pot	.20

H. O. McAbee
Manager of Dining Car and
Commissary Department
Baltimore, Maryland

DINING CAR SERVICE

THE MYSTERIOUS "MIDNIGHT LUNCHEON." This style of menu was found on B&O dining cars around 1940, but there is no indication of which train or trains offered this substantial late-night repast. Karl Spence collection

"Think of them as big doughboys"

All of you, I am sure, have seen trains of war weapons moving toward shipping ports. And you must be sensible of the tough job they must do to win this war. And when you see the big engines pulling their heavy loads, don't think of them merely as trains. *Think of them as big doughboys, with five thousand tons on their backs, on their way to help save our civilization.*

R. B. WHITE, *President of the B & O*

"THINK OF THEM AS BIG DOUGHBOYS." The term *doughboy* for a U.S. Army infantryman was passé by October 1943, so this characterization of one of the B&O's home-built T-3 Class 4-8-2s may seem a bit corny. This beautiful and patriotic menu cover belied a rather austere luncheon selection aboard the B&O's New York–St. Louis Diplomat. Tom Greco collection

A STUDY IN EMBLEMS. This B&O place setting uses a napkin with the road's pre-1937 emblem atop a tablecloth with the logo designed by Otto Kuhler and introduced that year. The ashtray displays the "Linking 13 Great States" emblem introduced in 1945. The B&O was proud of the bottled water from its Boiling Spring at Deer Park, Maryland. Jim Hart collection

What's Cooking ON THE B&O?

POPULAR RECIPES FROM
B & O DINING CARS . . .
and Tips about Safety in the Kitchen

A B&O CLASSIC. For nearly fifty years, *What's Cooking on the B&O?* remained the only readily available source of the road's dining car recipes. Twelve detailed recipes were given, along with tips for preparing seven breakfast dishes. Tom Greco collection

CRAB IMPERIAL. A Maryland staple, crab imperial was actually heated and served in the top shell of a crab by the B&O. Here the crab is presented with potatoes and a salad. *(See recipe in* Fish and Seafood Dishes *Section.)* Jim Hart collection

SOUTHERN STYLE FRIED CHICKEN. Shown here with boiled new potatoes, beets, and a corn fritter, this entrée was indicative of the Southern influence that pervaded many a B&O menu. *(See recipe in* Chicken Dishes *Section.)* Jim Hart collection

ALMOST TOO PRETTY TO EAT. This beautifully composed lettuce salad was certainly not picked from the road's famous "Help Yourself" salad bowl, but it does include at least a half-dozen ingredients. Jim Hart collection

THANKSGIVING DINNER. This remarkable photo graced the cover of the November 1957 issue of *Baltimore and Ohio* magazine. The à la carte feast includes a sumptuous helping of roast turkey with cranberry sauce, peas, hors d'oeuvres, dinner rolls, and a salad. Karl Spence collection

The Capitol Limited
Baltimore & Ohio Railroad

MENU

Official FLOWERS OF THE THIRTEEN STATES SERVED BY THE B&O

District of Columbia—American Beauty Rose

Maryland—Black-eyed Susan

Michigan—Apple Blossom

Pennsylvania—Mountain Laurel

Kentucky—Goldenrod

Ohio—Red Carnation

Missouri—Hawthorn

New Jersey—Illinois—Violet

Indiana—Zinnia

West Virginia—Gr. Rhododendron

Delaware—Peach Blossom

Virginia—Dogwood

New York—Rose

CAPITOL LIMITED DINNER MENU OF JUNE 12, 1958. This striking menu cover was used on the B&O's feature trains, having originally graced the cover of the November 1955 issue of *Baltimore and Ohio* magazine. Award-winning amateur photographer Earl France, an employee of B&O's Engineering Department, traveled across the system over a two-year period taking the photos and then worked with the magazine's staff to compose this montage. Tom Greco collection

BREAKFAST MENU, MARCH 9, 1961. "A pleasant tradition" is illustrated on the cover of this menu used on the Capitol Limited and the Columbian between Baltimore, Washington, and Chicago. It also recalls a time when smoking was more socially acceptable and allowed in most public places. This menu cover was used for approximately ten years, beginning around 1952. Karl Spence collection

BALTIMORE AND OHIO DINING CAR SERVICE *Menu*

Best Wishes of the Season

FROM THE MEN AND WOMEN
OF THE
BALTIMORE & OHIO RAILROAD

SEASON'S GREETINGS. The tradition of festive holiday menu covers was carried on for at least sixty years aboard B&O dining cars. This one was dated December 9, 1965. Karl Spence collection

menu

FRESH FRUIT CUP .60		CHILLED FRUIT JUICE .35	
SOUP OF THE DAY .35		TOMATO JUICE .35	

BROILED RIB EYE STEAK, FRIED ONIONS—2.85

ROAST YOUNG TURKEY, DRESSING, CRANBERRY RELISH—2.60

BAKED MEAT LOAF, MUSHROOM GRAVY—2.60

(Vegetable or Salad, Potatoes, Bread, Butter and Beverage Included)

SALADS

B&O SALAD BOWL	1.00	TUNA FISH, MAYONNAISE	1.25
LETTUCE AND TOMATO	.75	CHICKEN, MAYONNAISE	1.50

SPECIAL SALAD BOWL WITH JULIENNE HAM AND CHICKEN—1.75

SANDWICHES

HAM	.75	CLUB	1.75
TUNA FISH	.80	HAM AND EGG	1.25
CHICKEN	1.00	CHICKEN SALAD	1.00
FRIED EGG	65	CHEESE	.65

BACON AND TOMATO ON TOAST—.80

GOLDEN OMELET, CHEDDAR CHEESE
or
SEASONAL FISH, TARTAR SAUCE

POTATOES OR VEGETABLE   CHEF SALAD
Bread and Butter

Coffee   Tea   Milk
1.95

DESSERTS

FRESHLY BAKED PIE	35	PRESERVED FIGS	.35
A LA MODE	.60	CHEESE WITH SALTINES	.50
ICE CREAM	30	HALF GRAPEFRUIT	40

BEVERAGES

COFFEE, POT	35	SANKA, POT	.35
TEA, POT	35	INDIV. MILK OR BUTTERMILK	.25

A charge of 50c per person will be made for food service outside of dining car

Car In Charge of

J. B. Martin,
Manager, Dining Car and
Commissary Department
Baltimore & Ohio R.R.
Baltimore 1, Maryland
7-9-N-9-65

HOLIDAY REPAST. The festive menu of December 9, 1965, was used on Washington-Chicago Trains 7 and 9, the Diplomat and the Chicago Express, respectively. On the Diplomat, this would be a lunch menu offered while the train traversed northern Ohio and Indiana. It was the dinner menu to be served as the Chicago Express crested the Alleghenies at Sand Patch, Pennsylvania, and descended toward Pittsburgh. Steak and dinner omelet were traditional B&O dinner offerings, accented here by the seasonal turkey dinner and a real comfort-food item, baked meatloaf with mushroom gravy. Karl Spence collection

FISH AND SEAFOOD DISHES

CRABS

Deluxe Maryland Crab Cakes

Maryland Crab Cakes (Chef George Fulton)

Deviled Crab Cakes

Maryland Crab Flakes au Gratin

Imperial Crab (Recipe Number 10)

Crab Imperial

Crab Imperial à la Grady

OYSTERS

Capitol Limited Oyster Pie

Creamed Oysters, Baltimore Style

Oysters au Gratin

Oysters Bourguinonne

Oysters, Chesapeake Style

Oyster Fricassee, Baltimore Style

Oysters, Maryland Style

Panned Oysters on Toast

Ham and Panned Oysters on Toast

Shell Oyster Roast

Oyster Stew Recipes

Oysters with Macaroni

OTHER FISH DISHES

Broiled Boned Shad with Roe

Clam Pie, Individual

Delicious Codfish Cakes with Tomato Sauce

Finan Haddie Delmonico

Terrapin, Maryland Style

Panned Mountain Trout

DELUXE MARYLAND CRAB CAKES

From "Circular No. 1896," of July 27, 1943,
for menus effective August 1943

Follow the recipe listed below, which is somewhat different from recipe heretofore used:

1 pound Back Fin Lump Crab Meat
1 slice Bread, soaked in Water and Squeezed Dry.
   Break in Small Pieces
1 tablespoon Colman's Dry Mustard
¾ tablespoon Salt
1 teaspoon Pepper
1 tablespoon Mayonnaise
1 Egg, well beaten

Mix well, form into six cakes, and sauté in shortening. BE CAREFUL NOT TO BREAK UP THE LARGE LUMPS OF CRAB MEAT.

Chef's Comments

Before combining ingredients, wrap the crabmeat in cheesecloth and squeeze to remove as much liquid as possible.

In his book *Chesapeake Bay Cooking with John Shields,* Chef Shields refers to this dish when he writes, "The blue crab, along with the oyster, has been a major culinary influence on Chesapeake Bay regional fare. The crab cakes of the Baltimore and Ohio Railroad dining cars are legendary" (1998, p. 18).

B&O menus used several names over the years—Crab Cakes, Maryland Crab Cakes, Deluxe Maryland Crab Cakes—but the ingredients and amounts specified never varied, only the yield. By 1959, chefs were instructed to make seven cakes from this recipe, while

in the "General Notice" of July 5, 1960, is found this entry: "JUMBO CRAB CAKE: Recipe for this item is the same as that of Deluxe Maryland Crab Cakes with the exception to realize five (5) cakes to one pound of crab meat, instead of seven (7)."

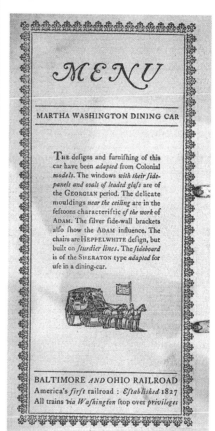

'MARTHA WASHINGTON' MENU (front). Each of the Class F-4B Colonial diners was named for a famous woman in American colonial history. This 1925 menu came from Car 1036, the *Martha Washington,* built in 1923. Tom Greco collection

MARYLAND CRAB CAKES
(CHEF GEORGE FULTON)

From *Dining by Rail* (Porterfield)

YIELD: 3 SERVINGS

1 pound Crabmeat
2 slices Bread
1 Egg
1 tablespoon Mayonnaise
1 teaspoon Dry Mustard
Few sprigs Parsley, chopped
Few drops Tabasco Sauce
Few drops Worcestershire Sauce
White Pepper and Salt, to taste

Clean and pick over crabs to remove any bits of shell. Trim bread of crust, and dice bread into small pieces. In a bowl, combine egg, mayonnaise, mustard, parsley, Tabasco sauce, Worcestershire sauce, salt, white pepper and diced bread. Using hands or a fork, mix until ingredients form a paste. Fold crabmeat into mixture. Shape into 6 or 7 individual cakes. In a large skillet over high heat, fry cakes in hot cooking oil about 5 minutes until browned, turning once.

Chef's Comments

This may be a case of improving on perfection. In his fine book *Dining by Rail,* Jim Porterfield cites this dish as B&O Chef George Fulton's "personalization" of the B&O's standard recipe (p. 316).

Be sure to dice the bread into very small pieces or substitute breadcrumbs.

Refrigeration after mixing will help the crab cakes stay together as they are shaped and cooked. Additional egg or bread can be added to accomplish the same result.

The late Tony Fulton, Chef George Fulton's son, gives us a poignant reminiscence of the hardships endured by the B&O's dining car crews and their families:

I was very angry as a young man growing up. I was angry that my dad was away. I was angry that he had to cook for Mr. [Howard] Simpson [president of the B&O]. I was angry that he had to work so hard. I was angry because of segregation. . . . But (now) I have a greater appreciation for life and what my dad wanted for me and why he was so tough on me. He didn't want me to be a chef cook. He didn't want me to work as hard as he had to work. (Tye 2004, p. 247)

DEVILED CRAB CAKES

From *B&O Chef's Notes*

4 pounds crab meat, 2 eggs well beaten, ¼ cup butter (melted), ½ teaspoon salt, ¼ teaspoon red pepper, ½ teaspoon celery seed, 1 cup milk, 1½ cup cracker crumbs.

Beat eggs. Add milk, pepper and celery seed. Melt butter and pour in. Add crab meat and the crumbs. Mold into shape and fry in deep fat. Drain on wax paper.

Chef's Comments

INGREDIENTS FOR 6 LARGE CAKES

1 pound Crab Meat
1 Egg, beaten
¼ cup Milk
⅛ teaspoon Salt
Dash Red Pepper

⅛ teaspoon Celery Seed
1 tablespoon Butter, melted
⅜ cup Cracker Crumbs

Beat the egg and add the milk, salt, red pepper, and celery seed. Add the melted butter, then the crabmeat and cracker crumbs. Mold into cakes without breaking up large lumps of crabmeat and refrigerate for up to one hour. Fry in deep fat and drain on a rack or on paper towels.

Here is yet another variation on the B&O's classic recipe. This one was written in longhand on a piece of B&O stationery and was actually titled "Crab Cakes Deviled Crabs" by the author.

There are as many recipes for crab cakes as there are people who cook them, with consistency and cohesiveness of the ingredients varying widely, from solid to barely holding together. If the crabmeat is still fairly moist after draining, or if a more cohesive product is preferred, try adding more cracker crumbs or beaten egg.

Although this recipe makes crab cakes, deviled crab as a casserole was "all the culinary rage" during the 1920s, when the ingredients would be heaped on an actual crab top shell and browned in a 375-degree oven (Shields 1998, p. 66).

MARYLAND CRAB FLAKES AU GRATIN

From "B&O General Notice," September 1, 1960

Sauté one pound of crabmeat in four tablespoons of butter until heated thoroughly. Mix one tablespoon of mayonnaise with four tablespoons of cream, pinch of salt and pinch of white pepper. Shake pan to equally distribute liquid so all pieces of crabmeat are coated. DO NOT BREAK LUMPS OF CRABMEAT. Top with buttered bread crumbs and pinch of grated cheese. Brown in oven. Four orders from each pound of crabmeat. If business does not warrant preparation of four orders, then use half portions of recipe.

Chef's Comments

INGREDIENTS FOR 4 SERVINGS

1 pound Crab Meat
4 tablespoons Butter
1 tablespoon Mayonnaise
4 tablespoons Cream
Pinch Salt
Pinch White Pepper
Bread Crumbs, buttered, as needed
Cheese, grated, as needed

Preheat oven to 400 degrees.
The term *au gratin* defines the manner of presentation. The *gratin* is the reduction of the sauce to a very thick consistency under the broiler or in the oven.

IMPERIAL CRAB (RECIPE NUMBER 10)

From *Old Standard B&O Recipes*

One pound of crab meat, mixed with four ounces of butter, cayenne pepper, tablespoon lemon juice, salt to taste. Chop one green pepper very fine and add to the mixture. Pack the crab shells, sprinkle with bread crumbs and bits of butter, and bake.

Chef's Comments

INGREDIENTS FOR 2 SERVINGS

1 pound Crab Meat
4 ounces Butter
Cayenne Pepper, to taste
1 tablespoon Lemon Juice
Salt, to taste
1 Green Pepper, chopped very fine
Bread Crumbs, as needed
Butter, thin slices, as needed
2 Crab Top Shells

Preheat the oven to 400 degrees.

If empty crab shells are unavailable, a small baking dish or ovenproof cup will do nicely.

Crab Imperial (or Imperial Crab, as this recipe was called) has been called "the *pièce de résistance* of Chesapeake Bay blue crab dishes" (Shields 1998, p. 63), and even within the B&O there were different ways to prepare the dish.

CRAB IMPERIAL

From *What's Cooking on the B&O?* (circa 1950)

1 pound Crab Meat
1 Egg, beaten
1 tablespoon Mayonnaise

Mix these ingredients together and salt and pepper to suit your taste—or your company's taste, if you know what it is. Fill crab shells with the mixture, dot with melted butter or margarine and brown in a hot oven.

It'll take from 6 to 10 minutes in a 400-degree oven. One pound of crab meat will make three Imperial Crabs—which probably won't be enough, they are so delicious.

CRAB IMPERIAL À LA GRADY

From *Baltimore and Ohio* magazine (August 1959) and *Dining by Rail* (Porterfield)

MAKES 3 SERVINGS

1 tablespoon Butter
1 tablespoon Green Pepper, chopped
1 tablespoon Celery, chopped
1 Egg
1 pound Backfin Crabmeat
1 tablespoon (heaping) Mayonnaise
2 tablespoons Heavy Cream
Dash Dry Mustard
Salt and White Pepper, to taste

Sauté lightly chopped celery and green pepper in butter. Mix ingredients and place in crab shells or in small Pyrex dishes. Bake in oven at 325 degrees for 30 to 35 minutes, or until brown.

Chef's Comments

On January 3, 1959, Alaska became the country's forty-ninth state. On July 4 of that year the B&O celebrated by flying 49-star flags on all passenger trains leaving Baltimore.

Joining the celebration was Baltimore's recently elected mayor, J. Harold Grady, and his wife, Pat, who was pictured in *Baltimore and Ohio* magazine handing this recipe, "a favorite of the mayor," to B&O Chef Dan Peters and Manager of Dining Car and Commissary Department James B. Martin.

Beginning July 9, the newly named Crab Imperial à la Grady was featured on the Capitol Limited's menu, and Pat Grady's photo graced the menu's cover. Inside were this recipe and the photo from *Baltimore and Ohio* magazine.

At $3.75, Crab Imperial à la Grady was one of the more expensive entrées, second only to a Broiled Selected Sirloin Steak, which went for a princely $4.75. These prices included an appetizer or soup, plus a salad, vegetable, and dessert.

CAPITOL LIMITED OYSTER PIE

From *Dining by Rail* (Porterfield) and "B&O General Notice," March 19, 1960

Oysters at all times should be prepared with utmost care, and particularly on the Baltimore and Ohio which operates through the territory where the finest oysters in the world are obtainable.

YIELDS 4 SERVINGS

4 tablespoons Butter
½ cup Flour
½ cup Milk
½ cup Oyster Liquor
2 cups Oysters, shucked
4 Carrots, ½-inch dice
2 Potatoes, ½-inch dice
1 tablespoon Parsley, chopped

4 tablespoons Onion, grated
2 teaspoons Green Bell Pepper, ¼-inch dice
Dash Tabasco Sauce
Salt and Pepper, to taste
½ recipe Flaky Pie Crust (no sugar) *(See* Desserts and Pie Crust *Section)*

In a large saucepan over medium heat, make a roux of the flour and butter. Add milk and oyster liquor, stirring until a fairly thick cream sauce forms. Put oysters in the sauce and cook over very low heat until the oyster edges begin to curl. Meanwhile, boil carrots and potatoes until tender, about 10 minutes. Drain and add them to the sauce. Add parsley, onion, green pepper, Tabasco sauce, salt and pepper. Stir to mix well and heat through. Put this filling in a deep casserole. Top with pie crust and place in oven for about 20 minutes, until crust is brown and filling bubbly.

CREAMED OYSTERS, BALTIMORE STYLE

From "B&O General Notice," February 4, 1964, for Menus Effective February 13, 1964

8 Oysters
1 tablespoon Butter
¼ cup Cream
2 tablespoons Bread Crumbs, fine
Salt and Pepper, to taste
1 slice Bread, sliced ¼-inch thick

Fry bread to golden brown in butter. Drain and pick over oysters. Melt butter, add cream and bring to a scald. Add oysters, salt and pepper, and heat until edge of oysters curl. Just before removing from stove, scatter in bread crumbs. Place fried bread in a shirred egg dish and pour mixture over it. Serve at once.

Chef's Comments

MAKES 1 SERVING

To bring the butter and cream "to a scald" means to heat them to just short of boiling.

OYSTERS AU GRATIN

From *Old Standard B&O Recipes*

Take six large oysters, put in an au gratin dish, season with salt and pepper, melted butter, grated cheese on top, cook in oven until brown.

Chef's Comments

INGREDIENTS FOR 1 SERVING

6 Oysters, shucked
Salt and Pepper, to taste
1 tablespoon Butter, Melted
3 tablespoons or as needed Cheese, grated

Before beginning, dry the oysters on a paper towel. The phrase "cook in oven until brown" means to bake at 350 degrees for about 20 minutes.

OYSTERS BOURGUINONNE

From *Old Standard B&O Recipes*

RECIPE NUMBER 41

Oysters on a half shell, season with salt and pepper, cover oysters with snail butter, sprinkle with bread crumbs, place in a hot oven to brown.

Snail butter; chop parsley and garlic very fine, and mix into soft butter, 3 beans of garlic to ¼ lb butter.

Serve 5 oysters as prepared above, on a bed of hot rock salt in a soup plate. The rock salt used in same manner as shaved ice in oyster cocktail, on the half shell. The service must be very hot and the oysters should be served immediately from the oven. It only takes a short time to prepare and must not be prepared in advance. Place rock salt in a pie tin and put in the oven or on top of the range, until it is very hot.

Chef's Comments

INGREDIENTS FOR 1 SERVING

FOR OYSTERS

5 Oysters, on half shell
Salt and Pepper, to taste
Snail Butter, as needed (*See below*)
Bread Crumbs, as needed

FOR SNAIL BUTTER

Parsley, chopped very fine
Garlic, chopped very fine
Butter, soft

It was hard to imagine why the butter in this recipe was called "snail butter" until we came across much the same formula in a French cookbook for a recipe called

Escargots à la Bourguinonne (Snails in Parsley Butter).
The bed of hot rock salt serves to keep the oysters warm and to hold them steady on the diner's plate.

OYSTERS, CHESAPEAKE STYLE

From "Dining Car Service, B&O Railroad," shown in *Eat, Drink, and Be Merry in Maryland* (Stieff)

Dry oysters on a towel, sauté in butter, sprinkle flour over them, sauté until brown, season with salt and pepper, then cook one slice of bacon, put on top, then put brown gravy around same on platter.

Chef's Comments

INGREDIENTS FOR 1 SERVING

1 tablespoon Butter
6 Oysters, shucked
1 piece Bacon, fried
Flour, as needed
Salt and Pepper, to taste
2 tablespoons Brown Gravy

OYSTER FRICASSEE, BALTIMORE STYLE

From "B&O General Notice," February 4, 1964, for Menus Effective February 13, 1964

Make a sauce of one tablespoon of butter and one-half teaspoon flour. Season with pepper. Add a pinch of minced parsley. Heat eight oysters in a little butter until edges curl. Add oysters to sauce. Serve on slice of toast. Garnish with fried bread crumbs and ¼ lemon.

Chef's Comments

INGREDIENTS FOR 1 SERVING

1 tablespoon Butter, melted
½ teaspoon Flour
Pepper, to taste
Pinch Parsley, minced
8 Oysters, shucked
1 tablespoon Butter
1 slice Toast
Bread Crumbs, fried, as needed
¼ Lemon

OYSTERS, MARYLAND STYLE

From *Old Standard B&O Recipes*

Simply plump the oysters in their own liquor. Use a nice rich cream sauce, season with salt, pepper and celery salt. Serve on toast as you would panned oysters, except use cream sauce for Maryland style.

Chef's Comments

INGREDIENTS FOR 1 SERVING

6 Oysters, shucked
¼ cup Cream Sauce
Salt and Pepper, to taste
Celery Salt, to taste
1 piece Toast

To "plump the oysters in their own liquor," put oysters and liquor in a saucepan and heat thoroughly.

PANNED OYSTERS ON TOAST

From *Old Standard B&O Recipes*

Blanche oysters, then put in hot butter to brown lightly, put on toast, mixing liquid and butter browned, over same season, sprinkle with salt and finely chopped parsley, serve on a tea plate under a glass cover.

Chef's Comments

INGREDIENTS FOR 1 SERVING

6 Oysters, shucked
1 tablespoon Butter
Salt, to taste
Parsley, chopped, to taste
1–2 tablespoons Oyster Liquor
1 piece Toast

Bring 2 cups of water to a boil and blanch the oysters by placing them in the boiling water for 30 seconds. Remove the oysters from the water and drain.

Place the butter in a frying pan to melt and bring to high heat. Place the oysters in the frying pan to brown. Place the oysters on the toast.

Allow the butter to cool somewhat and add oyster liquor. Stir together, heat and pour over the oysters and toast.

HAM AND PANNED OYSTERS ON TOAST

From "Dining Car Service, B&O Railroad," as shown in *Eat, Drink, and Be Merry in Maryland* (Stieff)

Serve a full slice of toast with a full cut from the horseshoe part of the ham. This is to be either broiled or fried and placed on top of the toast. Serve six panned oysters nicely arranged on top of this. Serve on a tea plate under glass cover, garnished with a cream sauce.

Chef's Comments

INGREDIENTS FOR 1 SERVING

6 Oysters, panned *(See recipe above)*
1 Ham, ¼-inch slice
¼ cup Cream Sauce *(See Sauces Section)*

SHELL OYSTER ROAST

From "Dining Car Service, B&O Railroad," as shown in *Eat, Drink, and Be Merry in Maryland* (Stieff)

Select eight large shell oysters and wash well. Lay them in a frying pan and set in a very hot oven for about ten minutes, when the oysters begin to open, serve them in the shell, place on a folded napkin upon a dinner plate. Cut a strip of bacon in two pieces, laying one small piece on each oyster, with parsley and half a lemon. Serve the liquor from the oysters with melted butter (hot), separate in a gravy boat.

Chef's Comments

INGREDIENTS FOR 1 SERVING

8 Oysters, in shell
4 pieces Bacon, fried
Parsley, as needed
½ Lemon
3 tablespoons Butter, melted

OYSTER STEW RECIPES

From *Old Standard B&O Recipes*

RECIPE NUMBER 13

Take a small part of oyster or clam liquor, put into a saucepan. To this add the equivalent of two pieces of butter, one-third teaspoon Worcestershire sauce, salt, pepper, celery salt and paprika to taste. Bring this to a boil, add your oysters and boil for a minute. Then add one half pint of milk and bring to a boil. Take off and put into a hot tureen, with a piece of butter and a dash of paprika added and served.

From "B&O General Notice," January 7, 1964, for menus effective January 9, 1964

Should contain 8 select oysters. Oyster stew with cream—made with half-and-half cream.

Chef's Comments

INGREDIENTS FOR 2 SERVINGS

1 cup Oyster or Clam Liquor
2 tablespoons Butter
⅔ teaspoon Worcestershire Sauce
Salt and Pepper, to taste
Celery Salt, to taste
Paprika, to taste
8 Oysters, shucked
1 cup Milk
1 pat Butter
Dash Paprika

B&O menus listed oyster stews made with milk and cream. Recipes are given here for both. "Oyster or clam liquor" is simply the liquid inside the shell before the oyster or clam is shucked. Canned oyster or clam juice or fish stock or bouillon may be substituted.

OYSTERS WITH MACARONI

From *Old Standard B&O Recipes*

Cook macaroni until tender, put in colander, and let cold water run over them, make a heavy cream sauce, mix with macaroni, season, put in chicken pie dish, then put five oysters on top, push them down a little, sprinkle with bread crumbs and butter over this, and brown in oven.

Chef's Comments

INGREDIENTS FOR 1 SERVING

3 ounces Macaroni
½ cup Cream Sauce
Salt and Pepper, to taste
5 Oysters, shucked
Bread Crumbs, as needed
Butter, as needed

Preheat oven to 350 degrees.
The B&O cooked and served this dish in individual ovenproof dishes, however, several servings can be made in a casserole dish.

BROILED BONED SHAD WITH ROE

From "B&O General Notice," April 6, 1964,
for menus effective April 9, 1964

All cars running this item, *will order it from the Baltimore Commissary ONLY.* The shad comes already filleted and boned. Cut each piece in half, making two servings to the piece. Generally, the roe will be 3 ounce sets—serve one set to an order. On occasions, you may receive roe weighing 6 ounces a set and, if so, serve one-half roe to the order. EXERCISE JUDGEMENT.

Garnish with wedge of lemon and sprig of parsley.

Chef's Comments

INGREDIENTS FOR 2 SERVINGS

1 Shad Filet
6 ounces (1–2 pairs) Shad Roe
Salt and Pepper, to taste
Butter, melted, or Cooking Oil, as needed
Lemon Wedges, as needed for garnish
Parsley Sprigs, as needed for garnish

FOR THE SHAD

Preheat broiler. Cut the filet in half, season with salt and pepper and baste with melted butter or cooking oil. Place on a broiler pan with skin side down and broil until lightly browned and cooked through. Do not turn the filet.

General note: Fish should always be taken from the oven or broiler just before it is done. The heat already in the fish will finish the cooking as it is served. Overcooking fish is all too common.

FOR THE ROE

Boil a pan of water and place the roe in a large wide bowl. Pour the boiling water down the inside edge of the bowl; avoid pouring directly on the roe. Roe will turn gray, and exposed eggs may "bloom" and pairs separate. Remove roe after 15 seconds. This "tempering" process will make the roe less likely to break while cooking.

Melt butter over medium heat in an ovenproof frying pan. Gently place the roe in the pan and baste with butter. Then place the pan under the broiler until lightly browned on one side. Gently turn over and brown the other side before serving.

CLAM PIE, INDIVIDUAL

From "Dining Car Service, B&O Railroad,"
shown in *Eat, Drink, and Be Merry in Maryland* (Stieff)

One cup of thinly sliced potatoes parboiled, six clams chopped fine. Place layer of potatoes in chicken pie dish, then layer of clams, sprinkle over this one teaspoon minced onion. Continue until dish is filled. Beat one egg into half cup milk and pour over the contents of the chicken pie dish. Make a biscuit crust to cover the pie and bake for thirty minutes. Serve hot.

From *Old Standard B&O Recipes*

One cup of thinly sliced potatoes parboiled, six clams chopped fine. Place layer of potatoes in chicken pie dish, sprinkle over one teaspoon finely chopped onion. Beat one egg into half cup milk, add the chopped clams, then another layer of potatoes and minced onion. Pour one quarter of the egg and milk liquid over the contents of the chicken pie dish. Make a biscuit crust to cover the pie, and bake for thirty minutes. Serve hot.

Chef's Comments

INGREDIENTS FOR 2 SERVINGS

2 teaspoons Onion, minced
2 cups Potatoes, peeled and sliced thin
12 Clams, chopped fine
2 Eggs, beaten
1 cup Milk
¼ recipe Flaky Pie Crust *(See* Desserts and Pie Crust Section)

Preheat the oven to 375 degrees.

The term *parboiled* indicates that the sliced potatoes will be boiled for five minutes to ensure that they will be fully cooked when the dish is served. For the same reason, the onions may be lightly sautéed beforehand as well.

After covering the dish with pie crust, make several holes in it with the tip of a knife to allow steam to escape.

One may, as this recipe advises, chop whole clams; however, 6½-ounce cans of chopped clams are available, perfect for one serving.

This recipe is intended for making individual portions in an ovenproof dish. Multiple servings can also be made in a casserole dish and covered with crust.

For a nice finishing touch, save a bit of the egg/milk mixture and brush it over the crust just before baking. This will give the crust a beautiful golden glaze.

The variation in these two recipes is slight but serves to illustrate and to clarify the ambiguity sometimes found in *Old Standard B&O Recipes*. Undoubtedly Stieff went to the B&O's Dining Car and Commissary Department for the recipes used in his book, while *Old*

Standard B&O Recipes appear to be notes made from the memories and experience of the author.

DELICIOUS CODFISH CAKES WITH TOMATO SAUCE

From *The Culinary Handbook* (Fellows)

Boneless codfish steeped overnight, boiled up, water thrown away, again boiled up using cold water; when done, taken up and drained, then pulled into shreds. The shredded codfish and an equal quantity of well-mashed fresh boiled potatoes, seasoned with salt, pepper and nutmeg, bound with a few yolks of eggs, mixed well, made into small flattened cakes, rolled in flour, fried in bacon.

Chef's Comments

INGREDIENTS FOR 1 DOZEN 4-INCH CAKES

8 ounces Codfish Filets, cooked
8 ounces Mashed Potatoes
1 Egg Yolk
½ teaspoon Nutmeg
Salt and Pepper, to taste
Flour, as needed
Bacon Fat, as needed
Tomato Sauce, 2 ounces per 3-cake serving

With a pair of forks, shred the filets in a large mixing bowl. Drain well. Add the remaining ingredients and mix thoroughly. Refrigerate for about 30 minutes, or until the mixture has stiffened. Form into cakes, coat in flour, and fry until brown. Ladle tomato sauce over cakes and serve.

The trick here is to get the mixture stiff enough to form into cakes. To remove as much liquid from the shredded filets as possible, the fish can be wrapped in cheesecloth and gently wrung out or wrapped in paper toweling to absorb liquid.

The B&O's menu item was titled Delicious Codfish Cakes with Tomato Sauce, but of course Fellows simply listed Codfish Balls or Codfish Cakes and had a separate recipe for tomato sauce.

FINAN HADDIE DELMONICO

From *Old Standard B&O Recipes*

Serve in a covered casserole. This should be skinned and soaked in warm water for half an hour, then take out and remove bones and cut up in half-inch pieces, wipe dry, sauté in butter, add tablespoon Sherry Wine, then supreme sauce, finish when taken off of the fire, with beaten yolk of egg and a little cream. Do not let it come to a boil after this. It should have a slight yellow color. Garnish with slices of hard-boiled egg in the center, pieces of shrimp on each end.

Chef's Comments

INGREDIENTS FOR 2 SERVINGS

1 pound Finan Haddie
1–2 tablespoons Butter
1 tablespoon Sherry Wine
1 cup Supreme Sauce (*See* Sauces *Section*)
1 Egg Yolk, beaten
2–3 tablespoons Cream
1 Egg, hard boiled
Shrimp, cooked, as needed

Finan haddie is a traditional cold-smoked haddock

from Scotland. Much more common "back in the day," it is now considered a gourmet food and is rather expensive when it can be found at all. The adventuresome chef will enjoy this dish with a variety of fish filets in place of the finan haddie.

TERRAPIN, MARYLAND STYLE

From *Old Standard B&O Recipes*

Terrapin meat simmered in butter, with liquor obtained from cutting up, flour added to form a roux, then moisten with boiling cream till like a fricassee, seasoned with salt, pepper and mace, finish by adding the eggs, simmer, then add Sherry.

HOW TO PREPARE TERRAPIN

From *Old B&O Standard Recipes*

To kill, plunge in boiling water and let it remain there twenty minutes, then take out and peel the skin off of the back and remove nails from the claws, remove the undershell by cutting with a sharp knife, where the lower shell joins the upper one, then remove the sand bag and gall bladder. Save the blood and remove all the meat and eggs. Cut off the head and use it with the shell for soups. Keep the meat, eggs and fat, found at the shoulders, in water until wanted for use.

Chef's Comments

This recipe was taken verbatim from *The Culinary Handbook,* further proof that the B&O used this as its "cookbook" for at least the first 30–40 years of the twentieth century. The preparation, however, was a

B&O procedure, much different from that shown in *The Culinary Handbook.* The blood that was saved in this recipe might be used as a thickening agent in sauces, gravies, etc.

PANNED MOUNTAIN TROUT

From "B&O General Notice," June 2, 1960, for menus effective June 2, 1960

These fish are of 10-oz. size. Rinse with cold water and dry. Cover with flour, salt and pepper to taste. Use sufficient shortening in frying pan to cover ½ of the fish. Shortening to be hot but not smoking. Place trout in frying pan so that one does not touch the other. After golden brown on one side carefully turn with a spatula and brown on the other side. Do not turn more than once. Serve on a hot dish. Waiters will ask patrons if they desire head and tail removed. Fish is already boned.

Chef's Comments

The menus of June 2, 1960, listed Panned Mountain Trout, Amandine. The lightly flavored amandine sauce *(see* Sauces *Section)* is a perfect complement to the delicate flavor of most fish.

The B&O offered a variety of fish "panned," and undoubtedly the process was the same as shown above.

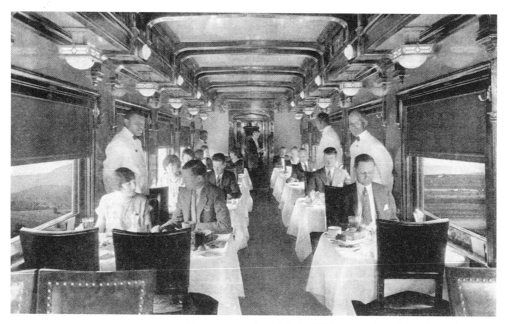

EARLY CAPITOL LIMITED DINER. From an envelope labeled "Photographs of the Capitol Limited" came this postcard showing dinnertime on a Class F-4A or F-4C car. Tom Greco collection

VEGETABLE AND PASTA DISHES

VEGETABLE DISHES

Asparagus

New Asparagus in Cream

Baked Beans, Baltimore and Ohio Style

Pan-Fried Bananas

Harvard Beets

Broccoli

Red Cabbage, Sweet and Sour

Diced Carrots and Peas

Stewed Celery

Egg Plant Creole

Boiled Onions, Parsley Butter

Peas

Potatoes
  Au Gratin Potatoes
  Baked Potato Recipes
  Browned Potatoes
  Creamed Potatoes
  Lyonnaise Potatoes
  Potato Salad, German Style

Mashed Hubbard Squash

Baked String Beans with Mushrooms

Sweet Potatoes Provençale

Marshmallow Sweet Potatoes

Baked Tomatoes au Gratin

Fried Tomatoes

RICE AND PASTA DISHES

Spaghetti Caruso

Shrimp and Spaghetti

Why Not Wild Rice

ASPARAGUS

From *Manual of Instructions Governing Dining Car Department Employees and Set Up of Cars and Service*, February 13, 1940

Serve on a small platter, triangular toast under large ends. Drawn butter or sauce over the vegetable.

Chef's Comments

INGREDIENTS FOR 1 SERVING

4–5 pieces Asparagus
1 large bowl or pan Ice Water
Toast, ½ slice per order, cut diagonally
Sauce, as desired

Remove the tough bottom end of each piece of asparagus, about 1–1½ inches.

Bring a pot of water to a rolling boil and immerse asparagus in the water for 30–45 seconds. Remove and immediately place in an ice-water bath. This blanching or "shocking" treatment will set the bright green color of the asparagus.

Boil asparagus for about 4 minutes. Longer cooking will make it mushy.

NEW ASPARAGUS IN CREAM

From *Old Standard B&O Recipes*

RECIPE NUMBER 20

A small portion of the hard end (about 1 inch of each asparagus spear) should be cut off. The asparagus should be peeled and cut into lengths not to exceed one inch. The cooks must be exceedingly careful in the cooking of this, so that the hard or butt end will be cooked evenly, with the top or blossom end, and consequently it may be necessary to boil this two or three ways, to get proper results. The blossom of the asparagus should be cut off and cooked separately, as this is more tender and does not require much cooking that it be done. Three stalks will fill a small baker. After placing in baker, pour cream sauce over same and top with chopped parsley. This will enable you to serve a generous portion to each person on table d'hôte meal.

Chef's Comments

INGREDIENTS FOR 2 SERVINGS

6 spears Asparagus
3–4 tablespoons Cream Sauce (*See* Sauces *Section*)
½ teaspoon Parsley, chopped

Place the asparagus, except for the "blossoms" (tips), in boiling water for 2½ minutes, then add the blossoms, boiling for an additional 1½ minutes.

BAKED BEANS, BALTIMORE AND OHIO STYLE (AKA BAKED BEANS, NAVY STYLE)

From *Old Standard B&O Recipes* and *B&O Chef's Notes*

SOAK BEANS 12 HOURS

5 pounds Navy Beans
1 ounce Tomatoes
1 cup Molasses
1 teaspoon Dry Mustard
½ teaspoon Baking Powder
1 Onion, minced fine

Let the beans simmer on the back of the range, four

hours, with two pounds of bacon and the above ingredients. When done, bake in a hot oven until brown. Salt pork could be used instead of bacon.

Chef's Comments

INGREDIENTS FOR 8 SERVINGS

1 pound Navy Beans
½ pound Bacon or Salt Pork, chopped coarse
3 ounces Tomatoes
¼ cup Molasses
¼ teaspoon Dry Mustard
⅛ teaspoon Baking Powder
¼ Onion, minced fine
Salt and Pepper, to taste

When simmering, start with enough water to cover the ingredients and be careful that all the water doesn't evaporate, allowing the beans to burn. Add water throughout the simmering process to achieve the level of moistness desired.

One can shortcut the 12-hour soaking step by placing the beans in a pot covered with cold water by 2-3 inches. Bring the water to a boil, and immediately turn off the heat. Cover the pot and allow the beans to stand for 1 hour. Drain the beans in a colander, rinse with cold water, then cook according to recipe.

The "hot oven" mentioned would be 450–500 degrees.

PAN-FRIED BANANAS
From *Baltimore and Ohio* magazine, January 1959

(Four firm bananas; four tablespoons butter or margarine, melted; use all-yellow or slightly green-tipped bananas.) Peel bananas. Keep whole or cut crosswise into halves. Fry bananas slowly in butter or margarine until tender—easily pierced with a fork—turning them to brown evenly. Sprinkle lightly with salt. Serve hot as a vegetable. Four servings.

Chef's Comments

The key to making this dish work is that first sentence; be sure the bananas are firm. Even the firmest bananas will soften as they are fried, so handle them very carefully. A plastic or rubber spatula can be used to turn them in the pan and move them to a plate.

Strange as this banana dish may seem, it was conceived with a specific purpose in mind. Let *Baltimore and Ohio* magazine explain . . .

Banana dishes of unusual appeal were featured on dining car menus of our through trains during December (1958), as a salute to the railroad's new multi-million-dollar fruit terminal, where banana boats of the United Fruit Company are docking. The pier was opened officially in Baltimore December 1.

To mark the event, B&O chefs came up with such exotic delicacies as Pan-Fried Bananas, prepared as the Latins enjoy them.

Having shifted the responsibility for such an unusual dish to the chefs, the article went on to explain that this dish and Banana Shortcake were being offered to guests on the Capitol Limited and the Columbian, running between Baltimore and Chicago, and the National Limited, which operated between Baltimore and St. Louis.

HARVARD BEETS

From "B&O General Notice," May 14, 1964

Order canned rose bud beets. Instead of using vinegar in preparation, substitute orange juice and do not use as much sugar.

Chef's Comments

INGREDIENTS FOR 4 SERVINGS

½ cup (scant) Sugar
1 tablespoon Corn Starch
¼ cup Orange Juice
¼ cup Water
1 can (15 ounces) Rosebud Beets
2 tablespoons Butter

In a 3-quart saucepan, combine the sugar and starch and mix well. Add the water and orange juice and simmer for 5 minutes.

Add the beets and hold over low heat for 30 minutes. Just before service, bring to a boil and add the butter.

If rosebud beets are unavailable, use any canned beets. If they are whole, slice them about ¼-inch thick.

BROCCOLI

From *Manual of Instructions Governing Dining Car Department Employees and Set Up of Cars and Service*, February 13, 1940

Serve on a small platter, triangular toast under large ends. Drawn butter or sauce over the vegetable.

Chef's Comments

INGREDIENTS FOR 1 SERVING

4 ounces Broccoli
1 large bowl or pan Ice Water
Toast, ½ slice, cut diagonally
Sauce, as desired

Blanch the broccoli by bringing a pot of water to a rolling boil and immersing broccoli for 30–45 seconds. Remove from the pot and immediately place in an ice water bath. Then boil or steam for 10–15 minutes to the desired tenderness.

The blanching or "shocking" treatment described will set the bright green color of the broccoli.

RED CABBAGE, SWEET AND SOUR

From *Old Standard B&O Recipes*

RECIPE NUMBER 45

3 pounds (1 head) Red Cabbage, chopped
1 Sour Apple, peeled, sliced thin
⅓ cup Bacon Fat
¼ cup Brown Sugar
⅓ cup Vinegar
½ teaspoon Cloves, ground
2 tablespoons Flour

Cook red cabbage with sour apple, heat bacon fat in frying pan, add flour, vinegar, sugar and cloves, cook until blended. Drain cabbage and pour the cooked dressing over the chopped cabbage. Salt and pepper to taste. This item appears on the menu as a vegetable.

Chef's Comments

INGREDIENTS FOR 6–8 SERVINGS

¾ pound Red Cabbage, chopped
¼ Sour Apple, peeled, sliced thin
2 tablespoons Bacon Fat
2 tablespoons Vinegar
1 tablespoon Brown Sugar
⅛ teaspoon Cloves, ground
½ tablespoon Flour
Salt and Pepper, to taste

To "cook" the cabbage and apple, simmer them in water until tender.

Make the dressing just before serving to maintain its fluidity. Add a little hot water if dressing becomes too thick.

DICED CARROTS AND PEAS

From *The Culinary Handbook* (Fellows)

New carrots cored with a column cutter, then cut in thin slices, stewed in consommé till tender; green peas boiled in salted water with a bunch of fresh mint. Strained off when done and mixed with the carrots; served as a vegetable.

Chef's Comments

INGREDIENTS FOR 2 SERVINGS

3 New Carrots, sliced thin
1–2 cups Consommé
1 cup Peas
3–4 sprigs Mint, fresh

A tablespoon of dried chopped mint can be used in place of fresh, however, the peas should be rinsed in a colander under hot water to remove the mint after cooking. Beef stock or bouillon can be substituted for the consommé.

This recipe does not mention draining the carrots after simmering them in consommé. However, most combination vegetable dishes are served without the cooking liquid.

STEWED CELERY

From *The Culinary Handbook* (Fellows)

Celery stalks all cut about the same size like asparagus, boiled tender in salted water, taken up and arranged in a sautoir, moistened with Veloute sauce, simmered; served with one end resting on toast, with some of the sauce poured over the ends.

Chef's Comments

INGREDIENTS FOR 2–3 SERVINGS

4 ribs Celery
1 cup Veloute Sauce
Toast, ½ slice per order, cut diagonally, crust removed

Boil the celery approximately 20 minutes to make it tender.

EGG PLANT CREOLE

From *Old Standard B&O Recipes* and *What's Cooking on the B&O?* (circa 1950)

1 Egg Plant
3 tablespoons Butter or Margarine
3 tablespoons Flour
3 Tomatoes, large, peeled, sliced
½ cup Green Bell Pepper, sliced thin
1 Onion, small, sliced thin
1 teaspoon Salt
1 Bay Leaf, small
2 Cloves, whole
1 cup Bread Crumbs

Slice the egg plant crosswise, peel and cut into one-inch cubes. Cook in boiling salted water for ten minutes. Then drain and put the egg plant into a buttered (or margarined) casserole.

In another dish, melt the butter, add the flour and mix until blended. Then add the tomatoes, the peppers, the onion, salt, pepper, bay leaf and cloves. Cook for five minutes, then pour this over the egg plant and cover with a thin layer of buttered bread crumbs.

Bake this in a 350-degree oven for ten minutes and serve hot.

Chef's Comments

What's Cooking on the B&O? advises that "in a pinch" you can use canned tomatoes instead of fresh.

Old Standard B&O Recipes ends by saying "This should feed about six people." That document also gave this recipe more of a French twist, naming it "Egg Plant à la Creole," a move that would certainly have raised the hackles on Charles Fellows's neck.

BOILED ONIONS, PARSLEY BUTTER

From *The Culinary Handbook* (Fellows)

Medium-sized onions, peeled, boiled well done in salted water, taken up and well drained, kept very hot; served with a spoonful of melted butter poured over them; used as vegetable.

Chef's Comments

INGREDIENTS FOR 4 SERVINGS

4 Onions, medium
4 ounces Butter
½ tablespoon Parsley, chopped

To make parsley butter, allow the butter to come to room temperature, then stir with a wooden spoon until creamy. Add the chopped parsley and continue to stir until well combined.

The parsley butter can be made ahead of time and placed on a sheet of plastic wrap. Roll it into a cylinder, twist the ends of the plastic wrap tight, and refrigerate.

"Pearl onions" or the slightly larger "boiler onions" can be used for this recipe; count on 2–3 ounces per serving. The B&O actually listed "Pearl Onions" as a menu item, but there is no evidence as to how these were cooked.

PEAS

From "The Epicure," Pittsburgh *Sun-Telegraph*, February 19, 1950

Green peas cooked in a little water to which a bouillon cube has been added.

Chef's Comments

INGREDIENTS FOR 6–8 SERVINGS

1 pound Peas, frozen or canned
¼ cup Water
1 Beef Bouillon Cube

Bring the water to a boil and add the bouillon cube, stirring until completely dissolved. Bouillon cubes are almost all salt; ¼ cup of beef stock may be substituted for the water and bouillon cube.

Reduce to a simmer and add the peas. Simmer 10 minutes, drain thoroughly, and serve.

This recipe was quoted by B&O dining car Steward J. J. "Jerry" Collins. A note from H. O. McAbee, Manager of the Dining Car and Commissary Department, to William C. Baker, Vice President of Operations, was attached to the clipping in the files of the Baltimore and Ohio Railroad Historical Society. He stated, "Here is a little publicity we got. The writer of the column 'The Epicure' rides regularly on the Capitol."

AU GRATIN POTATOES

From "B&O General Notice," June 3, 1964, for menus effective June 11, 1964

11 PORTIONS

4 pounds Potatoes, chopped, boiled
2 quarts Cream Sauce
2 ounces Bread Crumbs
½ pound Cheddar Cheese, grated
Salt and Pepper, to taste
Butter, as needed

Mix potatoes, salt, pepper and cream sauce together. Be careful not to make potatoes mushy. Pour into a buttered pudding pan. Sprinkle top with buttered bread crumbs and grated cheddar cheese. Bake in oven 30–40 minutes until brown.

Chef's Comments

Preheat oven to 350–375 degrees.

Boil the chopped potatoes for 5 minutes before adding them to the other ingredients.

Bread crumbs are easy to make. Put stale bread slices in a food processor and process to the consistency desired.

BAKED POTATO

From "Form 1875," *Manual of Instructions Governing Dining Car Department Employees and Set Up of Cars and Service,* February 13, 1940

AND

BAKED POTATO WITH SOUR CREAM AND CHIVES

From "B&O General Notice," March 6, 1964, for menus effective March 12, 1964

BAKED POTATO

Serve on small platter, potato to be split, with cut of butter and dash of paprika on top.

BAKED POTATO WITH SOUR CREAM AND CHIVES

Split the baked potato crosswise and squeeze at the openings, placing therein a dessert spoon of sour cream. Sprinkle with chopped chives. TO INSURE

FRESHNESS, POTATOES MUST BE BAKED AT INTERVALS DURING THE MEAL.

Chef's Comments

Perhaps all baked potato recipes are pretty similar, but this is how the B&O served and garnished theirs. Here are some cooking hints:

Before baking, puncture the potato with a knife or fork several times to allow steam to escape. Bake at 350–400 degrees until that same knife or fork slides easily into any part of the potato.

Although there is no evidence that the B&O used this method, coating the outside of each potato with olive or canola oil and rolling it in kosher salt before baking will ensure that the meat of the potato will stay nice and moist.

BROWNED POTATOES

From *Potato Cookery* (Suzanne and Senn)

Wash and peel neatly two pounds of medium-sized potatoes. When drained, arrange them on a baking pan, season with salt and add two ounces of dissolved butter or meat drippings. Bake in a moderately heated oven until done. Shake the pan occasionally so as to get the potatoes nicely browned. To serve, drain them from fat and dish up on a hot vegetable dish.

Chef's Comments

Preheat the oven to 400 degrees and shake the pan as described every 15 minutes. After 45 minutes, begin checking for doneness; a fork or knife should penetrate the potato easily.

Chef Mick Weis suggests placing the peeled potatoes in a pot of salted water, which is then heated. As soon as the water comes to the boil, remove the potatoes, pat dry, and place in the baking pan. This yields a much better product with more even color and texture.

CREAMED POTATOES

From *The Culinary Handbook* (Fellows)

Raw potatoes cut in very small dice, boiled till perfectly done, drained, put in a stew pan with a piece of good butter, seasoned with salt, covered with cream, simmered for two or three minutes, then served.

Chef's Comments

INGREDIENTS FOR 2 SERVINGS

2 Potatoes, medium
1 tablespoon Butter
Salt, to taste
Cream, as needed

Once again, Charles Fellows assumes that his readers are professional cooks. For those who are not, we would add that to cut something in "small dice" would mean into cubes ¼ inch on each side. So "very small" would be less than ¼ inch. Such finely diced potatoes must be watched carefully, however, to avoid overcooking. Better to have the water at a boil, add the potatoes, and check for doneness as soon as the water returns to the boil.

Lyonnaise Potatoes

From *The Culinary Handbook* (Fellows)

Cold boiled potatoes, either minced or sliced thinly, seasoned with salt and pepper, mixed with a little chopped parsley and fried onions; fried with butter in the form of an omelet.

Chef's Comments

INGREDIENTS FOR 4 SERVINGS

2 Potatoes, boiled, cold
3 tablespoons Butter
1 Onion, ¼-inch dice
4 tablespoons Parsley, fresh, chopped fine
Salt and Pepper, to taste

Peel the potatoes and place in a pan of cold water. Bring to a boil and reduce to a simmer for 10–20 minutes, depending on size. When the potatoes are tender, drain them thoroughly and cool. Then mince or cut into thin slices.

Melt the butter in a frying pan over medium-high heat and fry the onions until they are soft and beginning to turn translucent. Add the potatoes, chopped parsley, salt, and pepper to the pan and fry, turning with a spatula until evenly browned.

This recipe can be made without simmering the potatoes, but the frying time is a bit longer. Add the onions and potatoes to the pan at the same time, cover, and lower the heat for 10 minutes or so, then add the parsley, salt, and pepper. With the pan covered, cook until brown and tender.

Dried parsley can be substituted for fresh; cut the amount to 2 tablespoons. If the potatoes seem to be getting too dry while cooking, add a little more butter to keep them nice and moist.

Potato Salad, German Style

From *Old Standard B&O Recipes*

Boil potatoes in jackets, 2 tablespoons butter, 1 tablespoon flour, 1 tablespoon brown sugar, 1 half cup vinegar, 1 half cup water, 1 half cup dry mustard, salt and pepper. Melt butter, stir in flour and sugar, add water, vinegar and seasoning, cook until smooth. Cut potatoes and onions, pour dressing while hot over them.

Chef's Comments

INGREDIENTS FOR 8 SERVINGS

2 pounds Potatoes, ¾-inch dice
2 tablespoons Butter
1 tablespoon Flour
1 tablespoon Brown Sugar
½ cup Water
¼ cup Vinegar
½ teaspoon Dry Mustard
Salt and Pepper, to taste
1 Onion, minced fine

Starting in cold water, boil the potatoes for approximately 8 minutes. "Melt butter, stir in flour and sugar, add water, vinegar and seasoning, cook until smooth." Combine the potatoes and onions, pour the dressing over them while hot, and mix thoroughly.

The ½ cup of vinegar shown overwhelms the flavor of the other ingredients. About half that amount seems more appropriate. Likewise, the "1 half cup dry mustard" is certainly a typographical error; most recipes call for a small amount such as the half teaspoon shown in the ingredients list above.

This dish can be served hot or cold.

MASHED HUBBARD SQUASH

From *Old Standard B&O Recipes*

To be peeled and steamed, not boiled or baked, run through ricer or chinese cap.

Chef's Comments

INGREDIENTS FOR 2–3 SERVINGS

1 pound Hubbard Squash, peeled
3 tablespoons Butter
Salt and Pepper, to taste

Cut the peeled squash into pieces about one inch square (size is not critical). Steam for 20 minutes or so, until the pieces are fork tender. Put in a bowl and mash, adding butter until you reach the desired consistency.

The "General Notice" of January 6, 1961, for menus effective January 10 of that year, lists the following for Hubbard Squash: "This is mashed or whipped squash and should be the consistency of mashed potatoes. You will be furnished the frozen variety."

BAKED STRING BEANS WITH MUSHROOMS

From *What's Cooking on the B&O?* (circa 1950) and *Dining by Rail* (Porterfield)

½ pound String Beans, cut in slivers
½ pound Mushrooms
1 tablespoon Butter (or Margarine)
½ tablespoon Flour
1 cup Milk
2 ounces Buttered Bread Crumbs

String the beans, if necessary. Sliver them, cook in boiling, salted water until tender. Then drain them well.

Meanwhile the mushrooms must be peeled and sliced, and sautéed in butter with flour and milk added. Cook until thickened. Now add the beans and pour the combination in a baking dish. Over the top, sprinkle the breadcrumbs. Bake in a medium oven of 375 degrees just long enough to heat thoroughly and to brown the crumbs.

Chef's Comments

MAKES 4–6 SERVINGS

Many cooks will find that the 2 ounces of bread crumbs called for is much more than is needed. Start with 1 ounce and add more as desired.

On the other hand, this recipe called for one tablespoon of butter, and sautéing the mushrooms will nearly use that up. An extra tablespoon will provide for plenty of good rich sauce.

SWEET POTATOES PROVENÇALE

From *Old Standard B&O Recipes*

RECIPE NUMBER 24

Boil sweet potatoes, mash, season with salt, pepper, and butter and add a few seedless raisins. Form into cakes, fry in deep fat until browned, place in a dish. Pour one tablespoon of Maple syrup over cake and place in oven about 10 minutes, serve hot.

Chef's Comments

INGREDIENTS FOR 8–10 CAKES

2 Sweet Potatoes, peeled, rough chopped
Salt and Pepper, to taste
2–3 tablespoons Raisins
Fat for cooking, as needed
Maple Syrup, 1 tablespoon per cake

The cakes will retain their shape better if they are refrigerated for 30 minutes after being formed.

For an easier, and more healthful, approach, try baking the cakes at 350–400 degrees until brown.

MARSHMALLOW SWEET POTATOES

From *Old Standard B&O Recipes*

Prepare the same as for candied sweets, with the addition of a marshmallow placed on each piece of sweet potato, and place in the oven to brown and melt the marshmallow. This must be done just before ready to serve, as the marshmallow will not hold up properly if allowed to stand any length of time after removing from the oven.

Chef's Comments

INGREDIENTS FOR 1 SERVING

1 Sweet Potato
Brown Sugar, to taste
Butter, melted, to taste
½ teaspoon Nutmeg
½ teaspoon Cinnamon

Preheat oven to 350 degrees.

Peel the sweet potato and cut it in half lengthwise, arranging in a buttered baking pan. Sprinkle with brown sugar, then with melted butter and more brown sugar. Sprinkle on the cinnamon and nutmeg and bake until fork tender, about 40 minutes.

Put a marshmallow on the sweet potato and return it to the oven "to brown and melt the marshmallow."

BAKED TOMATOES AU GRATIN

From "B&O General Notice," April 6, 1964, for menus effective April 9, 1964

To each #2½ can of tomatoes use one slice of bread cut in half-inch cubes, one teaspoon sugar and salt, and place in a shallow baking pan. Top with bread crumbs and grated cheese and bake until top is slightly browned.

Chef's Comments

INGREDIENTS FOR 6 SERVINGS

1 28-ounce can Tomatoes
1 slice Bread
1 teaspoon Sugar
Salt, to taste

Bread Crumbs, as needed
Cheese, grated, as needed

A #2½ can contains 28 ounces of tomatoes, and this dish can be cooked with or without the liquid from the can with equally delicious results. Or, for a real treat, use thinly sliced fresh tomatoes. Note that the original recipe calls for a teaspoon of salt, which seems like quite a bit when one considers the amount of sodium in the canned tomatoes.

Be sure to mix the ingredients well for consistent flavor.

Preheat the oven to 350 degrees and figure on 20–30 minutes to brown the top of this dish to satisfaction. Depending on the type of cheese used, less salt may be needed.

FRIED TOMATOES

From "B&O General Notice," June 3, 1964, for menus effective June 11, 1964

Use tomatoes not too over-ripe. Cut ½-inch thick, sprinkle with salt and pepper, dip in crumbs, egg and crumbs again. Fry in hot fat, 6 to 8 minutes, to golden brown. Serve two slices with the omelet.

Chef's Comments

INGREDIENTS FOR 2 SERVINGS

1 Tomato, medium
Salt and Pepper, to taste
Bread Crumbs, as needed
1 Egg, beaten

As indicated by the last sentence of this recipe, in 1964, Fried Tomatoes were being served with omelets. In earlier years, however, they were a stand-alone dish.

SPAGHETTI CARUSO

From *Old Standard B&O Recipes*

Cook spaghetti in salted water, drain chicken livers cut about one inch square, sauté in butter, sprinkle with flour, fill casserole dish with spaghetti and chicken livers mixed with spaghetti, cover with spaghetti sauce, and place in oven to heat thoroughly; serving parmesan cheese in sauce dish on side.

Chef's Comments

INGREDIENTS FOR 4 SERVINGS

8 ounces Spaghetti (uncooked)
4–5 ounces Chicken Livers
8 ounces (or as desired) Tomato Sauce (*See* Sauces Section)
1 tablespoon Butter
1 tablespoon Flour

Preheat oven to 300 degrees and heat the spaghetti for 8–10 minutes.

This dish will need plenty of sauce to ensure that it is nice and moist after heating in the oven.

VEGETABLE AND PASTA DISHES

SHRIMP AND SPAGHETTI

From *Old Standard B&O Recipes*

Cook spaghetti same as macaroni, creole sauce, brown sauce, tomato sauce mixed. Chop some blanched sweet green peppers and finely chopped shallots or onions, little paprika salt, mix spaghetti and sauce, put in chicken pie dish, then top with five large pieces of shrimp, put in oven to bake.

Chef's Comments

INGREDIENTS FOR 3–4 SERVINGS

8 ounces Spaghetti (uncooked)
½ cup Creole Sauce *(See* Sauces *Section)*
½ cup Espagnole Sauce *(See* Sauces *Section)*
½ cup Tomato Sauce *(See* Sauces *Section)*
3 ounces Green Bell Peppers
3 ounces Shallots or Onions, ¼-inch dice
Paprika, to taste
Salt, to taste
Shrimp, cooked, shelled (5 per serving)

Preheat oven to 350 degrees and bring a large pot of water to a rolling boil.

Before chopping the bell pepper, place it in the boiling water for 30–45 seconds, then place in an ice water bath to cool completely. Then cut to ¼-inch dice. Place the spaghetti in the boiling water and cook for 10 minutes. Drain in a colander and run cold water over it.

Combine all ingredients except the shrimp and mix thoroughly. Place each order "in [a] chicken pie dish, then top with five large pieces of shrimp, put in [the] oven to bake" for 15–20 minutes.

For a "chicken pie dish," use any glazed ovenproof dish.

WHY NOT WILD RICE

From *Old Standard B&O Recipes*

Wash thoroughly through a sieve. Cover well with cold water, add a little salt, and boil steadily for about 15 minutes. Drain off water and dry the rice on the back of the range in open kettle for five minutes. Do not stir the rice and same will dry out and remain light and flaky. When used for stuffing it should be highly seasoned.

Chef's Comments

INGREDIENTS FOR 2 CUPS

1 cup Water
Pinch Salt
½ cup Rice

Bring the salted water to a boil, add the rice, reduce to a simmer, and cover for 15–20 minutes until the water has evaporated. Fluff with a fork before serving. This updated procedure is applicable to most types of rice. Modern "converted rice" need not be washed before use.

Where on earth did the name "Why Not Wild Rice" come from? Perhaps it was the name of a brand that the B&O used.

THIRD BIRTHDAY. Three candles decorate the cake of a little fellow—perhaps a budding railfan or an employee's son—celebrating his birthday. Big sister and brother look a bit envious of the gala event at Baltimore's Camden Station aboard a B&O observation car. Baltimore and Ohio Railroad Museum

DESSERTS AND PIE CRUST

MINCE MEAT COBBLER CAKE

From "B&O General Notice," January 6, 1961,
for menus effective January 10, 1961

For this item order Honey-N-Spice Cake Mix which comes in 5-lb. packages. Use 2½ lbs. cake mix, ¾ lb. mince meat and 3 cups water. Basic instructions: spread one-half of the dry cake mix (1 lb. 4 oz.) evenly over the bottom of a greased aluminum pudding pan (12 x 9 x 2 inches). DO NOT PACK MIX DOWN. Pour 1 cup of water evenly over the dry mix. Cover evenly with ¾ lb. of mince meat. Spread balance of dry mix (1 lb. 4 oz.) uniformly over the mince meat. Pour 2 cups of water evenly over the dry mix. Allow to set for 5 to 10 minutes and place in oven. Bake at 350 to 375 degrees F. for about 1 hour, or until center is set. Yield should be about 25 orders.

Chef's Comments

INGREDIENTS FOR 12 SERVINGS

1¼ pound Honey and Spice Cake Mix
6 ounces Mince Meat
1½ cups Water

A smaller baking pan should be used for the reduced recipe, but the 9 x 9 inch or 5 x 9 inch sizes usually found will yield cake of a different thickness.

GINGER BREAD PUDDING WITH COFFEE SAUCE

From *Old Standard B&O Recipes*

1 cup Butter
1½ cups Sugar
1 teaspoon Salt
1 cup Molasses
1 cup Sour Cream
½ cup Raisins
4 Eggs
1 teaspoon Baking Soda
1 teaspoon Baking Powder
4 cups Flour

TO THIS ADD

½ cup Cocoanut, grated
Rind of 1 Orange, grated

Mix all the ingredients together, beat until light, grease pan and set for five minutes before baking. Bake 30 minutes, in a moderate oven. To be served with coffee sauce.

Chef's Comments

Preheat oven to 300 degrees.
This "baked pudding" is actually a quick bread and bakes up like a small cake with a somewhat loose texture. Use one recipe of Coffee Sauce (*see* Sauces *Section*) with this recipe to make 20 servings.

FLAKY PIE CRUST

From Old Standard B&O Recipes

2 cups flour, 1½ cups Crisco, ½ teaspoon salt, cold ice water. Sift flour and salt in mixing bowl, then add the Crisco. Form lightly and quickly with the hand into dough, then roll out lightly as possible. Add gradually sufficient water to make a stiff paste.

Chef's Comments

	Double Crust Pie (1 recipe)	Lattice Crust Pie (¾ recipe)	Single Crust Pie (½ recipe)
Flour	11 ounces	8¼ ounces	5½ ounces
Salt	½ teaspoon	⅜ teaspoon	¼ teaspoon
Sugar (optional)	½ ounce	⅜ ounce	¼ ounce
Shortening	7¾ ounces	5¾ ounces	3¾ ounces
Ice Water	3¼ ounces	2½ ounces	1¾ ounces

To use this recipe for the crust of "meat pie" dishes, such as Chicken Pie, Oyster Pie, etc., do not include the sugar. To make the crust for a "dessert pie," sift the optional sugar into the mixing bowl with the flour and salt.

Proper mixing by hand will yield 1-inch chunks of flour and shortening, and much of the flour will still appear unmixed before the water is added.

Mind the advice to add the "cold ice water" gradually. Add only as much extra water as may be necessary to form a cohesive ball of dough.

Cover the dough and refrigerate for at least 4 hours, or place in the freezer for 20–30 minutes before use. Then roll the chilled dough to a uniform 1/8-inch thickness and place in a pie pan or dish.

The secret to a nice and flaky pie crust is to avoid overmixing the ingredients. The larger the chunks of flour and shortening when the dough forms into a ball, the flakier the crust will be when baked.

To ease the task of rolling the dough, place it between sheets of waxed paper or plastic wrap lightly coated with flour or cooking spray.

FRENCH APPLE PIE

From Old Standard B&O Recipes

Slice apples very thin, pour melted butter over them, put in oven until apples are soft, then make a nice flaky crust.

3 Egg Yolks
1 cup Sugar
½ teaspoon Vanilla
1 cup Milk
½ cup Raisins

Mix these ingredients together and pour over the apples and bake in oven until firm, then cover with meringue.

Chef's Comments

INGREDIENTS FOR 1 PIE

FOR THE FILLING

18 ounces Apples, peeled
3 tablespoons Butter, melted
3 Egg Yolks
1 cup Sugar
1 cup Milk
½ cup Raisins

FOR THE CRUST

½ recipe Flaky Pie Crust (with sugar) *(See recipe, above)*

FOR THE MERINGUE

3 Egg Whites
3 ounces Sugar

Preheat oven to 350 degrees.

"Slice apples very thin, pour melted butter over them, put in oven until apples are soft." When the apples are done, reset the oven temperature to 450 degrees. Mix the remaining ingredients and combine with the softened apple slices and butter and pour into a prepared pie crust.

Bake at 450 degrees for 15 minutes on the bottom shelf of the oven to set the crust, then move to middle shelf of oven and lower heat to 325 degrees and bake for an additional 20–30 minutes.

While the pie is baking, make the meringue by beating only the egg whites with an electric mixer, first at medium speed, then at high speed until soft peaks form. Add the sugar gradually with the mixer running and beat until stiff.

Spread the meringue over the top of the baked pie and return it to the oven for 10–15 minutes, until browned as desired.

Meringue can be made by hand (without a mixer), but it takes a lot more time and elbow grease.

MOCK CHERRY PIE

From *Old Standard B&O Recipes*

RECIPE NUMBER 28

3 cups Cranberries
1 cup Raisins
¼ cup Sugar
¾ cup Water
2 tablespoons Flour
¼ teaspoon Salt
½ teaspoon Vanilla

Chop cranberries and add other ingredients.

Chef's Comments

Of course these instructions imply that one already has a B&O flaky pie crust *(see recipe, above)* at hand. Be sure to add the sugar indicated in that recipe for this dessert pie.

Make an egg wash, with one egg beaten into a small amount of water, and brush this onto the exposed portions of the crust to give it a nice golden color.

Bake at 425 degrees for 30–40 minutes.

CRANBERRY PIE

From *Old Standard B&O Recipes*

1 pound Cranberries, chopped
1 ounce Flour
1½ cups Sugar
Pinch Salt
Butter, 1 tablespoon to a pie

Line pie plate with short flaky crust, chop cranberries and mix with the other ingredients, fill pie plate, place strips over top, bake in a moderate oven 30 minutes.

Chef's Comments

Make a ¾ recipe of Flaky Pie Crust *(see recipe, above)* and line the pie pan with dough for the bottom crust. Roll out the remainder and cut into ½-inch strips for the lattice top crust.

A "moderate oven" would be around 350 degrees.

FRENCH PEACH PIE
From *Old Standard B&O Recipes*

Butter inside before putting in bottom crust, then add the sliced peaches, spreading over peaches, one third cup of sugar. Yolks of three eggs, ¼ cup of milk, one cup of flour, 1 teaspoon baking powder, ¼ teaspoon salt. Bake until peaches are soft, cover with meringue, brown in a slow oven.

Chef's Comments

INGREDIENTS FOR 1 PIE

FOR THE FILLING

⅓ cup Granulated Sugar
3 Egg Yolks
¼ cup Milk
1 cup Flour
1 teaspoon Baking Powder
¼ teaspoon Salt
1 can (29 ounces) Peaches, sliced, drained

FOR THE CRUST

Flaky Pie Crust (½ recipe) *(See recipe, above)*

FOR THE MERINGUE

3 Egg Whites
3 ounces Granulated Sugar

Preheat oven to 450 degrees.
Butter a 9-inch pie pan, roll out the crust, and place it in the pan. Collect all ingredients except the peaches in a bowl and mix thoroughly. Place the sliced peaches in the pie crust and add the filling, spreading evenly.

Bake at 450 degrees for 15 minutes on the bottom shelf of the oven, then move to middle shelf and lower the heat to 325 degrees for 15–25 minutes.

While the pie is baking, make the meringue by beating only the egg whites with an electric mixer, first at medium speed, then at high speed until soft peaks form. Add the sugar gradually with the mixer running and beat until stiff.

Spread the meringue over the top of the baked pie and return it to the oven for 10–15 minutes until browned to suit.

PEACH PIE GLACE
From *Old Standard B&O Recipes*

4 cups Peaches, fresh, sliced
1 3-ounce package Jell-o, Orange
Dash Salt
¾ cup Sugar
1½ cups Water, boiling

Combine peaches and sugar and let stand ten minutes. Dissolve Jell-o in boiling water, add salt and pour over peaches, stirring occasionally as mixture cools. Chill until slightly thickened. Turn into cold pie shell, chill until firm. Top with whipped cream.

Chef's Comments

This recipe will require ½ recipe of flaky pie crust *(see recipe, above)* with the sugar included.

The authors' penciled notes on this recipe warn "follow these instructions, not those shown on Jell-o box."

PUMPKIN PIE

From *Old Standard B&O Recipes*

3 cups Pumpkin, steamed or canned
1½ cups Sugar, granulated
½ cup Butter, melted
1½ cups Milk
4 Eggs
½ teaspoon Salt
1 teaspoon Cinnamon
½ teaspoon Ginger
¼ teaspoon Nutmeg

First place the eggs, butter, and sugar in a mixing bowl and mix thoroughly, add the mixed spices, then add the milk. Last add the pumpkin. Then pour into a prepared pie dish.

Chef's Comments

INGREDIENTS FOR 2 PIES

Bake at 450 degrees for 15 minutes on a lower rack in the oven, then lower the heat to 350 degrees and bake until the filling sets, about 30–40 minutes more.

The term "prepared pie dish" means a pie pan or dish with a crust. Baking at the higher temperature for 15 minutes will help bake the crust and prevent it from getting soggy. Use one recipe of flaky pie crust (with sugar added) *(see recipe, above)*.

RHUBARB PIE

From *Old Standard B&O Recipes*

Fresh pink rhubarb, cut off root end, cut into one-inch pieces, without peeling, make a hot syrup of water and sugar, pour over the cut rhubarb, and set on back of the stove to simmer until done, without stirring. When cool put into a stripped top crust pie, sprinkle rhubarb with butter.

Chef's Comments

INGREDIENTS FOR 1 PIE

1½ cups Water
1½ cups Sugar
4 cups Rhubarb
¾ recipe Flaky Pie Crust (with sugar) *(See recipe, above)*
1–2 tablespoons Butter, melted

Line a pie pan with crust.

Cut off all green parts of the rhubarb, leaving only the pink. Cut into 1-inch pieces.

Combine the water and sugar to make syrup, then heat and stir until all sugar is dissolved. Add the rhubarb to the syrup and simmer without stirring until tender.

Place the filling in the pie crust and sprinkle with melted butter. Cover with a lattice made from strips of pie crust dough.

Bake in a 425-degree oven for 30–40 minutes.

To avoid burning the crusts, try baking the pie at 425 degrees for 10–15 minutes, then reducing oven temperature to 375 degrees. This will set the crust and prevent it from over-browning or getting soggy.

CARAMEL CUSTARD

From *Old Standard B&O Recipes*

Scald four cups of milk with one cup of brown sugar added. Stir until brown sugar is dissolved. Soak three tablespoons of gelatin, plain, in one-half cup cold water for ten minutes. Beat three eggs or five egg yolks until light, and add the hot milk gradually. Return to saucepan and add one teaspoon salt, and cook, stirring constantly for five minutes, add the soaked gelatin and remove from the fire, cool, stir in two teaspoons vanilla extract and pour into individual dishes, or one large to harden. Serve with cream.

4 cups Milk
1 cup Brown Sugar
3 tablespoons Gelatin
½ cup Water, cold
3 Eggs (or 5 egg yolks)

¼ teaspoon Salt
2 tablespoons Vanilla Extract

Chef's Comments

MAKES 6-10 SERVINGS

CHOCOLATE BLANC MANGE

From *Old Standard B&O Recipes*

1 quart Milk
Pinch Baking Soda
1 cup Sugar
4 tablespoons Cornstarch
4 tablespoons Chocolate, grated
1 teaspoon Vanilla

Beat the milk and add the soda. Into the milk stir the sugar, when dissolved add the cornstarch wet with cold milk. Cook until smooth and very thick. Add grated chocolate and cook for a minute before removing from the fire. Stir in the vanilla, turn into mould set with cold water, and set in a cold place to form.

Chef's Comments

INGREDIENTS FOR 10 SERVINGS

Chocolate chips can be substituted for grated chocolate. However, about twice the amount shown will be needed to get the same rich taste and color.

Stir frequently as the mixture thickens to keep it from scorching and sticking to the pan.

ORANGE CUSTARD PUDDING, MERINGUE

From *Old Standard B&O Recipes*

4 cups Milk
1 cup Sugar
6 Eggs Yolks
1 Orange, sliced
½ teaspoon Vanilla

Beat the eggs, sugar and milk together, then add the sliced orange. Bake in a medium oven until firm. Then add Meringue.

Chef's Comments

INGREDIENTS FOR 6 SERVINGS

6 Eggs, separated
1 cup Sugar
4 cups Milk
½ teaspoon Vanilla
1 Orange, sliced
12 ounces Sugar
Pinch Salt

Preheat oven to 350 degrees.

Beat the egg yolks, 1 cup of sugar, the milk, and vanilla together, then add the sliced orange. Place in ramekins or cups and bake until firm, about 30 minutes.

To make the meringue, place the egg whites, salt, and 12 ounces of sugar in the bowl of a mixer. About 5 minutes before the pudding is done, turn the mixer on high speed and beat until the mixture forms stiff peaks.

Add meringue to the top of each cup of pudding, finishing each with an artistic swirl. Return the cups to the oven until the meringue is lightly browned, about 6 minutes.

Do not overbeat the meringue and be sure that it is ready at the same time as the pudding. Otherwise, it will disintegrate and not hold its shape while being browned.

PRUNE WHIP

From *Old Standard B&O Recipes*

RECIPE NUMBER 12

Soak one pound of prunes overnight, stew one half an hour, adding one cup of sugar, when cool, remove pits and chop fine, then add whites of five eggs, beaten stiff, mixing with the prune pulp, pour into buttered dishes. Bake half an hour. Serve cold with whipped cream.

Chef's Comments

INGREDIENTS FOR 8 SERVINGS

1 pound Prunes
1 cup Sugar
5 Egg Whites
Whipped Cream, to taste

"Soak one pound of prunes overnight."

Place in a pot with plenty of water, bring to a boil and reduce to a simmer. Add the sugar, stir, and continue to simmer for 30 minutes. Drain and cool.

Preheat the oven to 325 degrees along with a pan with enough water in it to come halfway up the sides of the dishes in which the pudding will be baked.

Remove the pits from the prunes and chop the prunes fine.

Beat the egg whites until stiff, fold in the chopped prunes, and pour the mixture into buttered ovenproof dishes. Place the containers in the pan of warmed water and bake in the pan for 30 minutes.

"Serve cold with whipped cream."

PUMPKIN PUDDING

From *Old Standard B&O Recipes*

Prepare pumpkin same as used for pie *(see recipe, above)*, fill individual pie dishes, brown in oven. Serve topped with whipped cream and a teaspoon of honey on the whipped cream.

RICE OR BREAD CUSTARD PUDDING

From *Old Standard B&O Recipes*

FOR RICE CUSTARD PUDDING

6 cups Milk
8 Eggs
1 cup Sugar
1 teaspoon Salt
1 cup Raisins
1 cup Rice, boiled
1 teaspoon Vanilla
2 tablespoons Butter, melted
Nutmeg, to taste

Scald the milk, beat the eggs with the sugar, add salt in and pour the scalding milk over them, and put the mixture in a pudding pan. Grate a little nutmeg over the top. Set in a pan of hot water and bake very slow in a moderate oven until brown.

FOR BREAD CUSTARD PUDDING

May be made by the same recipe as above, except, use buttered toast cut in squares instead of rice.

Chef's Comments

INGREDIENTS FOR 12–16 SERVINGS

Preheat the oven to 300 degrees along with a pan with enough water in it to come halfway up the sides of the dishes in which the pudding will be baked and served.

Scald the milk by heating it slowly until small bubbles begin to appear around the edge. Stir frequently while heating.

Although the ingredient list calls for raisins, rice, and vanilla, the procedure fails to mention them. They should be added along with the salt to the beaten eggs and sugar. Stirring constantly, pour the hot milk very slowly into the egg mixture to avoid cooking the eggs. Then stir in the melted butter. Pour into a buttered pudding pan or individual dishes, sprinkling nutmeg over the top.

SHREDDED WHEAT PUDDING

From *Old Standard B&O Recipes*

Lay whole wheat biscuits in ginger bread pan or pudding pan, cover with mixture made of milk, eggs, sugar and cornstarch, season with vanilla, or just about the same mixture you would use for rice pudding. Pour the mixture over the biscuits, sprinkle lightly with nutmeg or cinnamon, then bake in oven.

INGREDIENTS FOR 5 SERVINGS

5 biscuits Shredded Wheat
6 Eggs, beaten
½ teaspoon Salt
½ cup Sugar
4 tablespoons Cornstarch
1 teaspoon Vanilla
1 quart Whole Milk
Nutmeg or Cinnamon, as needed
Hot Water, as needed

Fill a large baking pan with hot water that reaches halfway up the side of the pan or dish in which the pudding is to be baked. Place this in the oven and pre-heat to 325 degrees.

Place the pudding dishes into the heated water and bake for 1 hour.

Banana Shortcake

From *Baltimore and Ohio* magazine, January 1959

(Use fully ripe bananas—yellow peel flecked with brown.) Split homemade or baker's gingerbread, cake, cupcakes or biscuits into two layers. Place whipped cream and sliced ripe bananas between layers and on top. Garnish with a cherry if desired. Just before serving, peel and slice additional bananas and arrange them around the base of the banana shortcake if desired.

INGREDIENTS FOR 1 SERVING

1 Banana, peeled, sliced
1 piece Shortbread *(See* Shortcake Biscuit *recipe in* Baked Goods *Section)*
Whipped Cream, to taste
1 Cherry

Although the recipe offers a choice of shortbread-type items, note that there is a "genuine B&O" formula shown with the recipe for Strawberry Shortcake.

Like Pan-Fried Bananas, this dish was placed on the menus of the Capitol Limited, National Limited, and Columbian to celebrate the opening of the B&O's Locust Point banana import pier in Baltimore on December 1, 1958. *Baltimore and Ohio* magazine termed Banana Shortcake "long an American favorite."

The article continued: "Manager Dining Car and Commissary Department J. B. Martin reports that the promotion was an outstanding success, with many orders for the banana dishes being taken, and with many dining car patrons asking for the novel table tents as souvenirs."

These "tents" were freestanding cards listing the dishes along with an explanation of their significance and a photo of the newly opened pier. Unfortunately, the B&O's banana pier wasn't nearly as successful as these celebratory dishes appear to have been.

OLD-FASHIONED PEACH SHORTCAKE

From "B&O General Notice," June 3, 1964,
for menus effective June 11, 1964

Use frozen peaches. Make round shortcake biscuits, using one single biscuit with peaches over same. Serve in sauce Dish to cover "tab" service. For á-la-carte portion use two biscuits, placing one biscuit in bottom of oatmeal bowl, then some peaches, another biscuit on top with more peaches over same. In both "tab" and á-la-carte service use a portion of whipped cream to top off the service.

Chef's Comments

INGREDIENTS FOR 1 SERVING

1 or 2 Shortcake Biscuits *(See* Shortcake Biscuit *recipe in* Baked Goods *Section)*
Peaches, frozen, as needed
Whipped Cream, as needed

The term "tab" is short for table d'hôte, which is a complete meal, offered at a single price. A la carte denotes a menu on which each food or beverage is listed—and priced—separately. A la carte servings were often larger than those served "tab."

Canned sliced peaches are much more convenient than frozen, and fresh sliced peaches will make this dessert really memorable.

STRAWBERRY SHORTCAKE (RECIPE NUMBER 5)

From *Old Standard B&O Recipes* and *Eat, Drink, and Be Merry in Maryland* (Stieff)

AND

OLD-FASHIONED STRAWBERRY SHORTCAKE

From "B&O General Notice," April 6, 1964,
for menus effective April 9, 1964

Make round biscuits, using one single biscuit with strawberries over same. Serve in a sauce dish to cover "tab" service. For á-la-carte portion use two biscuits, placing one biscuit in the bottom of an oatmeal bowl, then some strawberries, another biscuit on top with more strawberries over same. In both "tab" and á-la-carte service use a portion of whipped cream to top off the service.

Chef's Comments

This dish was listed in *Old Standard B&O Recipes* and *Eat, Drink, and Be Merry in Maryland,* which provided the recipe for the shortcake biscuits shown in our *Baked Goods* section.

The only difference in the 1964 version was the use of whipped cream, which prompted the addition of the appellation "Old-Fashioned."

COUPE OF ORANGE AND GRAPEFRUIT

From *Old Standard B&O Recipes*

Equal parts of orange and grapefruit segments, serve in fruit cocktail glass.

FRESH FRUIT JELL-O

From "B&O General Notice," May 1, 1963

Be sure to use fresh fruits. DO NOT USE CANNED FRUITS OR FRUIT COCKTAIL.

Chef's Comments

This recipe allows for use of a wide variety of fruits, but there are some—pineapple and kiwi to name two—that can hinder the setting of gelatin or liquefy that which has already set. These contain actinidin, an enzyme commonly found in commercial meat tenderizers.

HAWAIIAN FRUIT CUP

From "B&O General Notice," August 13, 1959

Use equal parts of orange and grapefruit segments and pineapple chunks. Tint pink with grenadine.

MIXED FRESH FRUIT IN MELON RING

From "B&O General Notice," September 1, 1960, for menus effective September 1, 1960

Use care in preparing this item. Peel the melon and slice same into rings about ¾-inch thick. Place on a tea plate with orange and grapefruit segments, slices of peaches, etc., in center of ring. THIS MUST BE SERVED WELL CHILLED.

Chef's Comments

INGREDIENTS FOR 1 SERVING

1 ring Honeydew or Cantaloupe
Orange Segments, as needed
Grapefruit Segments, as needed
Peaches, sliced, as needed

That "etc." indicates that one need not be limited to only the fruits listed above.

RHUBARB JELLY

From *Old Standard B&O Recipes*

Prepare the rhubarb as above [i.e., for *Rhubarb Pie*]. Dissolve one package of lemon gelatin in a half cup boiling water, add the rhubarb, and pour into pan or mould to harden. Serve with cream or thin custard sauce. One pound of rhubarb to each package of gelatin.

Chef's Comments

INGREDIENTS FOR 8 SERVINGS

1½ cups Water
1½ cups Sugar
4 cups Rhubarb
1 3-ounce package Lemon Gelatin
½ cup Water

Cut off all green parts of the rhubarb, leaving only the pink. Dice into ¼-inch segments.

Combine the water and sugar to make syrup, then heat and stir until all sugar is dissolved. Add the rhubarb to the syrup and simmer without stirring until tender. Boil the water and add the gelatin, stirring until dissolved. Combine the gelatin and the rhubarb-syrup mixture and pour into a mold or pan to cool and harden.

"Serve with cream or thin custard sauce."

The name Rhubarb Jelly might lead one to expect something to spread on bread or biscuits. But this is actually what would be called Rhubarb Jell-o today.

END OF A PERFECT MEAL. Darkness has fallen and two couples are being served dessert aboard the Capitol Limited. Probably staged for publicity purposes, this photo highlights the B&O's famed Blue China designed for its centennial in 1927 and the prominently labeled bottle of Deer Park Spring Water from the railroad's own Boiling Spring in Deer Park, Maryland. A 1956 menu similar to that shown lists several tempting dessert selections but nothing that seems to describe the scrumptious concoction being served by the smiling waiter. Baltimore and Ohio Railroad Museum

GOOD MORNING

BREAKFAST

A la Carte

Table D' Hote

A la Carte

PLEASE WRITE YOUR ORDER ON CHECK; EMPLOYEES ARE NOT
PERMITTED TO ACCEPT ORAL ORDERS

(CHOICE OF)

Chilled Orange Juice .35		
Chilled Grapefruit, Tomato or Prune Juice .35		
Figs in Syrup .35 Stewed Prunes .35		Eggs (2), Fried, Scrambled
Half Grapefruit .40		or Boiled .80
Baked Apple .40	Half Grapefruit Apple Sauce	
	Stewed Prunes Baked Apple Figs in Syrup	Omelet, Plain .85
		Fancy Omelet 1.30
	Orange, Grapefruit, Tomato or Prune Juice	Poached Eggs on Toast .90

(A)	GRILLED HAM AND EGGS—2.00
(B)	SUGAR CURED BACON AND EGGS—1.90
(C)	EGGS, BOILED, FRIED OR SCRAMBLED—1.60
(D)	OMELET WITH CHEDDAR CHEESE—1.80
(E)	FRENCH TOAST WITH BACON—1.75
(F)	GRIDDLE CAKES WITH DAINTY LINK SAUSAGES—1.90
(G)	COUNTRY SCRAPPLE AND EGGS—1.75

Hot Cereal with Cream
or
Individual Package Cereal
with Cream .35

Broiled Ham
with Two Eggs 1.50

Rolls, Toast
or Muffins .25

Rolls   Corn Muffins   Toast

Bacon (4) Strips
with Two Eggs 1.40

Milk Toast .50
Cream Toast .60

Jelly   Apple Butter   Marmalade

(SELECT FROM TRAY)

Bacon (4) Strips .80

Broiled Ham 1.00

Coffee   Tea   Milk   Sanka   Postum

Coffee (Pot) .35
Tea (Pot) .35
Milk, Individual .25
Sanka, Postum
or Cocoa, Pot. 35

French Toast, Maple Syrup .75

Griddle Cakes (4) .75
with
Bacon or Sausage 1.50

MINUTE SAVER
1.00*
Large Glass Orange Juice
Rolls, Toast or Corn Muffins
Jelly Tray
Coffee   Tea   Milk
* with Cereal 1.30

Car in Charge of

BALTIMORE and OHIO Dining Car Service

J. B. MARTIN, Manager of Dining Car and Commissary Department, Baltimore 1, Maryland

5-25-6-26-C-9-1

A CHARGE OF 50c PER PERSON WILL BE MADE FOR FOOD SERVICE OUTSIDE OF DINING CAR

"**GOOD MORNING.**" Seven table d'hôte selections were offered on this breakfast menu, including that quintessential East Coast delicacy, country scrapple. In line with the dietary norms of the day, most meal selections included eggs, although a health-conscious passenger could also come away well filled. In the lower right-hand corner, the notation 5-25-6-26-C-9-1 indicates the trains and date for which the menu was printed. Trains 5 and 6, respectively, were the westbound and eastbound all-Pullman Capitol Limited between Washington and Chicago, while Numbers 25 and 26 were its all-coach running mate, the Columbian. The month of issue was given as C (third month of the year, shown by the third letter of the alphabet), followed by the day and last digit of the year. This menu was effective, then, on March 9, 1961. By this time the Capitol Limited and Columbian were combined into one lengthy consist (that is, the rolling stock, exclusive of the locomotive, making up a train) operated separately only during peak travel periods. Karl Spence collection

BREAKFAST DISHES

GRIDDLE CAKES

Buckwheat Cakes

Corn Cakes

German Pancakes and Apple Pancakes

Wheat Cakes

OTHER BREAKFAST DISHES

Service of Prunes

Fresh Sausage Patties

BUCKWHEAT CAKES

From *Old Standard B&O Recipes*

3 cups Buckwheat
½ cake Yeast, dissolved
3½ cups Cold Water
½ teaspoon Salt

Dissolve this, making a heavy batter, letting the same stand overnight, and in the morning you will add two basting spoons of dark syrup. One third teaspoon baking soda, dissolve in milk or water, one third cup of butter put in same.

Chef's Comments

INGREDIENTS FOR MAKING EIGHT 6-INCH CAKES

1½ cups Buckwheat Flour
½ teaspoon Yeast, dry active
1¾ cups Cold Water
¼ teaspoon Salt
½ tablespoon Dark Syrup
¾ tablespoon Butter
½ teaspoon Baking Soda
1 tablespoon Milk or Water

Melt some butter in a skillet or griddle and spoon in batter to make cakes the desired size. Cook at medium heat until bubbles appear and the top of each cake appears dry. Then flip and cook the other side. That "dark syrup" in the recipe could be corn syrup (like Karo), pancake syrup, etc. As mentioned in the original recipe, the batter for this and other pancakes made from scratch benefits from standing overnight.

From *Baltimore and Ohio* magazine, November 1928

March 20, 1928
Mr. E. V. Baugh
Manager, Dining Car and Commissary Department
Baltimore and Ohio Railroad
Baltimore, Md.

My dear Mr. Baugh:

I travel on the Baltimore and Ohio preferentially wherever I go its way. Yesterday morning I arrived at Washington, D.C. on The Capitol Limited; this morning I returned to Chicago on The Capitol Limited.

Both mornings I ordered buckwheat cakes, of which I am a devotee. Both mornings they were dark brown instead of the normal buckwheat gray, and both mornings they lacked the acid taste that belongs to a genuine buckwheat cake.

This morning I asked the steward why and he said: "Our recipe calls for syrup sweetening." That answers as to both the brown color and lack of the acid taste.

I used to get genuine gray, properly acidulated buckwheat cakes on the Baltimore and Ohio. I have not had them this year, nor last—ones that taste "like mother used to make." Alas, no more!

Yours,
Hungry for a Real Buckwheat Cake

CORN CAKES

From *The Culinary Handbook* (Fellows)

Batter for corn griddle cakes is made of half a pound each of wheat flour and corn meal mixed dry with a little salt and one ounce of baking powder, then moistened with a pint each of milk and water, two beaten eggs, a little syrup and two table-spoons of melted butter.

Chef's Comments

INGREDIENTS FOR 6 PANCAKES

4 ounces Flour
4 ounces Corn Meal
1½ teaspoons Baking Powder
1 teaspoon Salt
1 Egg
1 cup Milk
1 cup Water
1 tablespoon Dark Syrup
1 tablespoon Butter, melted
Butter (for cooking), as needed

Sift the flour, corn meal, baking powder, and salt together in a mixing bowl.

In a separate bowl, beat the egg and add the milk, water, syrup, and melted butter, stirring well. Add the liquid ingredients to the dry, mixing just until the ingredients are combined.

Melt butter on the griddle and ladle 2-ounce portions of batter onto it. As soon as bubbles appear on the pancake's surface and the bottom is browned, turn with a spatula to cook the other side.

As in the recipe for Buckwheat Cakes, the "dark syrup" called for could be dark corn syrup or any pancake syrup available.

GERMAN PANCAKES AND APPLE PANCAKES

From *Old Standard B&O Recipes*

GERMAN PANCAKES

½ Cup flour, ½ Cup Cream, Mix well and add two whole eggs, 1 Tablespoon melted butter, seasoned with a little sugar and a pinch of salt, have pan hot with a little butter in it, pour in dough to cover pan, and bake in a hot oven.

APPLE PANCAKES

Mix the same as above, after pouring dough into pan, place finely sliced apples to cover pan, and bake in a hot oven.

Chef's Comments

INGREDIENTS FOR 2 SERVINGS

½ cup Flour
½ cup Cream
2 Eggs
1 tablespoon Butter, melted
Sugar, to taste
Dash Salt
Apple, sliced fine (½ per recipe [Apple Pancakes only])

Place a large skillet in the oven and preheat to 450 degrees.

While the pancake is baking, remember to warm the syrup.

WHEAT CAKES

From *The Culinary Handbook* (Fellows)

Batter for wheat griddle cakes is made of a pound of flour, one ounce of baking powder, two beaten eggs, three cups of milk, a little melted butter, sugar and salt.

Chef's Comments

INGREDIENTS FOR 6 PANCAKES

4 ounces Flour
¾ teaspoon Baking Powder
½ teaspoon Salt
½ tablespoon Sugar
1 Egg
¾ cup Milk
1 tablespoon Butter, melted
Butter (for cooking), as needed

Preheat a griddle, skillet, or frying pan over medium heat and sift the flour, baking powder, salt, and sugar together in a mixing bowl.

In a separate bowl, beat the egg and add the milk and butter, stirring well. Add the liquid ingredients to the dry, mixing just until the ingredients are combined.

Melt butter on the griddle and ladle 2-ounce portions of batter onto it. As soon as bubbles appear on the pancake's surface and the bottom is browned to suit, flip with a spatula to cook the other side.

A tip from *What's Cooking on the B&O?* advises, "Don't overheat the griddle. It should be hot enough to make the cakes rise, but no hotter. Turning the cakes more than once makes them tough."

SERVICE OF PRUNES

From "B&O General Notice," February 4, 1964, for menus effective February 13, 1964

As outlined in our Standard of Dining Car Service on "Tab" meal, serve 5 prunes in sauce dish underlined with tea plate. On á-la-carte orders, serve 8 to 10 prunes in oatmeal bowl, also underlined with tea plate, individual pitcher of cream.

Chef's Comments

French terms abound in any culinary encyclopedia. *Tab*, short for *table d'hôte,* denotes the service of a complete meal at a fixed price (or prix fixe). This was a more economical option.

A la carte means that the guest chooses individual dishes, each priced separately. An á la carte meal would be more expensive, but portions were generally larger than those served "tab."

The Standard of Dining Car Service was a handbook published and updated regularly by the B&O's Dining Car and Commissary Department. Instructions covered such items as uniforms and deportment of the service staff, setup of tables, and, as outlined above, the china to be used in the service of various dishes.

FRESH SAUSAGE PATTIES

From "B&O General Notice," December 6, 1963,
for menus effective December 12, 1963

TO BE SERVED WITH GRIDDLE CAKES

This year we will change from the brown-and-serve sausage to the fresh sausage patties. It will be furnished in one-pound rolls and you will slice each pound into 8 pieces of equal size. Flatten the patties slightly, place in the skillet with sufficient water to come up half-way of the sausage cakes. Cover and steam slowly for 10 minutes, remove cover and brown. SAUSAGE SHOULD NOT BE COOKED AHEAD OF TIME. Be sure to drain the sausage patties well on a paper towel before serving. Serve 3 hot cakes and 3 sausage patties on a tab meal on the dinner plate, 4 cakes and 4 sausage patties á-la-carte. Hot cakes to have a chip of butter on top of same in addition to the regular butter service.

We want this hot cakes and sausage service to be good, and it is hoped that none of our chefs will be observed flagrantly cooking the sausage patties ahead of time. By actual test, the time needed is 10 to 12 minutes.

Watering Pancakes on the B&O, by Tom Greco

My interest in the Baltimore and Ohio Railroad's dining car service had a rather inauspicious beginning on the morning of July 24, 1964. As a 17-year-old, I was on my first "B&O vacation," eastbound on Train 8, the Shenandoah. Near Youngstown, Ohio, I went to the dining car for breakfast.

A bit of background information might prepare the reader for what happened next. My Dad is a great cook, and every Sunday morning after church, he would make pancakes for the family from scratch. Also from scratch he would make syrup for the pancakes that was as clear as water, albeit a bit thicker.

My table on Number 8 that morning was set in usual B&O fashion, including one glass of milk and another of ice water. In the center of the table was a beautiful glass carafe with a silver cap. All of my experience told me this was syrup for the stack of pancakes that was soon placed in front of me. With my knife I placed a pat of butter between each cake. Then came a liberal portion of syrup from the beautiful carafe.

I noticed an older couple across the aisle who seemed to be staring at me. I figured it was the stack of employees' timetables on the chair to my right that caught their attention, along with frequent jotting of times in my logbook as we passed stations along the way.

The pancake syrup didn't taste like much; certainly not like my Dad's. And it didn't look like Dad's syrup either, sloshing as it did with the movement of the train. A quick exploration of my table turned up a little dish full of plastic containers plainly labeled "maple syrup."

My newly aroused suspicions were confirmed seconds later when my waiter asked if I'd like a refill of my glass of ice water. "Yes, please," I said, and he deftly removed the silver cap and filled my glass from the beautiful carafe.

Years later we'd say "I knew that!" and that's just the way I acted, smiling and nodding politely at the couple across the aisle, jotting down passing times and notes as though I had fully intended to pour water on my pancakes.

Back home in Omaha several weeks later, I visited with my friends and mentors Bill Carder, Bob Downing, and Eddie Nelsen in the B&O's offline freight sales office downtown. The story "brought the house down," and it was good for months of friendly teasing!

The Diplomat Luncheon

"But you used to have such a variety!"

YES, that is true and we sympathize heartily with your disappointment. But, you see, our food is rationed, too, just as it is in your own home, and you know what a problem that creates. So, if we can't give you the wide selection available on B & O trains in peacetime, or if prices seem a little higher than before, please be indulgent. We assure you that the quality you expect of B & O food will remain, within wartime limitations, at its usual high standard.

We ask you to remember, too, that increased travel, both of civilians and of military and naval personnel, is taxing our dining-car facilities. We are sure you will be glad to co-operate with us and your fellow-passengers by leaving the Diner as soon as you have finished your meal. We will appreciate your assistance.

H. O. McAbee
Manager of Dining Car
and Commissary Department
Baltimore, Maryland
A4310

Steward of Car

Relish

Chilled Tomato Juice   Consomme

Omelet with Mushrooms - 1.25
Panned Fresh Fish, Lemon - 1.35
Poultry Entree (if available) - 1.50
Fried Tomatoes with Bacon - 1.25

Potatoes   Vegetable

Salad — Lettuce, Tomato, Green Peppers
Baltimore and Ohio Dressing
(Served on Request)

* Ice Cream   * Cheese   Pie

Coffee   Tea   Milk

* Rationed — Served when Available

Alcoholic Beverages Will Not Be Sold After 10.00 P. M.

Service of Meals Outside of Dining Cars 25c Extra Per Person

Service men on furlough, traveling at their own expense, will be afforded a 10 per cent reduction in charges for food when the total amounts to 50 cents or more. Please consult Steward.

"All prices listed are our ceiling prices, or below. By Office of Price Administration regulation, our ceilings are our highest prices from February 1, 1943, to April 10, 1943. Records of these prices are available for your inspection at Room 11, Camden Station, Baltimore, Md."

"**BUT YOU USED TO HAVE SUCH A VARIETY!**" Austerity and rationing were watchwords during the World War II era, and the nation's railroads were expected to sacrifice for the war effort like any other citizen. The four table d'hôte meals offered in this October 1943 menu look appetizing enough, but meat is conspicuous by its absence. Even the availability of the poultry entrée is uncertain, as is the method by which it would be cooked and served. B&O's Diplomat operated between New York and St. Louis and would be serving lunch in southern Indiana or Illinois on the westward run or between Washington and Philadelphia heading east. Baltimore and Ohio Railroad Museum

EGG DISHES

OMELETS

B&O Omelet Garnishes

Fluffy Omelet

Omelet, Plain or Golden

Golden Omelet with Chicken Livers

Golden Omelet, Fried Tomatoes

Spanish Omelet

POACHED EGGS

Poached Eggs on Toast

Poached Eggs à la Mornay

Poached Eggs à la Portugaise

SCRAMBLED EGGS

Scrambled Eggs

Scrambled Eggs au Beurre d'Anchois

Scrambled Eggs à la Dumas

Scrambled Eggs à la Lyonnaise

Scrambled Eggs au Jambon

Scrambled Eggs with Fresh Tomatoes

SHIRRED EGGS

Shirred Eggs au Beurre Noir

Shirred Eggs in Cream with Ham

Shirred Eggs with Sausage and Tomato Sauce

OTHER EGG DISHES

Deviled Eggs

Cheese Soufflé

B&O OMELET GARNISHES

From Menus, "B&O General Notices," *Eggs in a Thousand Ways* (Meyer), and *The Culinary Handbook* (Fellows)

Name	Type of Garnish	Type of Omelet
Asparagus Tips, simmered	I	P
Asparagus Tips, creamed	I, E	G, P
(simmered in Cream Sauce)		
Baltimore and Ohio Special	I, E	P
(See Chef's Comments)		
Cheddar Cheese, grated	I	F, G, P
Chicken Livers (See recipe)	I, E	G
Chicken Livers, Madeira	I, E	G
Creole (See Chef's Comments)	E	G, P
Fried Tomatoes (See recipe)	S	G, P
Jelly or Marmalade	I	G
Ham, cooked, diced,	I	F, G, P
chopped or minced		
Melba Toast	S	P
Mushrooms,	I	G, P
chopped or sautéed		
Onion Rings, French Fried	S	G
Oysters, stewed in white wine	I, E	P
or Cream Sauce, chopped		
Parsley, chopped	I	P
Plain (no garnish or sauce)		P
Rum (See Chef's Comments)	E	P
Shrimp, fresh	I, E	P
(See Chef's Comments)		
Spanish Sauce	E	G
Spanish Style (See recipe)	I, E	G, P
Vienna Sausage, sautéed	S	G, P
Western Style		G

NOTES: Type of Garnish: I = Internal, E = External, S = Served on Side. Type of Omelet: F = Fluffy, G = Golden, P = Plain

Chef's Comments

An internal garnish is added to the omelet before or during cooking; an external garnish is poured or sprinkled on and/or around the omelet after it has been plated.

A Rum Omelet has a little sugar mixed with the beaten eggs. On the plate it is dusted with powdered sugar; warm rum is poured over the omelet and set aflame.

The Shrimp Omelet was filled with chopped cooked shrimp with whole cooked shrimps attractively arranged around the omelet.

A Special Egg Menu, offered around 1920, described the following delectable offerings:

B&O Special Omelet filled with cooked hashed (i.e., finely minced) chicken in cream; Creole Omelet garnished with green and red peppers, ham and mushrooms hashed fine in tomato sauce (all cooked before mixing with the sauce).

FLUFFY OMELET

From *Eggs in a Thousand Ways* (Meyer)

The yolks of three eggs are gradually mixed with six tablespoons of powdered sugar and stirred until it becomes smooth and light; the whites of six eggs are whisked to a stiff froth and then mixed with the yolks and the sugar; this must be done gently but quickly, only taking a small part of the egg froth to commence with. A dish is buttered and bestrewn with powdered sugar, the egg mass put on it in an oblong shape, sprinkled with powdered sugar and cooked in a hot oven.

1 tablespoon Butter
3 Egg Yolks
6 Egg Whites
Salt and Pepper, to taste
Garnish, as needed (*See* B&O Omelet Garnishes,
    above)

Preheat oven to 500 degrees. On the stovetop, melt the butter in an ovenproof omelet pan over medium-low heat.

Add the salt and pepper to the egg yolks and beat well.

Beat the egg whites into a stiff froth and fold into the yolks. Pour into the warmed and buttered omelet pan. Add any garnish desired and place the pan in the oven for 3 minutes.

Remove from the oven, fold in half, place on a plate, and add exterior garnishes, if any.

Adolphe Meyer's procedure included powdered sugar for what he called a "sweet," or dessert, omelet. However, dessert omelets have not been found on B&O menus, so we opted to delete the sugar from the ingredient list.

Be careful not to overcook the omelet. With the extensive beating of the egg whites, it will rise like a soufflé (in fact, some sources call these soufflé omelets). Too much rising will prevent the omelet from being folded around the garnish.

Fluffy Omelets appear to have been more of a breakfast item and were seen on menus in the mid-1960s, at the same time that Golden Omelets were listed on dinner menus.

OMELET, PLAIN OR GOLDEN

From *Eggs in a Thousand Ways* (Meyer)

Break six fresh eggs into a bowl, add a sufficient quantity of salt and pepper, and for every three eggs add one tablespoon of thick cream; beat the egg well with an egg whisk, or a fork, and strain into another bowl. Put two ounces of butter into the omelet pan, and when it is melted without being browned, turn in the eggs; stir continually with a kitchen spoon so that all the eggs are equally well cooked and are of the same consistency, keeping it very soft; leave it for two or three seconds without stirring and then fold it into three layers, beginning with the side nearest the handle; this can be done with the spoon. Knock the bottom of the pan gently over the range so as to make the omelet move towards the outer part of the pan, and then fold the other part so that the omelet is a long oval shape.

All of this should take but three or four minutes, and at the same time exercising the greatest care not to overcook the omelet, as it is so much more difficult to fold when too greatly solidified.

Some persons like omelets of a golden hue, and to attain this it is only necessary, when the omelet is folded, to leave it over the fire for a few seconds.

Chef's Comments

INGREDIENTS FOR I OMELET

2–3 Eggs
1 tablespoon Cream, Water, or Milk
Salt and Pepper, to taste
1 tablespoon Butter
Garnishes, as needed (*See* B&O Omelet Garnishes,
    above)

Preheat an omelet pan over high heat.

Combine the eggs, cream, water, or milk, and seasonings in a mixing bowl. Beat well, but not to a frothy or foamy condition.

Melt the butter in the pan, being careful not to burn it. Then add the egg mixture.

With one hand, keep the pan over the heat, lightly swirling the contents while stirring with a fork or spoon in the other hand. The cooked edges of the omelet can be lightly pulled back allowing more liquid to come in contact with the pan.

When the eggs are almost completely set, add any garnishes desired inside the egg. With a fork or spatula, fold the egg in thirds, enclosing the garnish.

For a Golden Omelet, leave on the heat a few seconds to acquire a golden color.

To serve, turn the omelet over "seams down" onto a plate. Add exterior garnishes if desired.

Both Plain and Golden Omelets were found on B&O lunch and dinner menus intermittently starting in the early 1930s. Between late 1958 and the late 1960s, however, dinner omelets appeared on each month's menu.

The secrets of success with this dish are to have the pan as hot as possible without burning the edges of the omelet and to stir continuously to assure even cooking. Have the garnishes ready when the time comes to add them.

GOLDEN OMELET WITH CHICKEN LIVERS

From "B&O General Notice" for menus effective July 8, 1963, and January 9, 1964

JULY 1963

Poultry livers are to be floured and sautéed until brown. Chop livers, but not too fine. Fill omelet with some of the livers and garnish with same. Commissaries to utilize livers from spring chickens for this item.

JANUARY 1964

This should be a plain omelet filled and garnished with several pieces of livers. DO NOT CHOP LIVERS AND DO NOT SERVE WITH GRAVY.

GOLDEN OMELET, FRIED TOMATOES

From "B&O General Notice," June 3, 1964, for menus effective June 11, 1964

Use tomatoes not too over-ripe. Cut ½-inch thick, sprinkle with salt and pepper, dip in crumbs, egg and crumbs again. Fry in hot fat, 6 to 8 minutes, to golden brown. Serve two slices with the omelet.

Chef's Comments

INGREDIENTS FOR 2 SERVINGS

2 Omelets
1 Tomato, medium
Salt and Pepper, to taste
Bread Crumbs, as needed
1 Egg, beaten

SPANISH OMELET

From Old Standard B&O Recipes

Cook some finely chopped onions, green peppers in a little butter, pimentos, mushrooms, put tomatoes in same, and let it cook down (do not thicken) season, putting spoonful in omelet, and some around it, and serve on a medium platter.

Chef's Comments

INGREDIENTS FOR 2 OMELETS

1–2 tablespoons Butter
½ Onion, minced
½ Green Bell Pepper, minced
2 teaspoons Pimentos
2 teaspoons Mushrooms, minced
½ Tomato, diced fine
Salt and Pepper, to taste
2 Omelets

Melt the butter in a small frying pan and sauté the onions, peppers, pimentos, mushrooms, and tomatoes over medium-high heat for 2–3 minutes.

Lower the heat and simmer for another ten minutes.

Cook the omelet just as the filling has finished simmering. Place a spoonful of filling on the omelet and fold the omelet around the filling. Move the omelet to a plate and garnish with the remaining filling.

POACHED EGGS ON TOAST

From Eggs in a Thousand Ways (Meyer)

Poached eggs are nothing more nor less than eggs boiled without the shell.

The most important requisite is that the eggs should be fresh, as stale eggs will never poach well, even if the greatest care is used in handling them.

Have three quarts of boiling water in a shallow pan; salt it slightly, and drop into it three or four eggs; do not allow the water to boil any longer, and leave the eggs in it about three minutes, until the white is firm; then take them out, trim them, and serve on toast, or as directed.

Chef's Comments

To decrease the likelihood of breaking the yolks, break the eggs one at a time into a small cup or ramekin and gently slide them into the water. Keep the eggs from touching one another once they are in the water.

Serve on a tea plate (8–9-inch diameter) under a glass cover to keep warm.

To Meyer's caution that only fresh eggs be used we would add that they should also be very cold, which will help the egg stay together better when it hits the hot water.

The use of salt has its pros and cons. The salt adds flavor to the eggs, however, some chefs feel that it causes the egg yolks and whites to separate. Similar controversy is to be had about vinegar. Two tablespoons of vinegar can be added to the water to help keep the egg whites together as they cook, but Meyer felt that this only served to make the whites tough.

On B&O menus one serving consisted of two eggs.

POACHED EGGS À LA MORNAY

From *Eggs in a Thousand Ways* (Meyer) and
B&O Special Egg Menu (circa 1920)

Eggs covered with cream sauce mixed with cheese, and then gratinated.

Chef's Comments

INGREDIENTS FOR 1 SERVING

1 serving Poached Eggs on Toast
⅓ cup Cream Sauce *(See Sauces Section)*
Parmesan Cheese, grated, as needed

Preheat oven to 450 degrees and prepare one serving of Poached Eggs on Toast.

Place the Poached Eggs on Toast in an ovenproof dish, pouring the cream sauce over them.

Sprinkle with grated cheese, then place in the oven until nicely browned.

POACHED EGGS À LA PORTUGAISE

From *Eggs in a Thousand Ways* (Meyer) and
B&O Special Egg Menu (circa 1920)

Halves of tomatoes fried in oil, put on fried slices of bread; eggs on top and tomato sauce poured over.

Chef's Comments

INGREDIENTS FOR 1 SERVING

1 serving Poached Eggs on Toast
1–2 tablespoons Cooking Oil
½ Tomato
⅓ cup Tomato Sauce, heated *(See Sauces Section)*

Prepare one serving of Poached Eggs on Toast.

In a small frying pan, heat the oil until it begins to sizzle, then fry the tomato half as desired. Place the rounds of toast on a tea plate and top each with a tomato half and then a poached egg.

Pour tomato sauce over the eggs, place a glass cover over the dish and serve.

SCRAMBLED EGGS

From *Eggs in a Thousand Ways* (Meyer)

It should be remembered that the most important point in cooking eggs is never to overcook them. Scrambled eggs that are dried up when served are not only lacking in tastefulness, but they are also difficult of digestion. Here is a recipe that will give satisfaction if the directions are strictly followed out:

Butter a flat sauté pan liberally; put into it six well-beaten eggs, season with salt and pepper, and put on the fire. Keep stirring continuously with an egg whisk, or a wooden spoon, until the eggs become creamlike in consistency; when they are sufficiently done, add about two ounces of good butter and serve immediately. If scrambled eggs cannot be served as soon as cooked, a little cream, about one tablespoonful to two eggs, may be added; cooked this way they are more custard-like in appearance.

Chef's Comments

Modern taste and dietary concerns dictate that 2–3 eggs be used for one portion.

SCRAMBLED EGGS AU BEURRE D'ANCHOIS

From B&O Special Egg Menu (circa 1920)

Anchovy Paste, mixed with Butter, put on Toast and covered with Scrambled Egg, 50 cents.

Chef's Comments

INGREDIENTS FOR I SERVING

1 serving Scrambled Eggs
Anchovy Paste, as needed
Butter, as needed
1 slice of Toast

"Beurre d'Anchois" is French for anchovy butter. Anchovy paste is available in tubes at most grocery stores. It can be made from scratch by mashing anchovies until they form a paste.

SCRAMBLED EGGS À LA DUMAS

From B&O Special Egg Menu (circa 1920)

Served on Toast, Garnished Mushroom Sauce and Strip Bacon, 50 cents.

SCRAMBLED EGGS À LA LYONNAISE

From B&O Special Egg Menu (circa 1920)

Scrambled with Fried Onions, 40 cents.

Chef's Comments

INGREDIENTS FOR I SERVING

1 serving Scrambled Eggs
1 tablespoon Butter or Oil
1 tablespoon Onion, minced

In a small frying pan, heat the butter or oil until it sizzles. Then sauté the minced onions until slightly brown.
Add the onions to the scrambled egg mixture and cook.

SCRAMBLED EGGS AU JAMBON

From B&O Special Egg Menu (circa 1920) and *Eggs in a Thousand Ways* (Meyer)

Ham, cut in small cubes, fried in butter and mixed with eggs.

Chef's Comments

1 serving Scrambled Eggs
1 tablespoon Butter or Oil
1 tablespoon (heaping) Ham, ¼-inch dice

SCRAMBLED EGGS WITH FRESH TOMATOES

From *Eggs in a Thousand Ways* (Meyer)

Fresh tomatoes peeled, the seeds pressed out, cut in small pieces, cooked with butter and mixed with the eggs.

Chef's Comments

INGREDIENTS FOR 1 SERVING

1 serving Scrambled Eggs
1 tablespoon Butter or Oil
1 tablespoon (heaping) Tomatoes

To peel a tomato, first take a sharp knife and cut a large X on the bottom through the skin only. Be sure that these cuts wrap around the sides of the tomato.

Place the tomato in a pan of boiling water for 30–45 seconds, then in a bowl of ice water until cool enough to handle. The skin will peel right off.

SHIRRED EGGS AU BEURRE NOIR

From *Eggs in a Thousand Ways* (Meyer)

Eggs cooked plain, brown butter poured over.

BROWN BUTTER: Put two ounces of butter in a frying pan, turn the latter gently until the butter becomes brown, then add a tablespoonful of vinegar.

Chef's Comments

INGREDIENTS FOR 1 SERVING

1 tablespoon Butter
2 Eggs
Vinegar, to taste

Preheat oven to 325 degrees.

Lightly butter a ramekin or shirred egg dish and break the eggs into the dish. Do not break the yolks. Bake for 10–12 minutes, until the whites are firm and the yolks done to suit.

Meanwhile, heat the butter in a small saucepan over medium heat. Stir regularly and leave on the heat until the butter solids in the bottom of the pan take on a dark brown color.

Remove from the heat for a minute and add a few drops of vinegar, stirring to combine. Be very careful here, as the butter may spatter as the vinegar is added. Covering the pan will contain some of this.

When the eggs are done, pour the butter over them and serve.

Beurre Noir is French for black butter, but, as described above, it will actually be a very dark brown. The vinegar is added for flavor.

SHIRRED EGGS IN CREAM WITH HAM

From *Old Standard B&O Recipes*

Brown a slice of boiled ham in butter, place in shirred egg dish, top with two eggs, pour over two dessert spoons of cream. Place in oven until eggs are shirred.

Chef's Comments

Preheat oven to 350 degrees.

If a shirred egg dish is not available, any ramekin or ovenproof dish deep enough to keep the eggs together will do. Place the baking dish on a small sheet pan, which makes it easier to remove from the oven. A baking time of 8–10 minutes will result in translucent white and soft yolks, while 20 minutes will yield a hard-boiled consistency.

A dessert spoon is equal to two teaspoons.

The B&O service instructions from 1940 called for the shirred egg dish to be served on a tea plate with a cover.

SHIRRED EGGS WITH SAUSAGE AND TOMATO SAUCE

From *Old Standard B&O Recipes*

RECIPE NUMBER 46

Butter shirred egg dish, break two eggs in the dish, partly fry four links of sausage. Place two links of sausage between the eggs and one link on each end of the dish opposite the links in the center. Place in oven until the egg white is set, remove from the oven and cover the sausage with tomato sauce.

Chef's Comments

Preheat the oven to 350 degrees.

Most "shirred egg dishes" are oval or round bowls, 6–8 inches in diameter and an inch or so deep, with handles on either end.

DEVILED EGGS

From "B&O General Notice," July 5, 1960, for menus effective July 7, 1960

Recipe for deviled egg is as follows: Hard boil six eggs, cool, peel off shell, cut in half lengthwise and remove yolk. Mix yolk with a teaspoon of finely chopped parsley and one-quarter teaspoon salt. Add a dash of Worcestershire sauce and mix thoroughly. Refill egg whites with mixture. Two halves of egg with each order.

CHEESE SOUFFLÉ

From *Old Standard B&O Recipes*

MAKES 6 SERVINGS

12 Eggs
½ pound American Cheese, grated
1 cup Cream
1 teaspoon Salt
Dash Paprika
6 tablespoons Butter, melted

Separate egg yolks and beat, add other ingredients, then whip in whites of eggs. Boil in an oatmeal steamer until thick. Bake in a glass custard cup, about half full in a moderate oven, ten minutes, serve hot. Do not allow the batter to become cool before baking.

Chef's Comments

Here is an alternate set of instructions for those who do not have an oatmeal steamer (we have yet to see one).

Place a cookie sheet in the oven and preheat to 450 degrees. Butter six custard cups and allow the ingredients to come to room temperature. Carefully separate the eggs, making sure that no wisps of yolk remain in the separated whites. Such "goldfish" will prevent the whites from stiffening when beaten. Beat the yolks and add all remaining ingredients except the egg whites.

Immediately before baking, beat the egg whites until they form stiff peaks and fold them into the mixture. (This step is optional.)

Fill the custard cups ½–¾ full, place on the cookie sheet, and bake until the soufflés rise, are golden on top, and have edges that appear dry, about 10–12 minutes.

If desired, the combined ingredients can be placed into a buttered casserole or deep baking dish rather than individual serving containers.

Serve the soufflés straight out of the oven, before they have time to collapse.

CHICAGO BOUND. Author Karl Spence photographed trains in Silver Spring, Maryland, during the early 1960s and was often on hand for the departure of B&O Train 5, the Capitol Limited, for Pittsburgh and Chicago. Shortly after 5:00 p.m., dusk has already overtaken "the Cap" as its brightly lighted observation car slides by in this wintertime shot circa 1962. Karl Spence photo

EGG DISHES

SAUCES

MULTI-PURPOSE SAUCES

Bagarde Sauce

Béchamel Sauce

Cider Sauce

Cream Sauce

Creole Sauce

Espagnole Sauce

Hollandaise Sauce

Horseradish Sauce

Mushroom Sauce

Polonaise Sauce

Raisin Sauce

Robert Sauce

Supreme Sauce

Tomato Sauce

Veloute Sauce

BARBECUE SAUCES

Barbecue Sauce—Gourmet Sauce

Barbecue Sauce—Recipe Number 50

Capitol Limited Barbecue Sauce

DESSERT SAUCES

Chocolate Sauce

Coffee Sauce

SEAFOOD SAUCES

Amandine Sauce

Cocktail Sauce

Meunière Sauce

Tartare Sauce

BAGARDE SAUCE

From *Old Standard B&O Recipes*

Shred very fine the rind of two oranges, remove the white part of the rind before shredding, boil in water for 10 minutes and drain. Place the shredded rind in a saucepan with two tablespoons of currant jelly, glass of sherry wine, and half pint of brown meat gravy from the meat the sauce is to be served with. Let simmer until reduced one-third, served with meat hot.

Chef's Comments

INGREDIENTS FOR 2 CUPS OF SAUCE

Orange Rind from 2 oranges
2 tablespoons Currant Jelly
¼ cup Sherry Wine
2 cups Meat Gravy

Most cookbooks, including Charles Fellows's *Culinary Handbook,* list this as Bigarade Sauce. This sauce is best served with beef or duck dishes.

BÉCHAMEL SAUCE

From *The Culinary Handbook* (Fellows)

Into some reduced chicken broth, add some mushroom essence or purée, an equal quantity of rich milk or cream, a seasoning of mace; bring to the boil, then thicken with roux (flour and butter), strain. Used for boiled chicken, scalloped codfish, scalloped halibut, scalloped turbot, scalloped sweetbreads; chicken, turkey and sweetbread croquettes; also for mixing with green peas, asparagus points, macedoine of vegetables, etc., when used for garnishing.

Chef's Comments

INGREDIENTS FOR ½ CUP OF SAUCE

1 cup Chicken Stock
¼ cup Mushroom Essence or Purée
1 cup Milk or Cream
2 tablespoons Butter
2 tablespoons (heaping) Flour
Mace, to taste
Salt and White Pepper, to taste

In a small pan, melt the butter and stir in the flour, cooking over low heat for 10 minutes to make a roux. In another pan, combine the stock, mushroom essence, and milk or cream and heat almost to a boil. Gradually add the hot liquid to the roux, stirring constantly with a whisk to avoid lumps.

Bring the mixture to a boil, reduce to a simmer and cook for 30 minutes, stirring occasionally. Season to taste and strain.

This is an old-fashioned way to make Béchamel; modern cookbooks would leave out the stock and mushroom essence in exchange for half of an onion and two cloves heated in the milk and then removed—an *oignon pique.* For "mushroom essence or purée," simply use the liquid from canned mushrooms, or put mushrooms in a blender and purée until they become a liquid or paste.

Béchamel is one of the five "leading" or "mother sauces" of classical French cuisine. Although it certainly can be used on its own *(see recipe for* Chicken

Tetrazzini*)*, Béchamel, like the other leading sauces, is more often used as a basis for any number of "small sauces" such as Cream Sauce or Cheese Sauce.

CIDER SAUCE

From *Old Standard B&O Recipes*

Make a nice brown sauce, using essence of ham that has been previously baked, add ¼ cup of vinegar, strain and season to taste with sugar and lemon.

Chef's Comments

INGREDIENTS FOR 1 CUP OF SAUCE

2 tablespoons Butter
2 tablespoons Flour
1 cup Ham Stock or Drippings
¼ cup Cider Vinegar
¼ cup Sugar
½ tablespoon Lemon Juice

Make the brown sauce by melting the butter over medium-low heat. Stir in the flour and cook for 10 minutes. Stir in the stock or drippings, bring to a boil, and reduce to a simmer for 15 minutes, stirring regularly.

This is a great sauce to serve with a baked ham. For "essence," use the juice from the bottom of the roasting pan after removing the ham.

In researching recipes for cider sauce, we found the B&O's version to be unusual in its use of ham essence as opposed to apple juice or cider. The original recipe listed only "vinegar," which would have produced a "cider sauce" with no apple flavoring. Since other recipes used cider vinegar, it is a safe assumption that B&O chefs did so as well.

CREAM SAUCE

From "B&O General Notice," June 2, 1960, for menus effective June 2, 1960

4 tablespoons butter, 4 tablespoons flour, 2 cups turkey stock. Stir constantly until thick and smooth for approximately 10 minutes. Add one cup of milk, one cup of cream and 3 tablespoons sherry wine.

Chef's Comments

INGREDIENTS FOR 2 CUPS OF SAUCE

2 tablespoons Butter
2 tablespoons Flour
1 cup Chicken or Turkey Stock
½ cup Milk
½ cup Cream
1½ tablespoons Cooking Sherry
Salt and Pepper, to taste

Melt the butter in a saucepan and add the flour, stirring until thoroughly combined. Add the stock, bring to a boil, and immediately reduce to a simmer. Continue stirring constantly until thick, approximately 10 minutes. Add the milk, cream, and sherry; leave on the heat approximately 5 minutes to combine flavors.

Season to taste with salt and pepper.

CREOLE SAUCE

From *B&O Chef's Notes*

3 Green Peppers cut fine, 2 onions cut fine, 1 can of mushrooms with juice, ½ bottle of chili sauce, 1 can tomatoes, 2 tablespoons sugar, 2 oz butter, 1 teaspoonful salt, ¼ teaspoonful pepper, 1 teaspoonful Worcestershire sauce, small piece of ham to flavor. Cook the above-mentioned ingredients 3 hours.

Chef's Comments

INGREDIENTS FOR 1 QUART OF SAUCE

4 ounces Green Bell Peppers, ¼-inch dice
6 ounces Onions, ¼-inch dice
6 ounces Mushrooms, canned, with juice
1 teaspoon Chili Sauce
10 ounces Tomatoes, canned
1 teaspoon Sugar
4 tablespoons Butter
½ teaspoon Salt
¼ teaspoon Pepper, black
1 teaspoon Worcestershire Sauce
1 small piece Ham or Salt Pork

Combine all the ingredients in a large pot. Bring to a boil and reduce to a simmer. Simmer for 2 hours, up to 3 hours for larger amounts. Purée the entire contents of the pot.

There are several products that can be substituted for the canned tomatoes, including canned tomato purée. An 8-ounce can will work for this recipe.

ESPAGNOLE SAUCE

From *B&O Chef's Notes*

Take sauce pan and braise together some ham and raw beef trimmings with crisco, onions, carrots, turnips, and celery and fry until brown.

Then add enough flour to form a brown roux, then moisten gradually with a good strong stock and plenty of stock tomatoes with some whole mixed spice. Let the above simmer slowly for 1 hour, and then strain and it will be ready for service.

Chef's Comments

INGREDIENTS FOR 1 QUART OF SAUCE

¼ cup Shortening
2 ounces Ham and Raw Beef Trimmings
4 ounces Onion, ½-inch dice
1¼ ounces Carrots, ½-inch dice
1¼ ounces Celery, ½-inch dice
1¼ ounces Turnips, ½-inch dice
½ ounce Flour
5 cups Brown Stock
2 ounces Tomatoes

Melt the fat in a large saucepan and, when it is hot, fry the vegetables until brown. Stir in the flour and cook over low heat for 10–15 minutes. Gradually add the brown stock, meat scraps, and tomatoes. Simmer for one hour and strain. If the sauce is too thick, stir in a bit of hot water to attain the desired consistency.

Any shortening (or butter or oil) could be used to brown the meat trimmings and vegetables, as is hinted by the lower case "crisco," which apparently was used as a generic term.

"Brown stock" generally means beef stock or bouillon, but ham stock can also be used.

Espagnole is seldom used "as is." It is one of the "mother sauces" of classic French cooking that is used as the basis for many brown sauces. As such, this recipe is remarkable in that it yields a flavorful sauce in a relatively short time. Many basic Espagnole recipes call out an extensive list of ingredients, with a preparation time upwards of 5 hours.

HOLLANDAISE SAUCE

From *The Culinary Handbook* (Fellows)

One cupful each of white vinegar and butter, a half cup of lemon juice, two cupfuls of chicken stock, little salt and cayenne, boil, then pour it, beating all the while, to a liaison of egg yolks till thick like custard. Used with boiled seabass, boiled codfish and haddock, filets of codfish, boiled eels, boiled plaice and flounders, boiled halibut, boiled kingfish, boiled perch, boiled rockfish, boiled salmon, boiled sheephead, boiled weakfish, boiled sturgeon, boiled whitefish, cauliflower, asparagus.

Chef's Comments

INGREDIENTS FOR I CUP OF SAUCE

¼ cup White Vinegar
¼ cup Butter, melted
2 tablespoons Lemon Juice
½ cup Chicken Stock
2 Egg Yolks, beaten
Salt, to taste
Cayenne Pepper, to taste

HORSERADISH SAUCE

From "B&O General Notice," August 11, 1959

Make a roux with ½ cup of flour, kitchen spoon butter. Let cook ten minutes, then add a cup of boiling strained broth, stirring constantly, then strain. Add one kitchen spoon horseradish and a spot of vinegar. *Do not put sauce over meat.*

Chef's Comments

INGREDIENTS FOR 2 CUPS OF SAUCE

¼ cup Flour
2 tablespoons Butter
2 cups Beef Stock, boiling
2 tablespoons Horseradish
½ tablespoon Vinegar

Wait until just before service to add the horseradish and vinegar.

This recipe was shown just below Boiled Brisket of Beef, Horseradish Sauce, which accounts for the italicized admonition.

MUSHROOM SAUCE

From *The Culinary Handbook* (Fellows)

Into a Veloute or Béchamel sauce work a purée of mushrooms, and some sliced button mushrooms that have been lightly fried with butter; season with lemon juice and cayenne. Use with boiled chicken, capon, pheasant, partridge, sweetbreads, legs and saddles of rabbits, turkey wings, croquettes and rissoles of poultry, sweetbreads, veal, etc.

Chef's Comments

INGREDIENTS FOR I CUP OF SAUCE

1 cup Veloute or Béchamel Sauce, heated
   (See recipes, above and below)
Button Mushrooms, sliced thin, as needed
1 tablespoon Butter or Oil
Cayenne, to taste
Lemon Juice, to taste

Heat the butter or oil in a small frying pan until it sizzles and lightly sauté the sliced mushrooms. Place half of the sautéed mushrooms in the sauce and purée in a blender or food processor. Add the remaining mushrooms to the sauce and season to taste with cayenne and lemon juice.

POLONAISE SAUCE

From *Old Standard B&O Recipes*

Lemon juice, horseradish, chopped parsley and sugar added to veloute sauce.

Chef's Comments

INGREDIENTS FOR 2 CUPS OF SAUCE

2 tablespoons Butter
1 ounce Flour
2½ cups Chicken, Veal, or Fish Stock
1 teaspoon Lemon Juice
1 tablespoon Parsley, chopped
1 teaspoon Sugar
Salt and Pepper, to taste
4 teaspoons Horseradish

Melt the butter over low heat and gradually stir in the flour. Cook for about 10 minutes, stirring occasionally. Add the stock, bring the mixture to a boil, and reduce to a simmer for 30 minutes. Add the remaining ingredients, stir to combine, and serve.

This is an excellent sauce for fish or delicately flavored meat dishes.

RAISIN SAUCE

From *Old Standard B&O Recipes*

2 cups Water
1 cup Sugar
1 cup Raisins, chopped, seedless
1 glass Currant Jelly
½ teaspoon Salt
½ teaspoon Worcestershire Sauce
2 tablespoons Vinegar
2 tablespoons Butter
⅛ teaspoon Allspice, ground
⅛ teaspoon Pepper

Take a saucepan, add water and sugar, stir over fire until sugar is dissolved. Then add the chopped seeded raisins, butter, vinegar and salt, Worcestershire sauce and pepper. Last add the currant jelly and cook and stir for five minutes until the jelly is dissolved.

Chef's Comments

INGREDIENTS MAKE 1 QUART OF SAUCE

"One glass" of currant jelly would correspond to a
10-ounce jar.
This is an excellent sauce for pork or ham dishes, or
for bread pudding.

ROBERT SAUCE

From *The Culinary Handbook* (Fellows)

Minced fried onions, dry mustard, a little meat glaze
and white wine mixed into Espagnole or other brown
sauce. Used with roast pork, broiled or fried pork ten-
derloins, pork chops, and many entrées of pork.

Chef's Comments

INGREDIENTS FOR 1 CUP OF SAUCE

1½ teaspoons Butter
2 ounces Onion, ¼-inch dice
¼ cup White Wine
½ teaspoon Dijon Mustard
1 cup Espagnole Sauce, hot *(See recipe, above)*
Salt and Pepper, to taste

Sauté the onions in the butter until golden brown.
Slowly add the white wine and simmer until a third of
the liquid is left. Add to the Espagnole Sauce and simmer for 10 minutes.
Strain the sauce, stir in the mustard, and season to
taste with salt and pepper.

SUPREME SAUCE

From "B&O General Notice," June 2, 1960,
for menus effective June 2, 1960

¼ lb. Sliced mushrooms, 4 oz. sherry wine, 1½ to 2 qts.
milk. Butter roux (consisting of ¼ lb. melted butter
and ½ cup flour.) Stir roux well and bake in oven about
10 minutes, stirring frequently to keep smooth consistency. Sauté mushrooms, add sherry wine, let reduce.
Place this mixture on the side while you prepare the
following: Bring milk to a boil and add prepared Roux
gradually, stirring until it thickens. Let simmer about
5 minutes, then strain through a china cap. Add mushrooms and sherry wine mixture to sauce.

Chef's Comments

INGREDIENTS FOR 2 CUPS OF SAUCE

1 ounce Mushrooms, sliced
1 cup Milk
2 tablespoons Cooking Sherry
2 tablespoons Butter
2 tablespoons Flour

This method of making roux is rarely seen; more
often the flour is added to butter melted in a saucepan
and left on the stovetop for ten minutes. One could,
however, increase the amount of flour used to lessen the
chance of scorching if cooked in the indirect heat of an
oven.

TOMATO SAUCE

From *The Culinary Handbook* (Fellows)

Take equal quantities of good stock and tomatoes, a veal and a ham shank, a few herbs, sliced vegetables, and bay leaves; two or three cloves of garlic are optional; boil all till vegetables are done, thicken with roux, strain, add a little sugar.

Chef's Comments

INGREDIENTS FOR 1¼ QUARTS OF SAUCE

1 ounce Salt Pork or Bacon
1 Onion, ¼-inch dice
1 Carrot, ¼-inch dice
1 stalk Celery, ¼-inch dice
1 Bay Leaf
¼ teaspoon Thyme, dried
6 Peppercorns, crushed
3 Parsley Stems
2 Garlic Cloves, crushed
2½ pounds Tomatoes, fresh or canned
8 ounces Tomato Paste or Purée
1 Ham Shank
1 Veal Shank
2 cups Chicken or Veal Stock
2 tablespoons Parsley, chopped
½ teaspoon Basil, whole
1½ teaspoons Sugar
Salt and Pepper, to taste

In a large pot, render the salt pork or bacon. Add the onions, carrots, and celery and sauté, but do not brown. Add the remaining ingredients and simmer for 1–2 hours, or until the desired consistency is obtained. Remove the bones, process the sauce lightly in a food processor or blender, and season to taste. Do not process the finished sauce too much; the finished product should have plenty of "texture."

VELOUTE SAUCE

From *The Culinary Handbook* (Fellows)

Into some strong chicken and veal broth boil a small piece of pickled pork, a small bunch of garden herbs, a few carrots and onions, a little salt, sugar and pepper, simmer slowly till the pork and vegetables are done, then thicken with white roux; simmer gently, taking off the fat and scum as it rises till of a smooth velvet appearance; then strain through a hair sieve. It is used as a basis for other sauces.

Chef's Comments

The method shown above is much more involved than that used in contemporary practice. Here is a much simpler recipe that will yield 1 cup of excellent sauce.

1 tablespoon Butter
1 tablespoon Flour
1 cup Chicken Stock
Salt and White pepper, to taste

In a saucepan, melt the butter over medium heat and stir in the flour to make a roux. Continue to cook for 5 minutes or so, stirring regularly. Heat the chicken stock to a boil and pour into the roux, stirring constantly until smooth. Cover the pan and simmer gently for 30 minutes, stirring occasionally. Season to taste with salt and pepper. Go easy on the white pepper, which is a good deal more potent than black pepper.

BARBECUE SAUCE—GOURMET SAUCE

From *What's Cooking on the B&O?* (circa 1950)

⅓ cup Onion, minced
3 tablespoons Butter
1 cup Catsup
2 tablespoons Brown Sugar
2 teaspoons Mustard, prepared
⅛ teaspoon Salt
⅓ cup Vinegar or Lemon Juice
½ cup Water
2 tablespoons Worcestershire Sauce

Sauté the onions in butter in a saucepan until they are tender but not brown. Add all other ingredients, cover with saucepan lid, and let simmer for about 10 minutes. That's all. You'll now have two full cups of one of the world's great sauces.

Chef's Comments

That last sentence is some pretty tall bragging, and yet Jim Porterfield, author of *Dining by Rail* and *From the Dining Car,* says proudly that he always keeps a bottle of this sauce in his refrigerator.

Mick Weis, retired restaurant cook and B&O fan, suggests adding any of the B&O's barbecue sauces to canned navy beans or black beans for quick barbecue baked beans.

BARBECUE SAUCE—RECIPE NUMBER 50

From *Old Standard B&O Recipes*

MAKES ABOUT 3½ CUPS OF SAUCE

1 Onion, medium, sliced
2 tablespoons Butter
2 tablespoons Vinegar
2 tablespoons Brown Sugar
4 tablespoons Lemon Juice
⅓ bottle Catsup
2 tablespoons Worcestershire Sauce
½ tablespoon Mustard, dry
1 cup Water
½ cup Celery, chopped fine
Salt, to taste

Brown Onions in the butter, add the balance of the ingredients, and cook slowly for one hour.

Chef's Comments

This will be quite similar to B&O's much-vaunted Gourmet Sauce, adding only chopped celery and a twist of vinegar.

This is the last of the numbered recipes that appear only in *Old Standard B&O Recipes.* The significance of this system is unclear; some numbers, like this one, include only one recipe, while others include several. And, although all numbers from 1 to 50 are represented by one or more recipes, not every recipe in this document is numbered.

CAPITOL LIMITED BARBECUE SAUCE

A B&O Chef's Recipe, circa 1958

MAKES 2 CUPS OF SAUCE

3 tablespoons Butter
⅓ cup Onion, minced
1 cup Mustard, Grey Poupon
2 tablespoons Brown Sugar
⅛ teaspoon Salt
⅓ cup Vinegar, white
½ cup Water
2 tablespoons Worcestershire Sauce

Sauté the onions in butter in a saucepan until they are tender but not brown. Add all other ingredients, cover with saucepan lid, and let simmer for about 10 minutes.

Chef's Comments

This recipe comes from the papers of Robert W. "Bob" Gray, who lived in Willard, Ohio, and worked in train service for the B&O between 1940 and 1970, running west to Garrett, Chicago, and Toledo.

His son, Tom Gray, told us that his father "loved the Capitol Limited, and it was the only regular job he would bid on, but not because it was easy; you had to be on your toes on that run. But because it paid 73 bucks a round trip, and the service staff on it were such good people; he knew them all" (personal communication, September 10, 2006). In 1958, while working as a brakeman on Numbers 5 and 6, Bob Gray obtained this tangy alternative to the B&O's famous Gourmet Sauce from the chef on the Capitol Limited, and, for lack of another title, we have named this recipe after the train on which it was served.

When asked who this chef might have been, retired B&O waiter the late Jimmy Kearse mentioned that Chef Chester "Chet" Boyd was on the Capitol Limited at that time. He was, Kearse recalled, "a highly educated man" (personal communication, July 17, 2007). And indeed, Chet Boyd's name rang a distinct bell with Tom Gray.

CHOCOLATE SAUCE

From *Old Standard B&O Recipes*

1 pound Bakers Cocoa
1 pound Granulated Sugar
Pinch Salt

Mix together, pour in one pint of hot water, stir well. Then cool store in ice box, in covered glass jar. Take sufficient amount for each meal, place in saucepan in water to heat. If too thick add hot water to thin sufficiently. Flavor with vanilla.

Chef's Comments

INGREDIENTS FOR 8 OUNCES OF SAUCE

¼ pound Bakers Cocoa
¼ pound Granulated Sugar
Pinch Salt
½ cup Water, hot
Vanilla, to taste

This recipe would make a nice topping for ice cream, as well as for a variety of desserts.

When reheating the sauce, place it in a saucepan and hold that pan in a larger pan of boiling water (in effect, a double boiler). Stir gently as the sauce warms.

COFFEE SAUCE
From *Old Standard B&O Recipes*

1 pint Coffee
1 pint Water
¼ pound Butter
1½ cups Sugar
3 tablespoons Cornstarch

Let coffee and butter boil. Mix sugar and cornstarch, add the boiling coffee. Let cook for ten minutes over a moderate fire.

Chef's Comments

MAKES 20 SERVINGS

For this recipe, brew the coffee and melt the butter separately, then mix the sugar and cornstarch into the butter before adding the coffee.

This sauce will thicken up when cooled. Reheat it in a saucepan, thinning it with hot water as necessary.

AMANDINE SAUCE
From "B&O General Notice," June 2, 1960, for menus effective June 2, 1960

To ¼ cup butter add ½ cup blanched slivered almonds. Let simmer in butter until browned. Pour a portion of sauce over trout. Add a quantity of lemon juice and chopped parsley for flavor to the sauce. This is sufficient for 10 orders of trout.

Chef's Comments

The order of steps for preparing this sauce is correct. Squeeze or pour a small amount of lemon juice over each order and sprinkle with parsley. Go easy on the lemon juice.

It is clear that when this "General Notice" was published, the sauce was to be served with Panned Mountain Trout (sometimes referred to as Panned Mountain Brook Trout), but it would also be an excellent choice for any mild-flavored fish where there is a need for a sauce that will not overwhelm the taste of the entrée. The trout was to be served whole, with the guest choosing whether the head and tail would be removed before service. Given that, it is hard to imagine that this recipe would yield enough sauce for ten orders.

While trains serving Baltimore would normally have their diners stocked from the commissary there, the National Limited, running between Baltimore and St. Louis, was different. The "General Notice" opens with the following instruction for this dish: "Cars on Trains 1 and 2 running Panned Mountain Brook Trout, Almandine Sauce, will secure their requirements from the Cincinnati Commissary only."

This would also make a lovely sauce for fresh-cooked, uncut green beans.

COCKTAIL SAUCE
From *B&O Chef's Notes*

1 cup catsup, 2 cups tarragon vinegar, ⅛ teaspoon of Tabasco sauce, 1 teaspoon Worcestershire sauce, 1 tablespoon horseradish, 1 tablespoon finely minced celery, 1 tablespoon finely minced onion salt.

INGREDIENTS FOR 1½ CUPS OF SAUCE

1 cup Catsup
2 tablespoons Tarragon Vinegar
⅛ teaspoon Tabasco Sauce
1 teaspoon Worcestershire Sauce
1 tablespoon Horseradish
1 tablespoon Celery, minced fine
1 tablespoon Onions, minced fine
Salt, to taste

Mix ingredients thoroughly in a bowl and refrigerate until needed. This is a wonderful sauce to serve with most seafood.

MEUNIÈRE SAUCE (AKA FISH MEUNIÈRE SAUCE)

From "B&O General Notice," February 9, 1960, for menus effective February 11, 1960

INGREDIENTS FOR ONE PORTION

2 teaspoons Butter
1 teaspoon Lemon Juice
½ teaspoon Parsley, finely chopped

When fish is cooked squeeze lemon juice over it and the finely chopped parsley. Put butter in pan and brown lightly. Pour over fish and serve very hot.

Chef's Comments

Meunière is a classic sauce for seafood; the French term *á la meunière* translates to "in the style of the miller." It will enhance the flavor of fish without masking its delicate bouquet.

Despite the order in which the steps are listed, it is best to brown the butter first and have it ready when the fish is plated.

TARTARE SAUCE

From *The Culinary Handbook* (Fellows)

Into a mayonnaise sauce work some finely chopped parsley, gherkins, chives, capers and shallots. Used with breaded and fried filets of chicken and capon . . . frog legs . . . sweetbreads . . . eel cut in finger lengths . . . broiled salmon steak . . . fried calf brains . . . fried tripe . . . fried butter fish.

Chef's Comments

INGREDIENTS FOR 1¼ CUPS OF SAUCE

1 cup Mayonnaise
2 Gherkins, chopped fine
1 tablespoon Parsley, chopped fine
1 tablespoon Chives, chopped fine
1 tablespoon Capers, chopped fine
1 tablespoon Shallots, chopped fine

A Baltimore and Ohio Culinary Glossary

The final section of *Old Standard B&O Recipes* was this glossary, entitled "Terms adopted from the French in general use in cooking." By today's standards, many of these definitions are rather simplistic, and it is interesting how few are actually used in *Old Standard B&O Recipes*. Each term is quoted verbatim, with our comments or explanations shown in parentheses.

A la. In the manner of. (Designates a style of preparation or presentation.)

A la Carte. According to the menu. (A menu on which each food is listed and priced separately.)

A la Jardinière. Made with vegetables (*see* Jardinière).

A la Mode. In the manner of.

Aspic. Clear jelly, generally used as a garnish (or to coat and preserve foods for special presentations).

Au, Aux. With.

Au Beurre Noir. With black butter (*see* Beurre Noir).

Au Gratin. With grated cheese and brown bread crumbs (or any food with a browned and crusted top). (*See recipe for* Au Gratin Potatoes.)

Au Jus. With its own gravy.

Au Natural. Plain, simple.

Aux Rognons. With kidneys.

Barbecue. To roast any animal, generally outdoors.

Bard. A thin slice of bacon or pork laid over food to prevent drying (during roasting; *see recipe* for Roast Chicken).

Bearnaise. A rich egg sauce named after the town of Bearn (in the Basque Country of Southeastern France).

Béchamel. A white sauce made with stock. (One of the "mother sauces" of classic French cooking, made with milk thickened with a roux. *See recipe.*)

Beignet. A fritter.

Beurre Noir. Brown Butter. (Butter that has been cooked until dark brown; sometimes flavored with vinegar or lemon juice.)

Bisque. Cream (shellfish) soup; a rich frozen nutted ice cream.

Boeuf Bouilli. Boiled beef.

Boeuf Braise. Braised beef.

Bouches. Mouthfuls; applies to pancakes or patties.

Bouillon. A clear soup not quite as strong as consommé.

Bouquet. A small bunch of herbs used in seasoning, flavoring.

Braise. To cook in a covered pan so as not to lose flavor. (More completely, to brown in hot fat, then cover and cook in a small amount of liquid. *See recipe for* German Pot Roast with Noodles.)

Café au Lait. Coffee with milk.

Café Noir. Black coffee.

Canapés. Savory tidbits usually served on toast. *(See recipe for* Sardine Canapés.*)*

Caramel. A syrup of brown sugar named after Count Caramel, who discovered the seventh degree of sugar cooking.

Champignons. Mushrooms.

Chateaubriand. Center cut of filet of beef.

Compote. Fruit cooked in syrup.

Consommé. Clear soup (made from clarified beef broth or stock).

Crecy. With carrots.

Creole. With tomato, onions, and green peppers. *(See recipe for* Egg Plant Creole.*)*

Croustades. Fried pieces of bread to serve around meats.

Croutons. Shapes of bread toasted or fried.

Deviled. Highly seasoned (usually with mustard, vinegar, other spicy seasonings).

En Casserole. Served in the dish in which it was cooked.

En Coquille. Served in shells.

Entrées. Small savory dishes served between courses at (a French) dinner. (The main course of an American dinner.)

Escallop. Composed of alternate layers of meat or other ingredients, topped with bread crumbs and baked.

Fanchonette. A small pie or tart.

Farci. Stuffed with forcemeat.

Fermière. Braised with slices of vegetables; highly seasoned.

Filet Mignon. Small tender steaks usually served with sauce.

Filets. Strips of meat or fish with bones removed.

Foie Liver. Paté de foie gras, patty of fat liver, usually applied to goose liver.

Fondant. A boiled sugar beaten to a creamy paste (and used for glazing pastries).

Fondue. A preparation of melted cheese (plus wine and flavorings; used as a dipping sauce).

Fraise. Strawberry.

Frappé. Frozen water ice of thick consistency.

Fricandeau. Larded fried veal.

Fricassee. An essence of meat or other savory used as a basis for sauce. (A white stew in which meat is cooked in fat without browning before liquid is added.)

Fumet. Essence of meat or other savory used as a basis for sauces.

Galantine. Boned meat or fowl stuffed, cooked and glazed, and served as an aspic.

Glace. Frozen or coated with syrup.

Glaze. Stock cooked down almost solid, usually to brush over meats.

Hollandaise Sauce. A rich sauce like hot mayonnaise (made with butter, egg yolks, and other flavorings). (One of the "mother sauces" of classic French cooking.)

Hors d'Oeuvres. Savory morsels served at the beginning of the meal.

Jardinière. With mixed vegetables (often tomatoes, carrots, celery, onions).

Julienne. Vegetables shredded in fine strips (⅛ by ⅛ by 2 inches).

Koumiss. (A drink made of) yeast-fermented milk.

Lobster Farci. Stuffed lobster.

Lyonnaise. With onions and parsley. *(See recipe for* Lyonnaise Potatoes.*)*

Macedoine. Combination of vegetables or fruits.
Maigre. Meatless, fast-day dishes.
Marinade. Spiced liquor (in) which fish or meat are steeped before cooking.
Marrons. Chestnuts.
Maruite. Meat soup with bread crumbs.
Matolote. A fish stew served with wine.
Menu. Bill of fare.
Meringue. An egg white and sugar beaten to a sauce. (More like foam than a sauce.)
Mousse. Cream stiffened with gelatin, sweetened, flavored.

Nougat. A candy made from sugar and nuts.

Oeufs. Eggs.

Paprika. A Spanish sweet red pepper not as hot as cayenne.
Parfait. Whipped cream enriched with eggs, cooked with syrup.
Pate. A small puff pastry shell.
Piquant. Highly seasoned.
Poisson. Fish.
Pommes en Robe de Chambre. Potatoes in jackets. (See recipes for Baked Potato.)
Pommes Frites. French-fried potatoes.
Potage. Soup.
Pot au Feu. Stew.
Poulet. Chicken.
Printanière. With spring vegetables.
Purée. Mashed; a thick soup.

Quenelle. Forcemeat, with yolks of eggs and bread, richly seasoned, shaped in ovals and poached, and served as a garnish (for) meat.

Ragout. Savory (stew) dish made of meat, cut in small pieces with seasoning.
Rechauffe. Warmed over.
Rissoles. Roasted brown.
Roux. Flour and butter (cooked and) thickened for sauce or gravy.

Salmi. A hash of game stew.
Sauté. To fry lightly (in a small amount of fat, usually at high temperature).
Scallops en Brochettes. Scallops on skewers.
Soubise. A purée of white onion.
Soufflé. A lightly whipped pudding of eggs or cheese, baked. (See recipe for Cheese Soufflé.)
Soupe à la Reine. (A soup) to the Queen's taste.

Table d'Hôte. Dinner with a set menu (for a set price).
Têtes d'Oiseaux. Veal birds with bacon.
Timbale. Kind of a little pie in a (small thimble-shaped) mold.
Truffles. A dainty fungus found usually in France (used as) garnish.

Veloute. A rich velvety sauce. (One of the five "Mother Sauces" in classical French cooking, this white sauce is made with fish, veal, or chicken stock, thickened with a roux.)
Vinaigrette. Vinegar dressing.
Vol au Vent. A large pastry shell, filled with creamed oysters or chicken.

Zwieback. Twice-toasted bread.

BIBLIOGRAPHY

Anonymous. Undated. *B&O Chef's Notes.*

Anonymous. Undated. *Old Standard B&O Recipes.*

Baltimore and Ohio Railroad. Various Years. *Echoes from Colonial Days.* Baltimore: Baltimore and Ohio Railroad Company.

Baltimore and Ohio Railroad, Dining Car and Safety Departments. c. 1950. *What's Cooking on the B&O?* Baltimore: Baltimore and Ohio Railroad Company.

Fellows, Charles. 1904. *The Culinary Handbook: The Most Complete and Serviceable Reference Book to Things Culinary Ever Published.* Chicago: Hotel Monthly Press.

Hollister, Will C. 1965. *Dinner in the Diner: Great Railroad Recipes of All Time.* Los Angeles: Trans-Anglo Books.

Hungerford, Edward. 1928. *The Story of the Baltimore and Ohio Railroad.* New York: G. P. Putnam's Sons.

Meyer, Adolphe. 1917. *Eggs in a Thousand Ways: A Guide for the Preparation of Eggs for the Table.* Chicago: Hotel Monthly Press.

Porterfield, James D. 1993. *Dining by Rail: The History and Recipes of America's Golden Age of Railroad Cuisine.* New York: St. Martin's Griffin.

Ranhofer, Charles, 1920. *The Epicurean: A Complete Treatise of Analytical and Practical Studies on the Culinary Art by Charles Ranhofer of Delmonico's.* Chicago: Hotel Monthly Press.

Shields, John. 1998. *Chesapeake Bay Cooking with John Shields.* New York: Broadway Books.

Shircliffe, Arnold. 1926. *The Edgewater Beach Hotel Salad Book.* Chicago: Hotel Monthly Press.

Smith, Jeff, and Craig Wollam. 1991. *The Frugal Gourmet's Culinary Handbook: An Updated Version of an American Classic on Food and Cooking.* New York: William Morrow.

Stieff, Frederick Philip. 1932. *Eat, Drink, and Be Merry in Maryland.* New York: G. P. Putnam's Sons; Reprinted 1998, Baltimore: Johns Hopkins University Press.

Suzanne, Alfred, and C. Herman Senn. 1907. *Potato Cookery: 300 Ways of Preparing and Cooking Potatoes.* London: Food and Cookery Publishing Agency.

Tye, Larry. 2004. *Rising from the Rails: Pullman Porters and the Making of the Black Middle Class.* New York: Henry Holt.

DINNER A LA CARTE

MULLIGATAWNY SOUP, *Tureen* . . 30 *Cup* . . 20		
CLEAR GREEN TURTLE SOUP, *Tureen*		60
CONSOMME, *Cup*		20
CHOW CHOW . . . 20 SWEET GHERKINS . .		20
INDIA RELISH		20
INDIVIDUAL GREEN OLIVES		25
INDIVIDUAL KUKUMBER RINGS		30
EGGS, *Boiled, Fried, Shirred or Scrambled* (2) . .		30
OMELET, *Plain* . . . 45 *with Ham or Jelly* . .		65

Baltimore & Ohio Special Fish Dinner $1.25

Mr. K. H. Ackermann is Steward of this Car.

SPECIAL TODAY: D I N N E R .

Chilled Celery 30c   Sliced Tomatoes 35c
Soup - Clam Chowder 30c
Baked Chesapeake Bay Trout 65c
Creamed Crab Flakes on Toast 75c
Spanish Omelet 65c
Chicken Cutlets, Lima Beans, Tomato Sauce 80c
Commercial Travelers Club Dinner 75c
Roast Leg of Lamb with green Peas 90c
Roast Cochrane West Virginia Ham 90c
Baltimore and Ohio Special Dinner $1.25
Corn on Cob 30c   New Lima Beans 25c
Combination Salad 50c
Peach Pie (baked on car today) 25c
Honey Dew Melon 30c

FRENCH FRIED POTATOES	25
LIMA BEANS	20
GREEN PEAS	25
STRING BEANS	20

DEER PARK (MARYLAND) SPRING WATER IS USED
EXCLUSIVELY

Suggestions for the Betterment of the Service are Invited

DINNER A LA CARTE

CORN MUFFINS . . . 10 HOT TEA BISCUITS . .		15
BREAD AND BUTTER		10
MILK TOAST . . . 25 CREAM TOAST . . .		40
DRY OR BUTTERED TOAST		15
ICE CREAM . . . 25 NABISCO WAFERS . .		15
PRESERVED FIGS		35
INDIVIDUAL AIRLINE HONEY, *Liquid or Comb* . . .		20
INDIVIDUAL GRAPEFRUIT MARMALADE		25
INDIVIDUAL ORANGE MARMALADE		25
INDIVIDUAL FIG PUDDING, *Hard Sauce*		30

Hot Rolls, Colonial Style (2) 15

INDIVIDUAL ROQUEFORT CHEESE	35
AMERICAN CHEESE	25
INDIVIDUAL CAMEMBERT CHEESE	30
INDIVIDUAL MAC LAREN'S IMPERIAL CHEESE	25

Hard or Soft Crackers With All Cheese Orders

COFFEE, *per Cup* . . 15 *per Pot* . .		20
COFFEE, *Iced, per Pot* . 25 *per Glass* . .		20
INSTANT POSTUM, *per Pot*		20
TEA, *per Pot*		20
TEA, *Iced, per Pot* . . 25 *per Glass* . .		20
MILK		15
COCOA, *per Pot* . . . 20 CHOCOLATE, *per Pot* .		20
MALTED MILK, *per Glass*		20
CHOCOLATE BAR (*Almond or Plain*)		15

---

*An Extra Charge of 25c Per Person Will Be Made for
Meals Served Out of Dining Car*

E. V. BAUGH
*Manager of Dining Car and Commissary Department
Baltimore, Maryland*

INDEX

BREADS. *See* BAKED GOODS

BREAKFAST DISHES

Apple Pancakes, 133
Buckwheat Cakes, 132
Corn Cakes, 133
Fresh Sausage Patties, 135
German Pancakes, 133
Prunes, 134
Wheat Cakes, 134

CANDY

Sea Foam Candy, 24–25

CHICKEN DISHES

Breast of Chicken on Smithfield Ham, Mushroom Sauce, 69
Chicken à la Chef, 68
Chicken à la King on Toast, 68–69
Chicken Hash and Chicken Hash au Gratin, 71
Chicken Maryland, 71–72
Chicken Pie, Individual, 72–73
Chicken Tetrazzini, 75
Club Sandwich, 29
Curry of Chicken, 70–71
Roast Chicken, 74–75
Sauce for Chicken Pie, 74
Southern Style Chicken Shortcake, 75
Southern Style Fried Chicken, 70

CRAB DISHES. *See also* FISH DISHES

Crab Flake Cocktail, 22–23
Crab Imperial, 93. *See also* Imperial Crab
Crab Imperial à la Grady, 93–94
Deluxe Maryland Crab Cakes, 90
Deviled Crab Cakes, 91–92
Imperial Crab (Recipe Number 10), 92–93.
    See also Crab Imperial
Maryland Crab Cakes (Chef George Fulton), 91
Maryland Crab Flakes au Gratin, 92

DESSERTS. *See also* BAKED GOODS

Banana Shortcake, 126
Bread Custard Pudding, 125
Caramel Custard, 123
Chocolate Blanc Mange, 123
Coupe of Orange and Grapefruit, 128
Cranberry Pie, 120–21
Flaky Pie Crust, 119
French Apple Pie, 119–21
French Peach Pie, 121
Fresh Fruit Jell-o, 128
Ginger Bread Pudding with Coffee Sauce, 118
Hawaiian Fruit Cup, 128
Mince Meat Cobbler Cake, 118
Mixed Fresh Fruit in Melon Ring, 128
Mock Cherry Pie, 120
Old-Fashioned Peach Shortcake, 127
Old-Fashioned Strawberry Shortcake, 127
Orange Custard Pudding, Meringue, 124
Peach Pie Glace, 121–22
Pineapple Fritters, 28
Prune Whip, 124–25
Pumpkin Pie, 122
Pumpkin Pudding, 125
Rhubarb Jelly, 128–29
Rhubarb Pie, 122–23
Rice Custard Pudding, 125
Shredded Wheat Pudding, 125–26
Strawberry Shortcake, 127

DRESSINGS

B&O Cream Dressing for Fruit Salad, 36
Croutons, 38
French, 36–37
French, B&O Style, 37
Marshmallow Mayonnaise, 37–38
Nectar, 38
Russian, 38
Thousand Island, 38

Meet the Authors

TOM GRECO has loved the B&O since before his birth in a Baltimore row house overlooking the main line north of Mount Royal Station. During the summers in high school and college, he rode the B&O, pestering railroaders for employees' timetables and stories of the beautiful P-7-class steam locomotives. He graduated from Creighton University in 1969 with a B.S./B.A. degree in economics.

In 1971, Tom hired out on the Missouri Pacific Railroad as a clerk/telegrapher on the road's Omaha Division and became trainmaster in the Dallas Terminal in 1982. He helped found the B&O Railroad Historical Society in 1979 and now lives in Duncanville, Texas, where he works as Senior Code Enforcement Officer for that suburban Dallas city. Tom's interest in cooking began later in life and in 2004 he enrolled part time in chef's school at El Centro College in Dallas. He and his wife have one daughter.

KARL SPENCE lives in Clovis, New Mexico, the home of a hundred freights a day but not one B&O car in the lot. He has retired twice: first from the federal government, where he managed occupational safety and health programs for several federal agencies, and later as a commander in the U.S. Naval Reserve. Karl has had a lifelong interest in the B&O and grew up in Washington, D.C., where he spent many evenings at the nearby station in Silver Spring, Maryland, watching the Capitol Limited, Columbian, and National Limited on their westbound journeys. He also rode the B&O numerous times and enjoyed many of the recipes contained in this book. He is a member of the B&O Railroad Historical Society.

In addition to his mementos from railroading, Karl has a large collection of reference books and memorabilia from steamship lines and has published three books on identification of maritime china patterns used aboard merchant ships. He married a pretty blonde blind date he met at college forty-three years ago and now has a daughter and six grandchildren. The family owns and operates Weichert Realtors—The 505 Group—in Clovis.